Human Dignity

Human Dignity

George Kateb

The Belknap Press of
Harvard University Press
Cambridge, Massachusetts, and London, England
2011

Library of Congress Cataloging-in-Publication Data

Kateb, George.
Human dignity / George Kateb.
p. cm.
Includes bibliographical references and index.
ISBN 978-0-674-04837-9 (alk. paper)
1. Human rights. 2. Dignity. I. Title.

JC571.K343 2011
323—dc22   2010025821

To Sharon Cameron

Contents

Preface

The subject of human dignity is the worth of human beings or their high rank, or even their special place in nature. If we want to think about human dignity we should not remain content with a definition of the term or a short account that fails to acknowledge the idea's difficulty. The idea is difficult, even though it is rather casually used in many kinds of ceremonial or more substantial public speech, especially when such speech involves praising human rights. We can break down the difficulty into many difficulties, which are linked. One main difficulty is working out the distinction between the dignity of human beings in their relations with one another and the dignity of the human species in relation to other species and to nature as a whole. But there are other difficulties. Trying to deal with one difficulty may unsettle the conclusion we thought we had reached about another. I emphasize the conceptual or theoretical difficulties in this essay, not the formidable difficulties that stand in the way of the realization of the idea in practices and institutions or in taking the idea ever more seriously where it is already partly realized. No society fully realizes the dignity of the individual, though some societies come closer than others. In their awful luck, many societies have barely the beginnings and some have none. On the other hand, to say what the dignity of the species is will depend on trying to ascertain the human difference from the rest of nature.

The first part of the book takes up the dignity of individuals, or what

I refer to in the common phrase as the equal status of all persons. There may be advantage in aiming to work out what the idea of individual dignity requires in theory, despite all the obstacles that confront its initial realization or its further improvement. The idea is not in itself utopian, however distant past societies were from honoring what we now consider human dignity, and many present ones still are. Human individual dignity does not ask for much, but many of those who resist its claims act as if they are asked to give up everything.

The latter part of the book is driven by the wish to locate the dignity, or what I call the stature, of the human species in its unique qualities— capacities, and traits and attributes. These qualities, however, are not only uniquely human; they help to account for all that is valuable in the human species. Beyond that, these unique qualities form the basis for my contention that the human species is only partly natural. It is the only species about which that can be said. Every species is by definition unique, but only the human species achieves a partial break with nature; that is the reason that I call the human species the highest of all. But I try to suggest that such a position carries with it a tremendous duty toward nature—namely, to become ever more devotedly the steward of nature. This is a labor that only humanity can perform. Its unique break with nature makes it possible to serve nature because of such human responses to it as intellectual curiosity, awe, and gratitude, and also atonement for what human beings have done to it.

This essay is an exploration. It joins other works that have been devoted to understanding the idea of human dignity. It may seem presumptuous, however, for anyone to enter an assessment of the worth of human beings. I am sympathetic to that judgment. After all, what right do human beings have to act as judge in their own case? If we cannot have an absolutely trustworthy judge that is wholly external to us and that tells us what our worth is, what our dignity really is based on, are not we prey to either wishful thinking or misguided depreciation? I attempt to take on this question, but I am aware that people might remain skeptical of the whole effort. Or, in contrast, they may say that they know what human dignity amounts to on the basis of their assured belief in an absolutely trustworthy judge, some nonhuman entity or force greater than ourselves that has given us an explanation of what we are and a determination of what we are worth. We should proceed to correct our thinking about ourselves in this light. But suppose that there is no such entity or that we do not have indisputable communication from it or with it?

Of course, adherence to a system of theology appears to remove many of the conceptual difficulties that permeate the analysis of the idea of human dignity. By imputation, a divine entity can provide the right questions and answers on the subject of humanity, its nature and worth. A secular exploration of the idea of human dignity, like this essay, is undeniably harder to carry out than a religious exploration would be if we all could accept theological assistance as genuinely truthful. I try nevertheless to stay within the boundaries of warrantable speculation. If all the truth-claims in theological systems are refutable, the theologically based exploration of the idea of human dignity becomes not less difficult than the secular exploration, but impossible. It is better to refuse the temptation to claim, as some religious people do, that theology makes no truth-claims, and is instead an autonomous and self-enclosed language game. The trouble is that then these religious adherents slip back into basing speculation on what appear to be truth-claims in their several theologies, after all. Let us keep open the secular possibility of exploration, because if theology goes down, then in disappointment we might be moved to think that since there is no irrefutable theological system, there can be no idea of human dignity. We must be willing to think about human dignity with the assumption that it was not bestowed on us or imputed to us by some higher non-human entity, whether divine, demonic, or angelic.

I do not give an objective account. It is impossible to defend or attack such a charged idea as human dignity without commitment, whether it is a moral commitment or a theoretical commitment of some kind. The aspiration is to work with a commitment that is warrantable. This essay is not neutral, but it asks for no faith, and no trust in anything but our common ability to think through our positions without recourse to assistance from a more-than-human force or entity that we posit in the hope that we are able to do so, or out of an urgent wish to believe that we must do so, hope against hope.

If there are certain questions about human beings that must be addressed, as I think there are, I see no alternative to exploring the idea of human dignity. If it is presumptuous for human beings to discuss human dignity, then that would mean that much of the literature and philosophy of the world would be presumptuous. Few writers claim divine inspiration or access to divine revelation. Yes, there are scriptures; but their actual relation to divinity aside, the amount of scriptural writing is minuscule in comparison to all the rest. Yet a great deal of the world's writing does try to assess the worth of human beings, in one way or another. If some of the works we have rely on scriptures or assert that they do, many other works do not. I am not saying that the idea of human dignity as such usually figures explicitly; it rarely does. But we nevertheless read books that ask, if only implicitly, what it means to be human. Writers constantly enter judgments about how human beings treat one another, or treat nature. The underlying question is, do people, real or fiction, show awareness of the burdens of human dignity.

One must be tentative; that is why I speak of exploration. The conceptual difficulties are resistant to clarity or to agreement that is better than superficial. Other relevant explorations must be present to mind whenever any particular one, like this essay, is read. Readers without religious belief can learn in their own secular way from many religious writings. The bibliography includes a sampling of texts that offer help, by way of contrast or disagreement, on various aspects of the idea of human dignity.

I offer a defense of human dignity. To be sure, international documents in which human rights are declared appeal to human dignity to vindicate rights. But quite a number of thinkers find the very idea of human dignity unacceptable. They do so not only, or not even primarily, because they think it is mistaken for human beings to judge the worth or dignity of the human race but because they enter a harsh judgment that ridicules the supposition that humanity is so special or important as to justify an assertion of its dignity. Or these critics see nothing valuably distinctive or unique about human beings that other species lack; or they say that if other species lack these qualities, they make up for them with qualities that compare quite well with those that are uniquely human. Or critics think that the human race is manifestly aggressive and destructive in regard to nature, but also in regard to itself. How can such a species think well of itself when its record of moral wrongdoing is so extensive and intense, and when its exploitative and shortsighted treatment of nature is so dangerous to nature and itself? Up to a point, I grant the truth of these charges. Nevertheless, I still think that we can form an understanding of human dignity that perhaps survives the worst that people have done, and therefore the worst that has been said so far about humanity. We do not need a pessimistic theology to say the worst; we do not need to get entangled with sin as an affront to divinity. We have only to be honest about the immeasurable wrong that human beings have always done, still do, and will always do.

You do not have to love humanity in order to believe in human dignity. I must admit that I find the appeal of misanthropy not seductive but quite worth attending to, if for no other reason than the necessity to avoid excessive pride and consequently to accept the imperative to limit—whenever possible, whenever the truth allows—the claims we make about human dignity. But limiting the claims does not mean disowning the idea that human beings have dignity, a dignity that rests on a human uniqueness that is not only praiseworthy but manifests a break with nature. Of course, and inextricably so, we must often condemn human uniqueness. Perhaps a way can be found to believe that the praiseworthy considerations outweigh those that deflate or shame the human race and that sometimes even make a few thinkers imagine that they wish for its extinction.

Acknowledgments

John Kulka, Executive Editor-at-Large at Harvard University Press, suggested this book. His encouragement, as in the past, was indispensable, and I wish to acknowledge it gratefully. He also commented wisely and perceptively on the whole manuscript. David Bromwich read the manuscript with his usual acuteness and generosity; his many thoughts, coming from deep learning, were and remain continuously provocative. Stephen K. White made a number of penetrating comments about conceptual issues and valuable suggestions about various other aspects of the manuscript.

I benefited greatly from lengthy exchanges with Leo Marx on the subject of naturalist conceptions of human beings. Conversations with Peter Singer about his work and general moral questions were most productive. Kim Townsend gave unfailing support. For timely and in some instances decisive questions or animated scepticism, and for observations or bibliographical recommendations, I want to thank Lawrie Balfour, Corey Brettschneider, William E. Connolly, Bonnie Honig, Daniel Robinson, Jerome Schneewind, Morton Schoolman, George Shulman, Steven B. Smith, Anna Stilz, David Tubbs, and Jeremy Waldron.

Human Dignity

1

The Idea of Human Dignity

My aim is to defend the idea of human dignity. Does it need a defense? After all, the idea has become commonplace, especially since the end of World War II. In the name of human dignity, which now turns out to mean in its most common use the equal dignity of every person, charters of human rights are promulgated, and appeals to it are made when people all over the world struggle to achieve their claimed rights. Human dignity is thus perceived to be the basis for human rights. But not much is said about what human dignity is and why it matters for the claim to rights. It almost seems as if the idea of human dignity is axiomatic and therefore requires no theoretical defense. All it needs is to be translated into established rights, which are then preserved in the face of attempts to keep people down and deny them what they are owed.

When people have to struggle to establish or preserve or reestablish their rights, they contend with various interests that are threatened by the demand for rights and that have many kinds of power to repel such assertions, but these antagonistic interests have little theory of any weight to sustain their cause—they have only tenacious privilege backed up by alarms, and by lingering popular prejudice, superstition, and mental inertness, and the cry of security against the enemy always ready to hand. It can be thought that whatever was the case some centuries ago, the defense of rights at present requires little theoretical articulation. Why make trouble by defending rights at length and make worse trouble by claiming that human dignity is the basis, or part of the basis, for human rights? Theoretical defense invites philosophical skepticism, which is sometimes useful to stimulate thought, but there is these days not very much theory, though there is some, that comes out and says that human rights are, in Jeremy Bentham's phrase, "nonsense upon stilts," and that the idea of human dignity adds yet more nonsense.

The reason to go on with the theoretical defense of human rights is that opposition to them exists among thinkers who are on the side of the great majority of people and who do not support the established privilege that a system of rights threatens. One principal source of opposition to rights comes from those who think human rights are essentially bourgeois rights and therefore make too much of one particular right, the right of property. From the nineteenth century on, this opposition on the radical left has been prominent and sometimes revolutionary. The Marxist and other radical critics of the right of private ownership have gone so far as to call into question the value of almost all other rights because in an oligarchic or capitalist society the rich and their allies are so dominant as to make such rights as free speech, press, and religion into weapons useful to fortify the oppression of the subordinate classes. This analysis overshoots the mark, but retains the power to cause unease among those who are committed to human rights. Human rights are in fact conceptually and actually unsettled by widespread poverty, despite the strength of the case that the abolition of private property is not the way to reduce poverty in the long run. There are also other worries about rights that we will eventually attend to, including the critiques made by utilitarian and virtue-ethics thinkers. Like the oppositional left, these critics also write on behalf of the people, not the elite, though unlike the left, they rarely have much power. Still, we have to try to see what these theorists, who oppose rights because they either support the people or want to better the character of the people, say to defend their views, and what role, if any, the idea of human dignity plays in their arguments.

In any case, there is already a substantial theoretical literature in defense of rights. It begins in the revolutions in Britain in the seventeenth century, proceeds in revolutionary America and France in the latter part of the eighteenth century, continues in Kantian philosophy, and develops further in John Rawls's influential political philosophy and Ronald Dworkin's legal theory in the twentieth century. Add to all this work Western jurisprudence throughout. The truth is that the idea of human dignity figures in it only to a minor extent, if at all. The exception is Kant's political and moral philosophy, and he is of course a major theorist of dignity *(Würde)*. For him, dignity is a foundational idea, and his work remains a continuous source of profound instruction. My debt to him will be obvious. But why, it could be asked, make so much of Kant? Kant aside, why go on thinking about human dignity, especially when we see that, especially in the twentieth century, actual progress in realizing human rights (whether called by that name or called natural rights) has often come about without much need or use of theoretical assistance? Feelings of injury and insult have mattered most, especially when they come together to impel a leap of consciousness, in which a quickened expectation of decent treatment is combined with a more definite feeling of what human dignity in some simple sense is owed; and once emergent, these attitudes and passions disseminate themselves by ordinary if belated insight, by imitation, and by the attractiveness of gradually established example.

Can we at least say that there is no harm in thinking more about the idea of human dignity and its place in the theory of human rights? I hope that there is some good. It turns out, however, that the idea of human dignity encompasses more than a role in the defense of rights; there is place in it for the dignity not only of individuals but also of the human species as one species among all the others.

Dignity of the Individual; Dignity of the Human Species

The core idea of human dignity is that on earth, humanity is the greatest type of beings—or what we call species because we have learned to see humanity as one species in the animal kingdom, which is made up of many other species along with our own—and that every member deserves to be treated in a manner consonant with the high worth of the species. Since Pico della Mirandola's speech *On the Dignity of Man* (1486), in which the core idea is found early, there have been a number of revisions and elaborations. Yet doubt is sometimes expressed when human dignity is introduced into later discussions of rights, even when human rights are accepted as defensible and conducive to human interests. Several particular contentions stand out in supporting the thought that all theoretical discussion about human dignity is irrelevant to the cause of promoting the establishment of human rights, or may even be a distraction. The first contention is that, despite the efforts of Kant, the idea of human dignity adds nothing but a phrase to the theory of human rights; it surely does not provide, or help to provide, an indispensable foundation. The second is that the historical record shows such human savagery toward human beings that to speak of human dignity is to mock human suffering by refusing to make paramount the moral difference between victims and victimizers; we must grant dignity only to those persons who have acted morally. The only human beings who have human dignity are those who are morally blameless or at least much less guilty; violators of rights, the victimizers, have forfeited their chance to acquire dignity. The theory of rights must distinguish between those who have dignity and those who have (not yet) lost it. The third contention is that the affirmation of human dignity is dangerous because, when extended to the human species vis-à-vis other species, it leads to monstrous human pride, which drives people to exploit nature for human purposes and hence to ravage nature and ultimately make the earth uninhabitable for many species, including humanity. The fourth contention is that human species-pride is not only dangerous but false: there is no basis for thinking that the human species is anything special; or that it alone has dignity among all the species; or that if the human species does have dignity, that its dignity is greater than, or even incomparably greater than, the dignity of any other species.

Despite elements of truth or at least plausibility in these four contentions, my countercontention is that we should not repudiate the various attempts that have been made to defend the idea of human dignity, and that additional conceptual work is not necessarily wasted. There is more to be said. I cannot deny that any attempt should face the kinds of antagonism I have just mentioned and other kinds as well. I must try to show that the idea of human dignity adds something necessary to the theory of human rights; that though human history is a slaughter-bench, the scene of uninterrupted crimes and atrocities, human dignity must be affirmed, even the dignity of those who assault the dignity of others through wrongdoing, and thereby injure their own dignity also, implausible as that notion may seem.

As my discussion proceeds, I also wish to show, as I have said, that the idea of human dignity not only serves to help defend the theory of individual rights but also gives a perspective on the dignity of the human species. Still it is possible that the dignity of the species may be in tension with the theory of individual rights; the idea of human dignity may be at odds with itself, the claims to dignity of the individual with the claims to dignity of the species. However, to speak of the dignity of the human species as distinct from individual dignity is to invite more skepticism and even hostility. I nevertheless want to defend species dignity while admitting that human beings are generically given to mad presumption in their enterprises and exploits, whether at the expense of nature or of one another. I think that such presumption has actually been integral to species dignity. But now humanity should direct its energies, as no other species can, to the stewardship of nature and therefore curtail its mad presumption against nature. I wish to go to the extent of saying that the human species is indeed something special, that it possesses valuable, commendable uniqueness or distinctiveness that is unlike the uniqueness of any other species. It has higher dignity than all other species, or a qualitatively different dignity from all of them. The higher dignity is theoretically founded on humanity's partial discontinuity with nature. Humanity is not only natural, whereas all other species are only natural. The reasons for this assertion, however, have nothing to do with theology or religion.

I therefore work with the assumption that we can distinguish between the dignity of every human individual and the dignity of the human species as a whole. With that assumption in place, I make another assumption, that the dignity of every individual is equal to that of every other; which is to say that every human being has a *status* equal to that of all others. The idea of individual dignity thus applies to persons in relation to one another, and moves ideally in a progression from an individual's self-conception to a claim that other persons have no less than equal status. I, like anyone else, can insist on my dignity as a human being, in the face of others situated above me in power and prestige and who treat me in such a way as to fail to recognize my full humanity. I also see that what I insist on, which is universal in nature, I cannot claim just for myself or my group, but must claim for all human beings. Each person must claim for all, and all for each.

All individuals are equal; no other species is equal to humanity. These are the two basic propositions that make up the concept of human dignity. The idea that humanity is special comes into play when species are compared to one another from an external and deindividualized (though of course only human) point of view. When we refer to the dignity of the human species, we could speak of the *stature* of the human race as distinguished from the *status* of individuals. In comparison to other species, humanity has a stature beyond comparison. The reasons for speaking of individual dignity are the same as those for speaking of the dignity of the species: the same unique and nonnatural traits and attributes, characteristics, and capacities. I am therefore not saying that the species has a real existence apart from the individuals who make it up, or has a substance that is different from the substance of any individual or all of them, or has a collective agency different from the agency of individuals separately or in groups. Nevertheless, I talk about the species because the interdependence of individuals and groups is so extensive and deep, and so entangled, so hard, even impossible, to describe or trace, that for certain purposes we might just as well make the human species a unified entity or agent, even though we know it isn't. Most important, the human species also includes the nameless, countless, and unindividuated unborn. I do not see how the idea of human dignity can omit reflection on the human species, apart from named or nameable individuals or identifiable groups.

The historical record appears to indicate that thinking about humanity in relation to other categories of beings comes well before thinking about individuals as individuals. Affirmation of human stature, in one set of terms or another—the word *stature* rarely occurs—comes well before political and social concern for every person equally.

Conceptually, human stature precedes individual status; the greatness of humanity precedes the equality of individuals. Starting with Homer, Western literature dwells on individuals, but they are mostly of the upper rank and they tend to matter, except to Socrates, not as individuals but as members of a class, or as defined by role or function. What counts is that the few at the top demonstrate what humanity at its best is capable of.

Although Odysseus is remarkably delineated as a person, the standards are set even for him, and the gods have their own plans also for him. Priam and Achilles break out of their roles but into tears. Socrates, however, discovers the individual, the self-conscious and hence dissident and conscientious individual, who by thinking for himself acts to avoid being an instrument of injustice, not, like Sophocles' Antigone, to uphold mores or customary piety. To be sure, Socrates says that he pursues wisdom out of piety toward the god, and is put to death because he is accused of corrupting the youth by teaching gods other than those of the city. But he does not accept the accusation that he teaches other gods. Both he and Antigone can say in her bitter words about herself: "I stand convicted of impiety / the evidence my pious duty done" (*Antigone*, p. 190). What matters first is that Socrates would rather die than give up his pursuit of wisdom, which he began before the medium of the god Apollo at Delphi had answered no when asked whether anyone was wiser than Socrates, and second, that he would rather die than inflict injustice on another person. Condemned to death on the charges against him, he chooses to die for the safety of the laws of the city rather than escaping with the help of his friends. Death stalks him or he stalks it. Both his piety and his moral sense are therefore distinctively his and they dominate his bond to his fellows and his peculiar tie to his city. It is not necessary or even possible to say in which of the two qualities Socrates is more radical. In his *Confessions*, Augustine discovered the individual self, the largest continent, while looking for God within; what is amazing is that he not only believed that inside is where we should look for God, but with profound originality proceeded to map out the vastness of inwardness. Again, it is not necessary or even possible to say whether his theology grows out of the discoveries of his introspection or these discoveries grow out of his theology. Socrates in

Plato's *Apology* and Augustine in the *Confessions* are two principal landmarks on the way to finding that individuals can exist as individuals, and that as individuals they have equal status.

In these works, the individual as subject and the individual's subjectivity are presented in a way that still retains the power to inspire reflection. But until recent centuries, human stature was preponderantly thought equivalent to the dignity of the human species, and stature was owed to the exertions of a few. It would seem that, conceptually, human dignity was for a long time just a matter of stature, of humanity's superiority to all other beings on earth, although it was a superiority that only the few high and great ones proved or at least made vivid. The Socratic breakthrough, in a setting of Athenian democracy, which was itself a breakthrough, provides the earliest movement toward the notion of the equal status of every individual; but even so, in the background is the distinctiveness of the human race as the particular object of the gods' interest. Is it possible that for some of us, too, the idea of human dignity is equivalent to the notion of stature: the superior being of the few and the greatness of their achievements? Can human stature therefore do without individual status to fill out the idea of human dignity? In a turnabout, if we are committed to equal status, do we need the stature of the human species in order to defend it? As I will indicate, the element common to status and stature is uniqueness, but a uniqueness defined by its partial discontinuity with nature, unlike the uniqueness of all other species and of all their individual members. But perhaps, though I doubt it, the purported common element is only a loose analogy, relevant for some purposes but not conceptually essential for working out an idea of human dignity.

My rough determination is that equal individual status is shored up by the great achievements that testify to human stature because, in a remarkable, memorable, and graspable way, they rebut the contention that human beings are merely another species in nature, and thus prepare the way for us to regard every person in his or her potentiality. At the same time, the idea of human stature is helped by acknowledging the claims of equal status, if only because the theory of equal individual rights has set the old order on fire. But the better reason is that the notion of equal status deepens the idea of human dignity. It carries through on the attempt to establish the value of humanity by insisting on the value of every human individual. The theory of rights, however, must be more than partly, pragmatically, or grudgingly accommodated. The notion of equal status prescribes the imperative that role and function should not define any person, essentially or exhaustively. The potentialities of any person can become actualized unexpectedly, and jump over boundaries or, at a minimum, push the boundaries back by converting role and function into a vocation that is creatively pursued.

One implication of the equal status of every individual as a unique being is that no single person can stand for the species, whether that individual is average or is exceptional in various aspects. No one can represent (in the sense of embody) the human species in some imaginary congress of intellectual species in the universe. Equal status means that the question of which individuals in the human species are "best of breed," let alone "best in show," is out of order. Of course people vary in their talents and innate abilities, and in the manner of their acculturation, but that undeniable fact is irrelevant to human status. Most important, no person of whatever excellence could adequately incarnate such an unfinished and indefinite species as humanity; the potentiality of the species will always be incompletely disclosed as long as it lasts, and without any substantial change in its biological endowment.

Status and stature belong together in one concept of human dignity. But an important difference will emerge in our analysis. We know when individual status is respected when we determine that a state is not using or misusing the people, wasting or infantilizing them—in short, when the state honors their rights. The evidence is mostly in what the state does not do, in avoidance and noninterference. In contrast, we impute stature to humanity on the basis of the record of its achievements. The evidence is manifest. Status is a largely negative concept, defined by what assaults or even effaces it; stature can be defined only positively, by what is humanly achieved.

The concept of equal individual status is only part of the idea of human dignity; the other part is the stature of the human species. What is more, as I will suggest, status is only part of the defense of the theory of human rights; the other part is the public morality of justice. As we go along, these points will be developed.

Human Dignity Is an Existential, Not a Moral, Value

Human dignity is an existential value; value or worthiness is imputed to the identity of the person or the species. I stipulate that when the truth of identity is at stake, existence is at stake; the matter is existential. The idea of human dignity insists on recognizing the proper identity of individual or species; recognizing what a person is in relation to all other persons and what the species is in relation to all other species.

The truth of personal identity is at stake when any individual is treated as if he or she is not a human being like any other, and therefore treated as more or less than human. The truth of identity is also at stake when a person is treated as if he or she is just one more human being in a species, and not, instead, a unique individual who is irreplaceable and not exchangeable for another. These two notions seem to go in opposite directions—commonness and distinctiveness—but I think that they cooperate in constituting the idea of equal individual status.

In one sense, personal identity is not an achievement. I could not and did not choose to be born at all, or born a man instead of a woman; to be born on this date rather some earlier or later one, and born to these parents rather than some others. I could not have been some other person and still been myself, even though the society in which I grew up helped to shape me; the same me could of course have grown up in some other society, which would have shaped my beginnings differently. I am not a creature who has a destiny, but once I am in existence, certain features are what they are, and are more or less fixed. In another sense, identity is an achievement. Becoming or being oneself has meaning. One tries to realize certain potentialities rather than lazily leaving them dormant; one can try to resist imitating others or conforming thoughtlessly to the prevailing mores or fashions; one can work hard to avoid pretending to be what one isn't; one can change oneself for the better; one can take hold of oneself; one can aspire to be not the author but the editor of oneself and one's life; one can aspire to a measure or episode of authenticity.

For the time being, all that I want to say about the identity of the human species is that it is the only animal species that is not only animal, the only species that is partly not natural, and that is therefore unpredictable in its conduct despite its genetic sameness from one generation to the next. These are, I think, the most important considerations in regard to the identity of the human species.

Individual status is a major part of the idea of human dignity because it struggles against such notions as the natural or divinely ordained superiority or inferiority of some human beings in comparison to others or in relation to them; the idea of caste, or the natural slavery of some; the idea of hereditary rank; the idea of inherited curse; the idea of eternal damnation in itself, and also when it is posited for some but not others; and the belief that one may sacrifice the lives or conditions of life of the smaller number of persons for the larger number without seeing that acting from sincerely perceived necessity can nevertheless be doing evil. Actually, cynically asserted necessity is the norm. False metaphysics sponsors these and many other notions that war on equal individual status and thus fortifies the almost inveterate tendency that human beings have to divide the world up into pseudo-ontological categories. The pathetic fact is that the only enemies of human dignity are human beings.

When I speak of identity, I have in mind only individuals and species. I am skeptical of efforts that theorists make to give groups the same existential weight or dignity as individuals and the species. My skepticism extends to the concept of group rights, because under some versions of this concept, a group has rights that are not translatable into each member's individual right of free association and other rights, but rather are a sort of corporate rights that may abridge members' individual rights. The basis of my skepticism is the reason that if a person thinks of himself or herself first as a member of a group, that person has defined identity as affiliation, and not as first being oneself. To be affiliated with one's whole self is to welcome docility, to endorse the thought that one's possibilities are exhausted, perhaps from birth, and that one cannot change or be changed; all that one can do is play a part and at most make the part one's own by small differences of attitude or conduct. Indeed, cultural identity may be imagined as one's fated and irrevocable personal identity. Affiliation that is self-defining and life-defining with this intensity gives a person a hand-me-down identity, an identity that has completion and enclosure, which no personal identity that is free of self-mystification can possibly have. One's life becomes a vicarious experience, lived through the fate of the group. Group rights consign individuals to dependence sustained by their conformity. I know that a life-defining group affiliation can feel like an enlargement of the self, but it is actually a diminishment; it can feel like an intensification of the sensation of being joyously alive, but it is actually existential surrender.

I want now to make a contrast between existential values and moral values. The category of existential values, values of identity, includes such cherished aspirations and attainments as developed or distinctive selfhood, autonomy, authenticity, freedom, equality, power for its own sake, virtues for their own sake, perfectionism of character or style of life, honor, glory, and fame. All these values may pertain to individual uniqueness and hence are allied to the idea of human dignity; but they figure in uniqueness as a project, not as a given. They signify a desire for an enhanced identity or enhanced individuality. As such, these values can matter to the discussion of human dignity; some, like freedom and equality, have a place at its center; all can be and often are discussed, however, apart from the idea of human dignity. But as I will suggest when I discuss the value-ethics critique of human rights, the project of enhanced individuality or cultivated individual uniqueness is not essential to the defense of equal individual status. Every human being is unique and individual without having to try to be.

All existential values have a conceptual independence from instrumental practicality and most important from morality, despite the fact that freedom and equality, the core of human rights, are often defended as practically or morally necessary or useful. When I say that human dignity is an existential value, however, I do not deny its close relation to morality, despite its conceptual independence. (Not to say that all existential values—say, honor, glory, and fame—must bear a close relation to morality.) I mean that for many people, and rightly, morality has to do solely or principally with human suffering; but human dignity in its concern with status and stature has to do with the proper recognition of the identity of every human being and the identity of the human species. I also do not deny that the motives to inflict suffering and to assault dignity come from the same repertory of vices: the same appetites, emotions, and passions, whether they are inherent in everyday life or are inflamed by the eager adoption of the doctrine of necessity or by the appeal of ideology to the imagination. Still, being made to suffer, bodily and materially, is not conceptually the same wrong as being treated as if one is not a human being. Lastly, I believe that though a human being can never forfeit his or her dignity and thus become legitimately open to any kind of inhuman treatment, one assaults one's own dignity when one is a party to serious injustice, or systemic oppression, or to evil as a policy; one is acting as if one were more than human, or more human than those whose victimization one causes or calmly accepts as nothing untoward. The ties between moral values and existential values are often tight, but not always so; they are conceptually distinct, even in the idea of human dignity, and not only when tension between them appears.

Now, the deserved salience of Kant's moral philosophy in the theory of rights may lead us astray and make morality and dignity interchangeable terms. He holds that human dignity or worth lies in the uniquely human capacity on earth (to leave aside more-than-human entities) to act morally, which necessarily means to act from the correct moral disposition. First, only the good will shows respect for the moral law; emotions like love or pity do not belong to the correct moral disposition; and intrinsic to the good will is the resolve to be indifferent to the effects of one's moral action on human purposes. Second, Kant also thinks that we treat persons with the respect they deserve when we treat them as ends and not merely as means. They deserve respect as ends because as moral agents they are capable of respecting the moral law. To put the two thoughts together, we accord persons the respect they deserve as ends, when we treat them in a way that shows our respect for the moral law, not when we mimic morality out of one or another emotion or interest, much less when we immorally or disrespectfully use them as mere means. Kant ties respect for the moral law in one's actions and respect for persons as ends in our dealings with them into an unbreakable knot.

But suppose that we want to hold, instead, that there are additional bases for respecting human beings and hence their rights than their capacity to act morally. Free agency is a broader concept than moral agency. The moral and the existential are not interchangeable terms, and they cannot be tied into an unbreakable knot. We might also think that there are other praiseworthy sources of moral conduct, besides respect for the moral law, like pity or compassion. Then, too, we could believe, and as a matter of course, that anticipation of the consequences of our action is properly part of our disposition to act, just as the actual consequences are properly subject to moral judgment. All these objections to Kant are commonplace. We learn much from Kant, but not on moral motivation, and not on the place of morality in the larger scheme of human values, even when we take Kant's theory of the virtues into account.

The conceptual distinction between moral and existential values is interestingly made by Justice William Brennan in his concurrence to the per curiam decision that (temporarily) invalidated the practice of capital punishment (*Furman v. Georgia*, 1972). His discussion in this case is perforce framed by the specific kinds of pain and suffering (mental and physical) that punishment inflicts, rather than the many kinds of pain and suffering that a state that does not recognize and respect rights inflicts on the totality of a person's existence. But Brennan allows himself, when he is discharging his specific interpretative task, to reach a general principle. He says that more than pain is involved in "extremely severe punishment," and in capital punishment especially. "The true significance [of severe punishments] is that they treat members of the human race as nonhuman, as objects to be toyed with and discarded" and that they may "reflect the attitude that the person punished is not entitled to recognition as a fellow human being" (pp. 272–273). (The old Nazi phrase was "life unworthy of life.") He also says that severe pain like that of capital punishment can be degrading (p. 281), especially when it is inflicted arbitrarily on some but not all who have committed capital crimes; when the severity of the pain is unacceptable to contemporary society; and when a lesser punishment than death would be adequate for the deterrent or expressive function of punishment. The "paradigm violation" of human dignity is "torturous punishment," which capital punishment is, mentally more than physically.

His conclusion is that capital punishment is a cruel and unusual punishment and is therefore prohibited by the Eighth Amendment of the US Constitution.

It is excellent that somewhere on the highest level of US jurisprudence, the idea of human dignity appears to be doing irreplaceable work in the defense of human rights. In the Furman case, the target is torture or what is torture-like: living on death row for a long period and then enduring execution that is rarely free of serious pain. The trouble is that apart from the metaphor of the human being as an object that is toyed with and discarded, and the reference to the state's failure to recognize a prisoner as a fellow human being, the entire burden of Brennan's reasoning against capital punishment is carried by the view that the infliction of such severe pain is immoral, a great immorality committed by the state. He does not quite say that capital punishment makes the state no different from and certainly no better than a murderer, but he could have. Human dignity is frequently mentioned, but it is not clear what work the idea does. Elsewhere, he expands the notion of human dignity to require state provision for individual self-development. This idea is rather too custodial for the good of human dignity; the real force of his conceptualization lies in his principled aversion to capital punishment and other cruel or unusual punishments.

Brennan implies that deliberate infliction of severe needless pain is in itself degrading because it is the ultimate immorality; the infliction of such pain is the worst way that human beings treat other human beings. No one, no matter what they have done, ever deserves to receive the worst at the hands of the state. The treatment is inhuman. But Brennan does not hold on to his point that the infliction of severe pain can be an instrument of an intention that goes beyond pain for the sake of pain; namely, the reduction of a human being to the nonhuman status of a thing or animal. He keeps returning to the cruelty endured by the prisoner in capital punishment—that is, to the extraordinarily painful experience of a prisoner facing death and then undergoing execution. The severity of experienced pain is what holds Brennan's attention. He says that the United States believes that "the dignity of the individual is the supreme value"; but it is telling that he then calls this foundation "moral grounds" (p. 296).

I do not want to press Brennan too hard. I can see why it makes sense to hold that inflicted pain can be so severe that one wants to say that it is in itself an effacement, apart from intentions or effects, of the humanity and hence the dignity of the victim. What I would like, however, is a more definite indication that the violation of dignity has existential weight that is independent of the suffering in itself. Part of the intention of inflicting suffering is to re-identify groups of people as subhuman and do so through the kinds of suffering that degrade. In general, atrocities, crimes against humanity, are not merely immoral but evil. When evil in the form of the effacement of human identity is involved, the category of immorality seems inadequate. The moral concept of cruelty does not account sufficiently for the phenomenon of cruel and unusual punishments such as slavery.

I also think that what Brennan's opinion requires is a sharper distinction between pain (no matter how severe) and death. He hates the thought that a state would deliberately end the life of a human being and tries to make the awfulness of that act resemble as closely as possible the most extreme pain. By making so much of the cruelty, he is able to take refuge in the Eighth Amendment and thus see severe pain as in itself degrading and hence as violating human dignity. He believes that he cannot appeal to an absolute indefeasible right of life because the due process clauses of the US Constitution do not prohibit capital punishment, but assume its continued existence and only demand due process protections for the capitally accused person. Conceptually, he is left with the profound immorality of state-inflicted cruelty. Yet he sees that retributive moral arguments (secular and religious) are used to defend capital punishment: "a life for a life" has ancient standing. He consequently needs a kind of argument that is not only moral; so he continuously refers to human dignity, as if it were more truly moral than traditional morality, just because human dignity seems incompatible with, above all, the deliberate and punitive infliction of severe pain.

But why is death "an unusually severe punishment?" His answer is that it is "unusual in its pain, in its finality, and in its enormity" (p. 287). But he does not spell out the specialness of death as a punishment; he does not say why death is so bad that no one can ever be said to deserve it, even if it were inflicted quickly and painlessly. We need an existential argument for an absolute, indefeasible right of life, not a moral one, and I hope to give a sketch of it in a little while. In Brennan's concurrence, striking and praiseworthy as it is, morality actually does just about all the conceptual work; dignity hardly does any. The defense of human rights requires a more defined existential or identity component.

When we look, as we will, at the connection between pain and degradation outside the framework of legal punishment (capital punishment in particular), and with state-inflicted crimes against humanity in mind, the nature of the degradation that severe pain can cause becomes clearer.

Uniqueness and Dignity

In the idea of human dignity to recognize oneself as sharing in a common humanity with every human being is the primordial component of individual identity. Its positive center, however, is belief in one's uniqueness together with the uniqueness of every human being. Analogously, the dignity of the human species lies in its uniqueness in a world of species. I am what no one else is, while not existentially superior to anyone else; we human beings belong to a species that is what no other species is; it is the highest species on earth—so far. In a further step, we want to be able to say that the uniqueness in each case is commendable, not because any uniqueness whatever is commendable but because human individual and species uniqueness derives from capacities, from traits and attributes that are unique and commendable. All other species are more alike than humanity is like any of them; a chimpanzee is more like an earthworm than a human being, despite the close biological relation of chimpanzees to human beings. The small genetic difference between humanity and its closest relatives is actually a difference in capacity and potentiality that is indefinitely large, which actually means that it can *never* be fully measured. Only the human species is, in the most important existential respects, a break with nature and significantly not natural. It is unique among species in not being only natural. Of course, if the species breaks with nature, so must every individual member of it.

Does dignity really depend on uniqueness, on unique identity? In one sense of dignity, the answer is no. I mean that any creature or person or thing can strike an observer as having the dignity of being itself, worthy of perception, and able to arouse wonder at its mere existence. The concept of uniqueness does not have to be in play for us to feel this wonder at the suddenly vivid appearance of a particular thing, creature, or human being that is seen or found by the way; we know that species exist, but the particular is suddenly magnificent in momentary isolation and sufficiency. The creature or thing or person may be so little known to us that we do not have enough knowledge of it or him or her to make any claim of uniqueness. Or the concept of uniqueness can be in play as the momentary feeling that what is before us is the only one of its kind, when of course it isn't; its presence before us impels the feeling that nothing else is like it. Appearances and impressions count for everything. We observe as from a distance; the frame of mind is aesthetic.

But when we speak of human dignity as the status of the individual or the stature of the human species, we are reaching for another sense of dignity, the dignity of what is uniquely human in its identity. Human identity rests on unique traits and attributes, which make human beings capable of commendable works and ways of being, but also of wrongdoing of every kind and in every degree. If there were only or mostly wrongdoing, it would be nonsense to speak of human dignity. The existential values would be worthless without realized moral capacities. But there is more than wrongdoing. All (or almost all) and only (truly only) human beings have these commendable traits and attributes. (I will later discuss these traits and attributes at some length.) If we want people to be treated with the proper recognition and respect by means of a system of human rights, we must work to encourage the perception that each person's common human traits and attributes, in their individualized presence, make that person uniquely precious; and if we want the human species to serve as steward of nature, we are asking for people to direct, more than they have ever done, their uniquely human traits and attributes to activities that make up the great project of stewardship, which no other species could possibly conceive or perform.

We begin thinking about the human dignity of individuals, their equal status, when we impute to every person this thought: I have a life to live; it is my life and no one else's; it is my only life, let me live it. I exist and no one can take my place; I exist and though I do not owe my existence to fate or other superhuman necessity, I am not nothing. My birth may have been planned, but I was not intended as the specific person I eventually became. In some moods, I fantasize that everything that has so far happened in the world was needed to bring about my particular existence, and that my existence is therefore a necessary outcome of innumerable interlocking causal chains, although I know that the same could be said of all other persons and creatures. Anyway, I am not nothing, even if or even though I go to nothing at the end. I am not nothing, even if in my life I amount to nothing out of the ordinary.

There are people who are so disabled that they cannot function. Does the idea of dignity apply to them? Yes, they remain human beings in the most important respect. If they cannot actively exercise many or any of their rights they nevertheless retain a right to life, whatever their incapacities (short of the most extreme failures of functioning). They must be treated as human beings, not as subhuman or as animals or lumps of matter. Clearly, however, the idea I explore puts functioning human beings at the center. Nor do I wish to deny that the obvious differences between adults and children (potential adults) remain crucial.

Attacks on the Status of Individuals

Lodged in the idea of human dignity is the belief that the individual's status can sometimes be attacked—injured and insulted—painlessly, without suffering. People can be manipulated, controlled, or conditioned softly and subtly, or even invisibly, and not feel that they have been degraded or even wronged, that they have been existentially harmed. They may even find pleasure or numerous benefits in their situation, and feel grateful to those who rule them paternalistically or in such a narrowly regimented way as to withhold from them the contrasts and range of experience needed to create awareness of their dignity. It would take an outsider or an alienated subject to find their horizon arbitrarily closed in. To use a discredited term, people may live in false consciousness, and do so comfortably. One of the advantages of the idea of human dignity for the theory of human rights is to raise the possibility of painless oppression, whether in ostensibly rights-respecting societies or in successfully disciplined societies where the very idea of human dignity and the rights that flow from it are lacking.

The problem of painless oppression and the attendant problem of false consciousness, however, do not provide the most significant issue where the idea of human dignity does indispensable work. The greater the suffering that a society may inflict on people within or outside its domestic jurisdiction, the more urgent the question of human dignity becomes. But the suffering that a system may inflict on people in denial of their rights is not the whole story. The damage done to morality is crucial, but not an exhaustive account of the oppression. Beyond oppression, there are systems of suffering that are so extreme as to efface the personhood of individuals and leave only biological entities that do anything to survive, at whatever cost to those around them and to their own dignity. Degraded human beings therefore lose their identity as human beings and as particular persons, at least for a significant stretch of time. They have been forced to lose almost all uniquely human and personal characteristics. Thus through no fault of their own, they no longer manifest the reasons for which incomparable dignity is ascribed to human beings. Except in rare cases, they can no longer exercise free agency or moral agency. The assault on dignity has achieved its aim when the very possibility of the idea of human dignity is forced out of the mind of the victim by extreme suffering. One has been made to forget that one is a human being because those who do evil as a policy have already denied that those to whom they do it are human. This extreme will to deny the humanity of targeted groups grows out of ideologies and elaborated fantasies that congeal in revulsion and bottomless contempt for the afflicted groups and results in their degradation. The original denial of their humanity seems vindicated in a grotesque parody of proof. The effects of the atrocious policies reinforce the extremism of will. Crimes against humanity are the most serious crimes against human dignity as well as the most serious crimes against the morality embedded in human rights.

Deliberately effacing the person takes place in extreme situations like war, many prisons and forms of captivity, torture, slavery, concentration camps, induced or neglected famine, and death camps. But we should not speak as if at any time degraded human beings are no longer human; to do so would justify the treatment inflicted on them. They are human beings in ruins. Even if some captives are freed, their recovery of status may be only nominal, but it is something like resurrection to recover it more than nominally. Great suffering imposed by human decision, not by natural calamity, can thus impose the aggravated harm of the attempted destruction of existential status.

Yes, natural calamity may be so dire as to make human beings forget themselves in their efforts to save themselves at whatever cost to others, and prior or subsequent human neglect may worsen the effects of natural calamity, but nature has nothing in mind when it starts a catastrophic process. In contrast, the evil treatment of people—say, a totalitarian system of extermination—deliberately imposes on them the worst existential loss. The evil of inhuman suffering is a conceptually separate consideration from the inevitable existential loss that is sustained by most people when they are dehumanized, even if for only a while, by their suffering. The human loss has more than one dimension.

I am not saying that the idea of human dignity represents indifference to suffering. Rather it serves as a reminder that the harm sustained by a human being subjected to inhuman treatment is more than the experience of pain. In most cases (but not all, as we shall see), the existential perspective is not in competition with moral judgment. My complaint is that the existential loss, the loss of human dignity through extreme suffering, is not always taken into account. It is heartless but necessary to say that since the existential loss often ceases to register on the victim after the ordeal has gone on for a while, it is up to the observer to insist on it, precisely to highlight the compound nature of the experience of evil treatment, the total abrogation of human rights.

Moral and Existential Components in the Theory of Rights Compared

I propose the tentative thought that from a moral point of view human rights are instrumental in their value, while their value from an existential point of view is not instrumental. The fundamental moral advantage of rights is that they are supposed to reduce suffering by guarding against state oppression and wrongdoing. In contrast, the existential advantage is that the state's respect for rights shows that the authoritative source of laws and policies in society is constrained by its recognition of every person's identity as a human being equal in status to all others and as a unique self. For all its good effects on the psychology of a person, such recognition is not instrumentally valuable, because one's identity precedes any purpose one has. To be sure, a person finds that guaranteed rights create an atmosphere of freedom in which opportunities for action multiply. But I think that it is somewhat misleading to regard an atmosphere of freedom as only or primarily instrumental; it makes a new world. In exercising a right, one shows that one is aware of being free and also demonstrates what being free means. One exemplifies one's status as free and equal. I won't insist, however, on a sharp contrast between the instrumental and noninstrumental value of human rights, as if to say that what is noninstrumental must always rank higher.

The hope, perhaps futile, is that the question should not arise as to the comparative importance of moral and existential components in the theory of individual human rights. At first sight, we can say that both are necessary, and neither is sufficient. A second look indicates, however, that since there can be painless degradation where no right but life is respected (discussed again later), the existential component is occasionally necessary and sufficient to condemn such an infantilizing system where rights are comfortably absent because they are thought unnecessary. The moral element has failed to cooperate with the existential element in upholding human rights.

There is one last stumbling block. Does morality actually require a prior existential element? I mean that a committed champion of animals could ask why the prevention or reduction of human suffering counts as an absolute moral purpose, while animal suffering is at best, and rarely that, a minor consideration. One way of dealing with this question is to say that individual members of the human species matter existentially more than members of all other species; human beings have an incomparably higher dignity. They matter more because of what they are: members of the human species, with the unique and incomparable traits and attributes of the species. In being partly and commendably nonnatural, a human being has an incomparably higher status than any animal. If human beings matter more, their suffering matters more.

I know that what I have just said is not a strict entailment; it may even be a mistake. But I just do not see that animals are existentially equal to human beings when they are not existentially similar to human beings. The infliction of needless suffering on any person is wrong not only for the pain that it causes but also for the failure to recognize a shared humanity that it demonstrates. What makes the precept that no person should suffer needlessly into a *moral* precept of the highest order is thus a prior existential consideration: persons are to be treated in some ways and not in others. To cause them needless suffering is to treat them in a way that denies them their dignity. It would therefore seem that only the idea of human dignity can be the starting point for the claim that human suffering matters more than animal suffering, even though the needless suffering of any animal that is not immediately threatening is always deplorable. (It is also right but regrettable to have to kill a lion to save a human being.) The alternative way of defending the priority of human suffering is simply to plead species-solidarity: us against them. This is a neat solution but a bad one because it comes down to the adage that might makes right, which is not a moral principle. It is instead a debased existential idea: since human beings are usually able to overpower other species they are permitted to make them suffer for any purpose human beings have.

Let me ask again: should we judge the comparative importance of moral and existential elements in the theory of rights? Is this theory only a branch of moral philosophy and not of existential philosophy as well? Later, we will take up more fully the subject of existential values in the theory of rights; so I will delay addressing this question (to the extent that I am able to discuss it) until then. But I will say that, in my judgment, the highest value is morality and always deserves at least prima facie precedence in our practice in the present and future, whatever we may think about the more remote past, that assessment does not establish, by itself, that whenever there is a moral consideration involved morality is a sufficient guide for thinking about the issue.

Secular Affirmation of the Dignity of the Human Species

It has been said that the earth would be better off without human beings living on it. I think that after a set of steps, we can reject that contention and affirm the unique contribution that humanity can make to nature. The stewardship of nature is a contribution that only humanity can make, and would exemplify human stature most gloriously. From nature's point of view, even though nature has no point of view, the human species is irreplaceable because its stewardship depends on commendably unique traits and attributes that help to make human beings partly not natural. Before humanity perished we could not pass on to any other species, not even our closest relatives, our knowledge and appreciation of nature. Only the partly not natural can serve nature in certain ways that it deserves and cannot provide for itself.

This essay will thus concentrate on the place of the idea of human dignity, in the form of equal individual status, in the theory of human rights; and on the dignity of the human species, in the form of human stature, which is based on unique nonnatural capacities. But in the affirmation of the dignity of the species, the record of human atrocities will not be forgotten; nor will the affirmation be turned into a counsel of forgiveness. Furthermore, the standing of the human species vis-à-vis other species is not the only form of stature that counts; nor is the stewardship of nature the only active expression of stature. Stature is also tied to the repeated demonstration that humanity has made, at any given time, if not the most of itself (who can say what the most is?) then something astonishing and unexpected; that its achievements are great and have shown that at any given time there could be no foreseeable end to the realization of unsuspected human potentialities. Human stature is essentially an existential, not a moral, value.

My essay is a secular attempt to discuss human dignity. I do not rely on traditional answers that any religion gives to the question of humanity's rank. A common Christian answer is that humanity finds its place in a scale of entities with divinity at the top, angels below the divinity, and humanity "a little lower than the angels" (Psalms 8:5), with all animals beneath humanity and intended to serve it. But we are not in the eye of any divinity. I do not assume that there is a religious answer to the question of the worth of humanity. It would be flattering to think, for example, that only human beings are in the image or likeness of the divinity and that therefore we have the dignity of kinship with some entity immeasurably greater than us but nevertheless not utterly removed from us in its nature, not "wholly other." If we could first believe in the more-than-human entity of monotheism, there would then be no problem about the nature of and reason for imputing dignity to every individual and to the species. Who could deny it? Then, too, Greek myths include stories in which the gods feel lust for human beings (whom the gods did not create out of nothing) and sometimes mate with them. There is literal if selective kinship. Christianity teaches that being human is a good enough (though temporary) condition for God. But we should try to do without such props; they can always give way to enlightenment. Furthermore, given the extent of suffering in human history, much of it owing to human wickedness, God the creator has endured a perpetual legitimation crisis all through the history of theological reflection. Secularism relieves us of his burden.

I am aware that a case can be made for perceiving much of Western religion as existing not to make truth-claims about more-than-human reality, but by artful means to promote human dignity in the only ways that could establish a foothold and that then perhaps could eventually be discarded as a theological husk. I mean that Greek and Roman polytheism, Jewish theism, and Christian theism invent deities to provide a standard that is supposedly not humanly devised and yet pretends show that humanity—in its god-like resemblances or creative achievements or even in its capacity for wickedness—has a dignity, an importance, that humanity does not have to claim for itself. Who could doubt the centrality of humanity in the eyes of the deities when one reads Homer and Sophocles, the Jewish scriptures, and the Christian Testament? We must learn to manage without the literalness of such assistance, if we can. But suppose human beings can respect one another only as creatures of a god or as mortal (though rather feeble) copies of the gods and grow to hate one another as shriveled worthless beings against the assumed background of a godless world? Imagine having to lie to people to persuade them of the truth of their dignity.

It would also be comforting to posit the existence of the soul as an answer to the question of the identity of every individual. In one version, the soul of any individual has existed immaterially, without a body, from the beginning; it has a necessary existence because of God's purpose; it bears an identity known fully only to its maker. Incarnation is the soul's prison; the soul, one's identity, needs no body. In some accounts, any soul could conceivably have been given any human or animal corporeality (or more than one) and retained the same identity, the same essence; it is, if not eternal, then immortal. However, as long as we have no continuity of consciousness between incarnations, no recollection of earlier embodiments, the idea is a nonstarter. I may as well be only one self-aware person as be many persons and animals, linked who knows how—charming as that thought perhaps is, and fertile in suggesting human kinship with all nature because humanity, like everything else, came from matter, or suggesting the inclusion within every individual of traces of many animal species. (Chromosomal similarities are irrelevant to the doctrine of reincarnation, which is not a metaphorical anticipation of molecular biology.) Some who believe in the soul think that one could have been born at some other time or place and somehow still be the person one is now; one's existence is not merely the outcome of a chance coming together of progenitors at one time in one place. Perhaps the oddest notion is Christian: the resurrection of the dead body into immortality and the reawakening of the immortal (not eternal) soul on Judgment Day. The secular theory of dignity does without such unwarrantable claims about the soul and should content itself with the concept of mind, a uniquely human possession, which is not dissociable from the body, is not immortal, much less eternal, but, rather, infinite, despite its meager life-span.

Nor do I posit a nonhuman or more-than-human audience for speculation about the standing and worth of humanity. If we accept religious teaching, these problems receive solutions, diverse as they must be. One problem is surely solved: the posited divinity is the measure of all things. But humanity must perforce be the measure: it introduces measure into the universe. Humanity must be the judge in its own case, with all the strains and perplexities such a condition engenders. It is also the only audience or interlocutor for the discussion. There is no arbiter or sponsor. Humanity talks to itself about itself, it judges itself, it invents the questions and answers, it alone worries about human dignity. There is no appeal beyond itself. But the discussion must go on because there are certain questions that must be answered, and can only be answered by reference to the idea of human dignity. Or we can say more modestly that the idea of human dignity supplies the least unbelievable answers.

We will return to these questions later. But let us now develop some thoughts about the place of the existential element in the theory of human rights and its relation to the moral element.

2

Individual Status and Human Rights

⚭

My assumption is that the major human rights are found most purely and economically stated not in recent charters but in the US Constitution, where the phrase *human dignity* does not appear and neither does the phrase *human rights* (or *natural rights*). Yet we now can see regard for human dignity in some provisions found in the original seven articles; the first ten amendments (the Bill of Rights) that guarantee freedom of speech and press, freedom of religion, and the freedom of association, together with due process of law, and the definition of the US government as based on rights and hence on limitation of state power (Ninth and Tenth Amendments); the Civil War amendments that abolished slavery, guaranteed the equal protection of persons and their right to due process, and enfranchised all races (Thirteenth, Fourteenth, and Fifteenth Amendments); and the amendment that enfranchised women (Nineteenth). When government recognizes and adheres to these rights, they make up the fundamental protections of human beings from the tyranny of one or a few and from systemic despotism. The separation of political powers and the independence of the judiciary reinforce the rights. Protection against tyranny and despotism is what all persons are owed.

We should also notice that the US Constitution teaches that state establishment of any religion, race, or ethnicity delegitimates a government prima facie because such establishment defines government's highest mission not as the recognition and respect for equal individual rights but as the proclamation of exclusivity and superiority of a particular group identity. The state consolidates its illegitimacy when establishment is not merely nominal and the state actively promotes one group identity at the expense of or by the subordination of others.

I have no wish to deny the continuing theoretical interest and fertility of the French Declaration of the Rights of Man and the Citizen, in both versions of 1789 and 1793. Nor do I wish to tarnish the importance of the Universal Declaration of Human Rights (1948) or of the European Convention on Human Rights (1950). It is good that the right of privacy and a number of welfare rights are explicit in both these later documents; but the shortcomings in comparison to the US Bill of Rights are substantial. The most general deficiency in both documents, especially the European Convention, is that they are rather statist *(étatiste)*: they enshrine the state's authority to abridge rights in the name of morality, order, welfare, and unspecified national purposes. These exceptions seem to leave rights vulnerable to any opportune occasion that presents itself to an impatient or cynical government. Rights lose the nature of rights when subject to so easy a rationalization of necessity. Yes, rights under the US Constitution have suffered abridgement, but the burden has always been on the government to defend the proposed abridgements, and the burden has not always been met. As big an advantage as any to starting with the US Bill of Rights (and relevant statements in the original Constitution) is the immense accumulation of jurisprudence and commentary (in clear continuity some of the time with English statutes and common law) that explores the meaning of rights in various and often novel circumstances—not to say of course that judicial reasoning can always be counted on to enhance rights and not shrink them or validate their political shrinkage.

Rights Are Absolute

Inherent in human rights is a commitment to the equality of all human beings. They count equally in the sense that the state must grant "equal concern to all," in Ronald Dworkin's term in *Freedom's Law*. They are not guaranteed substantive equality of wealth or of satisfaction, neither of which could be the purpose of a constitutional government. But each one must be treated as if he or she mattered equally; the state is not to overlook or disregard any person, or treat a person as a second-class citizen or practice discrimination against any group by law. No one's rights are of lesser importance than anyone else's.

Two kinds of equality are involved when the state recognizes and respects human rights. First, there is moral equality, and second, there is the equal status of every individual. Moral equality and existential equality usually mean the same thing in practice: the state is not to abridge or deny the rights of any individual. But the same treatment serves two kinds of equality: the principle of moral equality is served when no person is made to suffer or endure morally cognizable pain by abridgement or denial of his or her rights, and the principle of existential equality (equal individual status) is served when the state does not damage anyone's human dignity, anyone's identity as an equal human being. The two kinds of equality converge on the fundamental conviction that the rights of every person are absolute, or have the presumption of absoluteness, because every person is of absolute value. Every person's absolute value is not merely presumptive: the rebuttal to absoluteness is not to be expected, but must come as a shock, and it must not rest on a pragmatic—that is, a shortsightedly shrewd—balancing.

Absoluteness of protected rights registers what a human being is worth and how he or she deserves to be esteemed. When we speak in this way, the inference is likely to be that the status or existential component in the theory of human rights is what sustains the claim that human rights are absolute. The moral component can sometimes be better accommodated when rights are compromised: that is, suffering can be more effectively handled in the short term if the state abridges one right or another and thus treats all citizens or some of them as mere means to an undeniably good end. In contrast, the existential component requires that we discountenance this calculation. Though rights can be seen as instrumental, they are still absolute. They should not be abridged because persons should never be seen as instrumental.

Naturally the story of rights in the United States and in any comparable society is marked by their recurrent betrayal, while the interpretation of what any particular right means and what it entails for practice can engender dispute and even genuine perplexity. But let us consider these rights as ideals that are always in need of attention and often repair; and that other rights may be offered for consideration in due time, in one society or another.

When we say that rights are absolute, we mean that every individual is entitled to hold rights that are not subject to routine compromises or abridgements in the mode of cost-benefit analysis. Justice Brennan, John Rawls, and Thomas Nagel have all spoken of the "inviolability" of the person. I construe that concept to say that anyone's rights are incommensurably valuable because each person is incommensurably valuable: not to be sacrificed to others or thought interchangeable or replaceable, or part of a majority or minority that should be allowed to gain some advantage at the expense of the inviolability of others. To be sure, two rights of the same person may conflict or appear to conflict: a common example is the clash between security and liberty. Or, a particular right of one person may clash with a different right of others. I think, however, that these two kinds of conflict occur less often than advocates of state interests would have us believe or that melodramatic imagination would prefer. Tendentious interpretation makes rights conflict. We should always be especially suspicious when officials or media experts tell us that abridgements of the rights of one person, a group of persons, or all people, for the sake of security (the right of life) is called for. Nothing is more elastic than national security or gives a better cover to reason of state; nothing is more real than an abridgement of the rights of particular individuals and designated groups. Of course, the right of life is the precondition for all other rights, even if preservation of one's life may not be one's highest value; but rather regularly the judiciary has erred on the side of caution against liberty. But the right of life can swallow all other rights. Concern for security nearly always exaggerates and often lies. Rights do not characteristically interfere with one another.

What of abridgement of rights in time of war or other emergency? I think we don't need a close look to see that many abridgements actually served no purpose beyond gratifying the paranoia, excitement, vengefulness, or other inflated passions that erupt in war, or that were, in the name of being serious about the war effort, stage-managed by the state for dramatic effect. At the least, abridgements are quite in excess of any need. War gives an opportunity for its agents to experiment on their prisoners as well as on their own civilian population, play with their technology of domination, exercise their cleverness, and test their martial prowess. The initiation of war depends on fantasy, which is not given to respecting limits. When there was real need, as, say, in the years of the American Civil War, even then there was surplus abridgement; it is always to be expected.

The general lesson is that the center of the defense of human rights is the will to protect individuals. Both the moral and the existential components look to this purpose. The superior component in supporting the absoluteness of rights is existential because, as I have said, it sometimes seems that the moral component, the concern with suffering, could be facilitated by abridging or denying rights, and thus making them subject to frequent instrumental *calculations*, not merely to an overall instrumental moral perspective. But if rights are absolute, such calculations are not allowable, even when morality appears to demand them. Actually, the right of property includes the duty of assistance to others in dire need.

Furthermore, the will to protect individuals does not go well with a defense of human rights that looks to the general benefits to society of upholding a system of rights. In order to cajole his readers to support individual freedom of speech, press, and conduct, Mill in *On Liberty* offers arguments for the usefulness to society of these freedoms by appealing to the values of truth and progress, which he assumes will be attractive to people otherwise disposed to be intolerant. To be sure, these instrumental arguments may tend to be right, but then again they may be rebutted on the grounds that greater restrictions on freedom could lead to more truth or progress. Every instrumental defense of rights is vulnerable to circumstantial rebuttal. Look at the great achievements of past societies that did not recognize and respect rights, but nonetheless produced much beauty, some truth, and some sort of progress. I am willing to accept an instrumental component in the defense of absolute rights when we consider the moral end of reducing suffering at the hands of the state. But I think that other instrumental defenses of rights in the name of positive benefits to society are to be discouraged when we agree that the purpose of human rights is the protection of individuals. Of course, we are not thereby excluded from noticing the effects in society at large of a system of rights.

The Moral Component in the Defense of Rights

There are two components, then, in the defense of human rights: the moral and the existential. It is obvious that I think that the moral component is necessary but insufficient. But I would like to see how much work the moral component does on its own, because for many people, the defense of human rights is exclusively moral, and the moral defense is at the same time the defense of morality as such, with perhaps some minor adjustments forced on morality by the nature of political life. I accept the belief that the heart of morality is concern for human suffering. But I cannot accept the inference that such concern, when worked out, can provide by itself a sufficient defense of human rights; that morality could not possibly need assistance to defend rights. It is said that when moral agents hold office in government, their moral burden is an enlargement of everybody's daily burden: in their decisions and the measures of execution, officials must try to avoid inflicting pain or suffering as much as possible, to prevent others from inflicting it where possible, and to remedy it where possible, or at least to mitigate it. When the state respects human rights, supposedly the *only* thing that matters is that the state is, by and large, acting by positive policies or by avoidance and restraint to reduce human suffering, whatever else the state may imaginatively do for the good. In disagreement with a solely moral theory of human rights, I will explore it in the hope of uncovering problems caused by the omission of the existential component, and some other problems as well.

Now, a state's recognition of and respect for rights is called constitutionalism, which is both a set of limitations on political power and a set of imperatives to guide state action and abstention from action. Rights are essential to political legitimacy. Without constitutionalism, no state has a title to govern; it is based on force or docility or both. How an unconstitutional state acts or restrains itself may sometimes coincide with constitutionalism, but such coincidence is selective, if not random, and not to be depended on. Even the good deeds and procedures of an illegitimate state seem capricious and are largely undependable.

Where there is no constitutionalism, there is likely to be either personal tyranny or systemic despotism with or without the tyranny of one or a few. These states are principal sources of human suffering all through history; the suffering is intrinsic to them. The suffering they inflict is intentional or unscrupulously indifferent or by the way. Of course legitimate governments make people suffer for no good reason and impair their own legitimacy by such policies. A government that claims to be legitimate because it respects rights may nevertheless recognize the rights of only some groups and behave despotically toward other groups; a legitimate government may also impose despotism on people outside its borders through colonization and aggressive war. In both types of selective anticonstitutionalism, I would say that the originally legitimate (even if imperfectly legitimate) government has lost its legitimacy altogether: imperfect legitimacy has turned into forfeiture of legitimacy. Supposedly constitutional governments deny that they are imposing tyranny or despotism when in fact they are, and thus show a peculiarly vicious moral blindness.

What happens to the citizen's duty to obey when legitimacy is forfeited or severely compromised by an ostensibly constitutional government's terrible policies and practices? In the sphere in which the government systematically acts anticonstitutionally—as in upholding a practice like slavery, legal segregation or discrimination, or in conducting an aggressive and atrocious war—allegiance disappears, prudent obedience replaces duty in regard to the laws in other spheres of life, and nonviolent disobedience and resistance become morally right. Some of the time at least, constitutional governments allow for their own correction. Indeed, the procedures and processes of legitimate government, which incorporate the recognition and practices of human rights, are methods of correction of state action as much as they are devices for innovation; innovation itself is often abusive or morally reckless. In any event, constitutionalism, despite its all-too-frequent violation of rights, does in actuality tend to prevent, reduce, or eliminate a good portion of human suffering, thanks to its adherence to rights.

Tyrannical and despotic rule causes many kinds of suffering. People can get used to it and are helped in their adjustment by tradition, inhibition, conditioning, or inculcation. They may not know how much they had been putting up with until they are released, if they are released. But let us look at the situation as if people felt the whole force of their mistreatment. Immorally inflicted suffering may be felt because of some or all of the following features. These kinds of domination often lack the rule of law—they have only a corrupt or arbitrary system of criminal law that dispenses with due process and substitutes for justice the pleasure of the rulers and their agents; they may create a thoroughgoing system of surveillance and induce people to spy on one another; they suppress free speech and press and might allow only official utterance in public; they might police as much private communication as possible; they might persecute one religion or all religions; they might restrict education; they might restrict travel; they will exploit some or most people or steal from them; they will rule by lies; they might make base chauvinist appeals to their people; they might wage wars for the sake of social solidarity; they might carry out massacres or, at the totalitarian extreme, will commit mass murder of certain groups; and they will engage in the casual expenditure of lives of subjects and foreigners, supporters and enemies alike. There are degrees of completeness and intensity in various tyrannical and despotic systems. The denial of rights aspires to be as nearly total as the apparatus of tight control requires, while the apparatus manufactures its own necessities and the necessities expand to use the capacities; the development of capacities produces its own momentum. To be sure, some of these methods will be found in societies that ostensibly recognize and respect human rights, but in tyrannies and despotisms the whole system is a concerted and deliberate denial of rights.

The whole society becomes "carceral," in Michel Foucault's useful term but not in his exact sense. Under this control, people endure constant apprehension and some of them experience the actual pain of harsh penal treatment and other disadvantages and penalties. People are thwarted in their most natural inclinations and desires. One must constantly watch one's step. Life is abundantly supplied with superfluous negation, restraint, and limitation. Lives are not only circumscribed by apprehension but permeated by it. Matters are made worse in some cases by regimented frenzy and hollow enthusiasm.

The Need for an Existential Component in the Defense of Rights

Is it then, a sufficient defense of human rights to show that the tyrannical and despotic denial of human rights causes so much needless pain and suffering that any such system is condemnable as grossly immoral? Isn't it enough to show that these systems are guilty of denying most people equal moral consideration in order to give a few others disproportionate and hence immorally excessive consideration? What is added by saying this denial also grossly offends human dignity? If our wish is to condemn the systematic denial of human rights not only as grossly immoral but also as grossly injurious to the equal status of every human being, we are dealing after all with the behaviorally same political phenomenon. What is the point of giving it two conceptually different descriptions or interpretations, one of them moral and the other existential, especially when the moral perspective seems adequate? The answer is that we should want to highlight two issues: the attitudes toward human beings that the infliction of suffering by means of the denial of rights manifests, and the diminishment or deformation people undergo when they endure harsh and needless suffering at the hands of those who have superior power and manage, at least for a time, to keep the people either acquiescent or intimidated or both. The same political phenomenon, tyranny or despotism, has a double meaning.

Look not only at the suffering but also at the human diminishment. Behind the diminishment lie tyrannical or despotic attitudes. Contempt for human beings is intrinsic to the mentality of officials who rule rights-denying states. (Not to deny that some officials in an ostensibly rights-respecting state—especially but not exclusively in executive and administrative agencies and bureaucracies—show contempt episodically or selectively.) But more than contempt, bad as that is, is being expressed when rights are denied. We can say that the pain of suffering is the most important fact, more important than any existential loss induced by suffering. But we still should pay attention to that existential loss.

For those who are denied their rights as well as for those in power who are the cause of this denial, the existential loss, the assault on human dignity can be charged with significance. The victims feel assaulted, while the rulers are delighted by their power to assault. People do not have to be told that they are in pain; severe pain blots out everything else in the world. But the pains inflicted by tyranny and despotism—arbitrariness and repression, neglect of poverty and deliberate deprivation, frustration and suffocation, constant apprehension and menace—may register themselves on human consciousness with a heightened meaning and therefore with a heightened intensity when there is the sense, if only incipient, that these pains are undeserved and unbefitting. The reason is not so much that the victims are innocent and that they are being treated unfairly as that they have a dignity just by being human that has been violated. Human beings should not be treated in this way; they should not be treated as if they are not human beings but something other or lesser.

In unconstitutional systems, rulers and their agents are moved to deny people their rights by contempt, yes; by sadism, yes; but also by a determined refusal to look on their population (or populations beyond their borders) as equally human to themselves. Actually, it is often the case that the worst denials of and assaults on human rights are impelled by an ideological commitment to the view that the subject populations are existentially inferior by nature or in their nature. We can add that when apologists for the established order do not claim, as they sometimes do, that the injustice and oppression they cause is actually justice or a higher justice, they rationalize their domination instead by religion or science, tradition or fate, all of which are purportedly higher in importance in the scale of values than morality, while equal human dignity is untrue or unreal. These subject populations are treated as means or impediments to purposes that are not their own, not as people with ends of their own. The tendency of illegitimate states is to regard people as if they did not have lives to live but existed on sufferance, only to serve, or to fill a function, or to languish in neglect or impotence, or to be cleared away.

When we study oligarchic or absolute governments, we notice recurrent particular habits and methods of illegitimate domination. Rulers treated their own populations as mere resources or weapons for making war, or as beasts of burden that were worked as slaves, serfs, and proletarian near-slaves to sustain society and its institutions, or as machines suitable only for fulfilling specified functions, or as children that could never grow up. People were narrowed into hands, or bodies, or dwarfed into single-purpose creatures. They were treated as means only. Or they were regarded as too incompetent to define their lives for themselves. Foreign populations were transformed into prey, or vermin, or slaves, or objects of experimentation. But there was only a difference of emphasis in the treatment accorded native populations and that accorded foreign ones; there was a migration of habits and methods from abroad to home and from home to abroad. From the ruler's perspective, all people, at home and abroad, were merely means or obstacles or impurities or orphans. (Of course among the unconstitutional rulers there were some who mitigated their power, if only out of prudence.) I have mentioned just some of the pathologies that infect all governments, but illegitimate governments with special virulence. And these pathologies work to deny the humanity of human beings—that is, their unique capacity to be agents with purposes. Among the keenest pleasures of power is to violate human dignity. Perhaps using power to keep people under tyrannical or despotic control is as important to the mentality of unconstitutional rulers as extracting from people their labor or service at whatever cost to them in pain and suffering. Mastery in itself is as important as exploitation and is known in other ways than by exploitation; by inducing pervasive fear or reflexive submission, for example. Love of power for its own sake is gratified best by violations of human dignity. This is not to deny that quite a few of those ruled often led pleasurable lives, provided they took nothing for granted, did what they were supposed to do, and kept quiet.

We see that rulers who have recognized no rights inflict pain and suffering in the course of converting people into something less than human, or something smaller or less distorted than they could be if their rights were respected. To the moral sense, it is the pain and the suffering that count and that therefore condemn rulers throughout time. Probably that is the first thing that should be noticed, even by a student of human dignity. But we should also think that it is often true that what came first, in time and in importance, were the denial of equal human dignity, of equal individual status, and the consequent reduction of human beings into the not-fully-human (or the never-to-be-adult). This reduction facilitated the infliction of pain and suffering. A predisposition to reduce or eliminate the human status has always existed in those who wield unconstitutional power. This diminishment—dehumanization at worst—is condemnable in itself, not only for the immorality, or the infliction of pain and suffering, that is yoked to it or ensues from it. The upshot is that for the most part, the moral and the existential (dignity) components of the defense of rights cooperate in the critique of anticonstitutional government, with each component doing indispensable work.

Now, there is one right whose denial matters not because of the suffering it causes but because it means death. (I here resume my discussion of Justice Brennan's concurrence in *Furman v. Georgia*.) If human rights are absolute and indefeasible, can the basis on which we affirm the right of life be anything but moral? We often say that killing is the most immoral deed. There is no harm in speaking in this way; indeed to be killed is to be dispossessed of what justly belongs to a person. But if immorality is the infliction of needless suffering, and death is the end of a person's suffering, isn't there a better way of condemning the taking of human life than calling it immoral? I think we have to say that taking life is not merely immoral but evil. The word *immoral* is not strong enough to encompass the wrong, except in the case of a fetus, a potential person, where *immoral* is an adequate word for taking its early life and the word *evil* is in my judgment excessive except near the end of pregnancy. I cannot bring myself to believe that ending a fetus's entire chance to live a human life is as bad or worse than killing a person: there is so much waste of life-matter in the conception of any person, let alone in the incalculable amount of nonprocreative sex. (I will say more about abortion later on.)

To end a person's existence prematurely does not matter because a person's future pleasures are foreclosed, as it is sometimes said; so are his or her pains. Of course, it does matter that, by imputation, every person has an intense desire, often unrationalized, to stay alive; we generally respect a person's desires when they do not harm others. But desire in itself is not an argument, when rightful life is in question, but rather when rightful freedom is in question. Needless premature death matters most because it means that a person's selfhood has not been allowed to realize itself more completely. That is one kind of evil, though of a different sort from the deliberate dehumanizing degradation before death that is inflicted in totalitarian camps and in state torture. The loss of a fuller selfhood through premature death, violent or not, is an incalculable existential loss. The value of a person's life is immeasurable and not commensurate with any other value. The reason for which we object to the state's infliction of needless premature death, whether in war, neglect of poverty, or capital punishment, might therefore be not so much moral as existential. In that respect, the right of life is unlike other rights, where considerations of pain and suffering are significantly implicated in the justification. But since protection of the right of life is the precondition for the exercise of all other rights, the indispensable role of the existential component in the defense of human rights becomes all the more established.

I realize, however, that there is something not quite right in trying to give reasons for why taking life is wrong; even moving killing from the category of immorality to that of evil does not end the unease one feels. A life is a life; there it is; if anything is sacred, a life is. The question: Of what value is a human life? is indecent. The question: Why do you want to stay alive? is a tyrant's question. It should not be asked; any answer will always be off the mark; the words will fill in poorly for the appropriate silence.

How Serious Is the Tension between the Moral and Existential Components in the Theory of Human Rights?

The relation between the moral component and the existential component in the defense of rights stops being cooperative and becomes tense when, as I have already noticed, people can be well treated in certain respects, and endure no suffering beyond what is incurably present in human life, and still be injured in their human dignity, in their equal human status. Aldous Huxley's futurist novel *Brave New World* (1932) is an ingenious account of a society in which the various classes are perfectly adapted to their lives by genetic manipulation and the system's all-competent conditioning. With few exceptions they are happy; they do not have longings to be other than they are; they have no imagination and hence no aspirations; they are free of self-doubt; and they have no need for conscience and no capacity for introspection. They have little use for free agency in general and moral agency in particular. But above all they are spared material misery and have more than adequate prosperity. Only a few rebel against their happiness in order to become more fully human, or as I would say, to insist on their human dignity, even at the cost of pain and suffering, with the chance of danger and various other painful risks. (Some people want to read the fall of Adam and Eve in this way.) To be sure, these costs are self-incurred, not initiated by abusive power. Huxley has imagined, under Plato's influence, a world in which there is a systematic denial of human rights and yet the immemorial pathologies of tyranny and despotism have been transmuted into a dreadful kindness. Tocqueville's analysis of democratic despotism in the second volume of *Democracy in America* (1840) dwells on the problem of state kindness, more overbearing than dreadful, and suggests that a democratic polity is likely to show actual evidence of the tendencies that Huxley's imagination showed at their extreme.

I do not believe that we could call Huxley's world immoral. The right of life is protected; servitude is made to feel like liberty; everyone has a properly rationed and allocated purpose in life; all wants are satisfied and no vague longings possess the spirit. The question of human dignity does not arise, except implicitly in a few subversives. To condemn this society, we would have to call it dehumanized, but in a sense different from that inflicted by acute sufferings. We would have to assert existential values. It is not that we disregard morality and prefer existential values to moral ones. Rather, in some circumstances, moral values have no place in the defense of rights, because suffering is not the issue; suffering is so little the issue that its absence accounts for the people's unawareness of the assault on their human dignity.

For the defense of rights, the idea of human dignity is indispensable in all circumstances, even if, as we shall see when we take up virtue ethics, a different idea of human dignity is used to qualify or abridge rights in the name of improving the character of human beings. Virtue-ethics must be challenged in the name of the idea of human dignity, which helps to support human rights. In any case, morality cannot condemn a general condition of happiness—or at least a painless existence—that comes at no morally cognizable physical or material cost to human beings. No one's pleasure causes anyone else any morally cognizable pain.

Thus the idea of human dignity is indispensable when we wish to condemn a society or some aspects of it and have no moral complaint against it. People remain unaware of their loss of individual status because they are content and so do not recognize the degradation in their condition, unless they are awakened by a few in their midst who are perhaps abetted by outsiders. I do not deny, however, that the idea of human dignity is also and more urgently needed when the denial of rights inflicts pain and suffering in the course of treating people as means for the purposes of a few, or when people are deliberately dehumanized by pain and suffering as the result of an atrocious master-scheme. The existential element in these cases of severe or even terrible suffering fills out the moral case, which would otherwise be incomplete.

Huxley's satire of utopia is an extreme case because its presents a picture of a whole society that combines happiness and degradation—a city of pigs, for the most part. But any society, whether technologically advanced or not, promotes by control, manipulation, and conditioning the degradation of unthinking and complacent happiness in various degrees among the contented classes. The situation cannot be completely otherwise. Immorality enters the picture when this contented degradation is accompanied by moral blindness—that is, inattention to the suffering of others or parasitical benefit from it. Every society is partly barbarous in its many cruelties. There is a two-way flow between (on the one hand) the barbarism involved in the moral harm inflicted in everyday life or by the state (in society's name) on selected groups at home or abroad and (on the other hand) the degradation involved in the self-inflicted injury to the dignity of those who acquiesce in the injury done to the dignity of others, as if nothing important was happening. The self-inflicted degradation is made yet worse when those who are contented assert their superior existential status and thereby make absolute their denial of the equal status of others.

Morality, Relativism, and Skepticism

I have so far spoken of morality as if it were a simple or uniform concept. Now I want to look at some of the complexities in morality that I have so far disregarded. Nothing in what I am about to say changes my contention that even though moral considerations figure with great importance in the defense of human rights, they do not sufficiently, by themselves, provide the basis for human rights, and the basis for the insistence that people are to be treated by the state in some ways only. Given the importance of moral considerations in the theory of rights, some elaboration of morality is called for. I think that one of the best and most sensible general discussions is in Schopenhauer's *On the Basis of Morality* (1841). He says that only "actions of voluntary justice, pure philanthropy, and genuine magnanimity" have genuine moral worth (1965, p. 130). He goes on to say that "compassion, as the sole nonegoistic motive, is the only genuinely moral one" (p. 167). Pain and suffering are the center of moral concern, and the efforts to prevent or reduce it preoccupy moral agents. Yes, the center of morality is remedy, where possible, for humanly caused suffering that seems needless and dispossesses human beings of what is theirs or that neglects to preserve them in it. But there are problems that need our attention.

Let me say first that I will not try to justify morality against relativists. I will only try to indicate why no justification is needed. Relativism is the view that what any group of people say (or otherwise indicate) morality is, then that is what morality is. (A rather evasive synonym for relativism is moral pluralism.) The plain meaning of relativism is that there is no such thing as morality; there are only different codes. The group is right if it thinks it is. There are no principles of morality that are universally accepted or nearly so, and there is no way of proving that one set of principles is correct and the other sets are mistaken.

However, I think that there is sufficient continuity throughout recorded history in what counts as fundamentally right or moral, despite differences in interpretation and application. The precept *To each his own* (preserve each in his own or give to each his own) appears nearly universally, and the precept *Do not treat others as you do not wish to be treated* appears commonly. These two precepts have kinship; perhaps the second is derived from the first. To be sure, each elicits important differences in interpretation and application. Different times and places stretch or narrow the meaning of the terms. There is such variety that it seems easier just to say that they are right if they think they are. But that is the wrong way out of moral dispute. There can be no other proof of the validity of a moral precept than the quite common and fairly steady acceptance of it by peoples all over the world, for as long as there has been moral reflection, if only its rudiments. No transcendental instruction is needed; it is not even a question of human discovery, but a sensitive awareness of the obvious that gradually accumulates adherence.

Nietzsche's genealogy is relevant for our discussion of relativism. The plain but ironic fact is that he actually undermines moral relativism just because he is trying to undermine morality. If he is an antirelativist, it wouldn't matter if anyone else is a relativist. He is so little a moral relativist that he offers a genealogy of morality as such. It is important to see that he does not challenge the assumption that morality is a universal concept, applying in its required duties and entitlements to all people equally, whatever their group. He knows that the defense of morality is an appeal to universal principle against the particular, against the mores of any particular society and the codes of conduct that are specific to different castes and classes, and even against religion when religion is not already universal. If a system that aims to guide conduct is not universal, it is not morality. Mores and codes belong to a genus different from morality. Morality guides conduct when the basic entitlements of all people are at issue, but otherwise is silent; mores and codes, though local, constitute a detailed and comprehensive guide to conduct in a society. Nietzsche therefore accepts the view that morality means one basic thing: all people, equally, should be spared as much preventable suffering as possible or helped in their need. He blames

Christianity for inventing universal morality—that is, for inventing and promoting the idea that a guide to conduct (of whatever scope) can be universal. (He ignores Stoicism.) Obviously, he is keenly interested in the great diversity of mores between classes and societies in order to single out those mores he admires for favoring his idea of life as amoral vitality or immoral exertion. I should add that the absence of moral relativism in Nietzsche's thinking is fully compatible with his defense of perspectivism in knowledge, which I will discuss in the next chapter.

His genealogy of morality is of course intended to discredit morality by tracing its original motives, located in early Christianity, not to brotherly love and fellow feeling but to resentment and envy toward rulers and the few. But he knows that it would be odd indeed if people did not resent and even hate those who oppressed them; what he finds remarkable is the force of those devices that transform hatred of oppressors into the self-blame of the oppressed. In any case, at a certain point, a doctrine—morality—emerged that spoke generally about suffering, not merely locally, but spoke acquiescently rather than rebelliously. Political rebellion in the name of universal morality would come much later. Morality's appeal must be to the universal because the particularity of mores and codes usually tends to favor the few against the many and the conquerors against the conquered. Or if these categories are too crude, let us say instead that a given system of mores often has more than one division between the few and the many; rather, there is a hierarchy in which there are quite a few gradations that give numerous people a chance to take advantage of and look down on classes or groups beneath them. The few at the top will of course take advantage of and look down on everyone. Thus, mores and codes often entrench immorality: Nietzsche is sure of that. Only the intelligently led underclasses need to appeal to a universal standard. And with time, all classes gradually see the point of it, no matter how much they resist it in practice.

On easier ground, Nietzsche's critical genealogy also attempts to show that all through the Christian centuries up to the present time, many of those who have struggled to propagate and defend Christianity in the name of its founder have used immoral methods of coercion and mendacity. Such methods of conversion to religious doctrine, not settled motives of acceptance of the morality enclosed in its doctrine, stamp the historical origins of Christianity with a profound and inveterate hypocrisy. (But why should Nietzsche the immoralist worry so much about purity of methods and wish to get his readers to worry? He could feel disgust at hypocrisy only if he himself is still committed to uncoercive and honest persuasion, and he is.)

The ever-present truth of Nietzsche's genealogy is that those who rank morality as the supreme value or who otherwise make too much of it may, to an appreciable degree, resent or envy any kind of superiority and encourage others to do so; they partake of the original motives of those people who spread or embraced universal morality. The worst of it is that sometimes their professed love of humanity is hatred of life. Morality then becomes compensation for slaves and the slavish. In the name of hierarchy and its promotion of the will to sustain an un-Christian life not sickened by moral scrupulousness and not driven by resentment toward life, Nietzsche, at his most zealous, in *The Anti-Christ,* endorses Manu's code of caste and its associated mores (sometimes sickening even to Nietzsche?). To be sure, Nietzsche tried to clear the concept of justice from the imputation of resentment and envy, but his effort to separate utterly the motives of morality from those of justice is not persuasive. What matters in any event is that Nietzsche, supposedly the great friend and even sponsor of moral relativism, knew that morality means universal and egalitarian precepts for the guidance of conduct, when conduct affects the vital interests of others; and hence that morality is not to be conflated with mores or codes, which are local, diverse, mutually incommensurable, and usually slanted toward the preservation of hierarchy.

But skepticism is different from relativism, and a response to skepticism about the nature of moral judgment could help advance my argument by illustrating the theme of uniquely human characteristics. Hume famously taught that we cannot derive a moral judgment from a description of the alleged source (theist, in the first place) of the moral command; as it is usually put, we cannot derive *ought* from *is* (*Treatise,* pp. 468–469). In what follows, I am more interested in the skepticism that Hume helped to start up again after the Greeks and Romans than in the details of his teaching. The logical positivists of the twentieth century were the last ones to push hard for the contention that *ought* cannot be derived from *is,* that facts cannot lead to correct moral judgment, only to subjective or arbitrary preference. So let us direct our criticism at the positivist view, while not forgetting Hume. In fact, we should remember that in his essay on judging works of art, "Of the Standard of Taste" (1757), Hume produces a complex argument, devoid of skepticism, that we can extend to any sort of evaluative judgment, including moral judgment.

Whatever its standing these days among academic moral philosophers, the positivist version of moral skepticism flourishes (if only as a reflex) in the world at large—perhaps among undergraduates more than anybody else. The positivist claim is that reason stops with descriptions and analysis of matters of fact, whereas moral response to matters of fact has nothing to do with reason but only with feelings of praise and blame that are aroused in the observer by matters of fact. In general, evaluation adds qualities to the facts that the facts themselves do not possess; they are imposed on facts by subjective response from the outside. Reason ascertains the facts and analyzes them. Feelings (Hume usually said sentiments) and reason are thus entirely separate; reason cannot cross the boundary that separates it from feelings, and all that feelings can do is to encroach irrationally on the integrity of facts. The skeptics are not saying that feelings distort evaluation of the facts; they are saying that evaluation as such distorts analysis of the facts.

What is true of scientific facts, however, is false about human relationships. Even if evaluative judgment is nothing but the expression of feelings, where's the damage? Such moral feelings as pity, compassion, sympathy, empathy, fellow feeling, and so on are required to make sense of the morally relevant facts. A lack of feeling in responding to certain facts would show not reason's presence but its absence; a kind of derangement or solipsism. Then, too, feelings are not merely bodily sensations but are entwined with thinking and imagination and would not exist without them.

Hume makes a radical suggestion. If it were obvious that God existed and he commanded us to act in certain ways and abstain from acting in other ways, the mere fact of his command would not entail a moral obligation to obey his word; there can be no normative "deduction" from a description of God's authority, no matter how certain beyond a reasonable doubt one is that he exists. However, if God turns out to be in reality as he is described by pious people in the West, and if he unmistakably presented himself, it would seem to me foolish not to feel an obligation or even a feeling stronger and more imperious than obligation. I do not refer to fear of his power to punish as the appropriate motive, but to the belief that he is of an inconceivably higher order of being than humanity and, what is more, created humanity and is the author of its existence. How could we not feel psychologically compelled, not only conscientiously obliged, to obey him and trust him to command us in what we should do? He would give us an unanswerable prescription for what we should do, no matter how much we would be disposed to question its moral correctness. Job was overwhelmed by God's rhetoric of majesty, and rightly so, not convinced of his own guilt or outargued and outreasoned. Then again, God ordered Abraham to sacrifice what was most precious to him, his son, Isaac, a human being. No *is* can sensibly be made to go to that *ought*; as Kierkegaard taught, some convulsion of the spirit—not amenable to analysis—is required to comply: a sudden and provoked willingness to perform the "teleological suspension of the ethical," as he put it nervously.

I am offering a secular account of human dignity and its relation to morality. I am trying to base human dignity on an interpretation of some facts—their traits and attributes—about human beings. In general, there is no *ought* without *is;* there is no way to *ought* except from *is;* no way to a moral judgment except from a view of facts. As long as there are human beings, there will be facts; and as long as there are facts (events, situations, long-lasting conditions and structures), there will be human interpretations and judgments of them, in the realm of morality or outside it. For human beings, evaluation is as inevitable as seeing colors, and as little to be wished away. Most human phenomena, and not only performances, are meant to be evaluated and would be senseless without evaluation. What is usually involved is not strict entailment but a persuasive and defensible inference that withstands other inferences that are less persuasive and defensible to those who take the trouble to think through the nature and meaning of the facts before them. There are bound to be doubts and perplexities in many cases, as we constantly see.

Reasoning about moral evaluations is not expressing a preference in regard to physical sensations like the taste of food; giving reasons for evaluation is not mere rationalization. The audience is made up of human beings exercising their considered judgment of human beings. Moral judgments must rest on an interpretation of facts or claimed facts. The facts are those that people cannot help responding to by interpretation; moral judgment takes place in one of the main sectors of life in which human powers of interpretation are exercised. Interpretation is stimulated by the daily occurrence of human conduct in the face of countless opportunities and predicaments. Social facts are not often allowed to go uninterpreted and unjudged. Imagine what it would mean if extermination of peoples, massacre, torture, slavery, induced poverty or famine, administered despotism, and corruption of the rule of law were to go unjudged, or criticized but with a feeling of embarrassed presumptuousness. Imagine what it would mean when these policies and activities are condemned, if masses of people thought that reason was being abandoned and mere subjectivity was replacing it, and the condemnation misrepresented the activity in question or denatured it.

No doubt, there is sometimes room for hesitation, because the facts are not entirely clear, or there seems to be more than one plausibly defensible side in a contest, or the phenomenon to be judged is too novel to be perceived without misleading preconceptions. For the time being, hard cases produce no right answers. (There are some hard cases that never do.) Hume's philosophical point about *is* and *ought* comes out of a very distorted conception of reason as a mere instrument to achieve a person's ends, which are mere preferences that can never be judged, and which from an external perspective have equal standing; scratching one's finger and letting the world be destroyed: it's all the same. It is an irrational conception of reason that does not even permit a person to understand that one's finger would not survive the destruction of the world. After Hume, the logical positivists are besotted by their extension of the model of scientific knowledge and method to areas of human life where it is out of place. There are, however, no tenable grounds for suspicion or disparagement of evaluation as such, whatever the merits of any given act of evaluation may be.

In his magnificent book *The Individual and the Cosmos in Renaissance Philosophy* (1926), Ernst Cassirer quotes Nicholas of Cusa to the effect that without the human intellect there would be no value in the world. There would be no evaluation. No apology is needed for the fact that there cannot be a world without evaluation in which there are human beings. Nicholas says, "When God wanted to give value to his work, he had to create, besides the other things, the intellectual nature" (1963, p. 44). That is a theological way of saying what can be said in an entirely secular manner. Human beings are such that they cannot live and make a world without a continuous flow of evaluations, moral and otherwise.

By now there is wide consensus in the world as to what morality is. It is when diverse mores, especially but not only religious ones, usurp the place of morality that irreconcilable disputes take place. These disputes obscure the moral consensus. Yes, it is also true that consensus can be found mistaken at any time. For example, for millennia the consensus was that slavery was unobjectionable. In a matter-of-fact way, and quite stupidly, people inflicted on others manifest pain and suffering that they would never have wanted inflicted on them. It suited them to be blind to what was most obvious. But there are moral precepts and certain interpretations of them that, once sent into the world, manage to last; they withstand critique, even though they often cannot withstand betrayal. They become self-evident in Jefferson's sense. Of course there will always be disagreements about what the facts are and how to construe them and act on them, but though the problems of morality are given to these kinds of indeterminacy, the indeterminacy is not on the deepest level. Not everything goes; not much skepticism and no relativism can pass muster, intellectually useful as these irritations are to moral seriousness.

The Differences between Personal and Public Morality

We must now distinguish between the morality that should be practiced among persons in everyday life and the morality that is present when the state recognizes and respects those rights that persons are owed and that the people have learned to claim. We have so far been talking primarily about morality as it is present when the state upholds rights. I think that true morality among persons in everyday life adheres to the golden rule, but the justice of constitutional rights is the morality required in the dealings of the state with the people. Adherence to the golden rule is unmediated by the state, though remedial state action can make the occasions of the golden rule less frequent, but can never eliminate them. The two kinds of morality—for short, personal (or private) and public—are not totally discontinuous, but their motivations and scope are substantially different. They have in common the most general maxim: *to each his own.* Its meaning is that no person should be made to suffer through being dispossessed of what he or she owns or is otherwise properly entitled to. This maxim entails that the first duty, a duty as high as any, is that human agents, whether private or public, must abstain from any action that improperly invades or seizes or destroys or damages or culpably neglects what belongs to a person. Not only material possessions belong to a person but also life, liberty, safety, and bodily integrity are in justice owed to all persons as a matter of right. There is thus a measure of commonality between the respect a person gives, thanks to self-restraint, to the moral rights of all other persons in everyday life and the respect for human rights that the state shows when it fully accepts constitutional limits on its conduct. The reason is that the first duty in private and public life is negative: avoidance of the wrongs of dispossession in its several kinds.

I realize that claims to an absolute right of property, of the sort associated with property libertarians, bedevil many discussions of human rights. In *The Rights of Man*, Thomas Paine distinguishes between those rights "in which the power to execute is as perfect in the individual as the right itself" and those rights where "the power to execute them is defective" and the "enjoyment of which [a person's] individual power is not, in all cases, sufficiently competent" (p. 68). "The rights of the mind" do not need the material support of the state to be realized, whereas "security and protection" require the support of the "civil power" (p. 69). It seems to me that we could extend Paine's conception to say that the right of property is different from other rights because its very existence depends on a network of detailed rules and conventions for its definition, maintenance, and promotion, and the ever-vigilant state for its protection, unlike rights of speech, press, and religion, which are unregulated because they are self-executing. The right of property is not self-executing and can therefore be subject to regulation, provided the very right of ownership is preserved. The Fifth Amendment of the US Constitution acknowledges that property is not quite the same kind of right as other rights when it states that private property shall not "be taken for public use without just compensation" (Fifth Amendment). That is to say, it can be taken, subject to the constraints of fairness. There is, however, no compensation for abridgement of the rights of mind, like free speech, press, and religion.

The right of ownership of an object cannot be derived exclusively, as in Locke's theory, from either inheritance or the labor one has expended on the production of that object. For one thing, many people are not independent farmers or artisans. The point is that no extreme and theoretically unacceptable claim to a completely unregulated and barely taxed right of property can be used to discredit the very idea of human rights, or, in particular, the right of ownership itself. Here nevertheless is a brief assertion: the right of life can be the basis to circumscribe the right of property, so as to help many stay alive and in conditions that are not miserable, and not die before their time from preventable causes. This assertion goes beyond Locke's acknowledgment of the duty of people with a surplus to use it to keep others from starvation. And because the right of property is not quite the same kind of right as other rights, taxing property for reasonable purposes, but especially for relief of the poor, is not a genuine case of conflict of rights. Paine in fact advocates a quite extensive transfer of wealth to the needy. In this case, the right of life is not swallowing other rights. People have rights that allow them to act unvirtuously, but do not allow them to harm others deeply by culpable neglect.

In any event, my main point here is that the golden rule (on the one hand) and the state's respect for rights (on the other hand) are different moral phenomena. I think that the golden rule, which incorporates and then supplements *to each his own,* is the best private morality and that the constitutionalism of rights is the best public morality.

The Best Personal Morality Is the Golden Rule

Let us look first at the golden rule and some of its assumptions and implications. In the Gospel of Luke, Jesus says: "And as ye would that men should do to you, do ye also to them likewise" (Authorized Version, Luke 7:31; see also Matthew 7:12). The whole sense of the golden rule goes against conditional reciprocity. We are supposed to treat others as we would be treated, not as they have treated us, if such treatment has been bad. The golden rule therefore repudiates the common assumption that we ought to treat others well only as long as they have treated us well, and treat them badly if that is how they have treated us, provided we can retaliate with impunity. By returning good treatment for bad, our act implies that the bad treatment never occurred, and so facilitates reconciliation. We act as if we had been treated well. Then again, if another person treats us morally in a situation that calls for it, we act in the spirit of the golden rule when we have a chance to reciprocate and we do so happily and in gratitude. If our benefactor never needs us, we act in the spirit of the golden rule if we treat others with whom we have no history of relationship in its spirit. The expectation of favorable reciprocation sullies the sprit of the golden rule, not that one desires to be treated badly. The phrase "as you would be treated" means as you think anyone should be treated, yourself included. The Good Samaritan did not expect reciprocation from the wounded person he helped; nor did he expect that his own good treatment of a stranger would inevitably be accorded him by another stranger.

The golden rule does not ask for heroic self-sacrifice or saintly forbearance. It asks, instead, that we be better, if only by a little, than the level we might see around us, despite all the risks of priggishness or self-righteousness, and better than we may have been in the past. To be better is to be prepared to run some risks and make some sacrifices (none of them heroic) in order to help others, even if we cannot count on them to help us in some future need. Subsumed under the golden rule is the primary will to avoid harming others as one wishes not to be harmed, but then the rule adds a positive duty to help others, even when there is some loss or risk to oneself. The motive of the golden rule can never be prudential or, in Tocqueville's phrase, self-interest rightly understood. I think it is fair to say that the unhindered ability to imagine oneself in the position of another person is a large part of the very foundation of the golden rule and even plays an imperfect role in one's moral life when one does not aspire to go out of one's way to be good but only to keep out of trouble.

The Good Samaritan exemplifies the golden rule. We know of the Good Samaritan from one act, which defines his whole moral personality. Is samaritanism, however, ordinarily only a one-act morality? That would be too easy. Samaritanism must be a disposition; still, it can be tested too often. The Samaritan does not live to be good, but will be good when he must be, and will have many things to occupy him other than moral goodness. But what does samaritanism call for when, say, you find a baby at your doorstep, and there are no nearby people able to help? Or, suppose that a persecuted person asks you to take him in, and you don't know how long he will need you, though you do know that the risks to yourself and your family are appreciable but not great? The golden rule would say that you cannot leave them to die, which is the essence of the Good Samaritan's deed. But as soon as possible, you could, consistently with the golden rule, hand over the baby or the persecuted person to others who, you are sure, will protect them. A samaritan obligation of indefinite duration stretches the golden rule to the breaking point; it asks for moral heroism.

Of course people act in the spirit of the golden rule every day and think nothing of it: for example, in relations of inequality, like those between parents and children, and in relations of equality, like those between spouses and partners, friends with friends. People often give more than they receive, depending on circumstantial need and temporary inequality of strength, resources, or position. In these relations, people ideally do not expect to be paid back, even though they sometimes need to be helped; but they don't act with the expectation of being paid back or feel they have lost out when they're not paid back. I do not think, however, that these are essentially moral relations. They are relations of love or affection and hence go beyond morality, even though in countless cases these relations trespass so badly that they fail to rise to the level of morality. Abuses and betrayals, boredom and neglect, indomitable selfishness or vanity: all of them plunge what is ideally beyond morality into trauma and disgrace.

Despite the injunction to love another as one loves oneself, the realm of love is not, by its nature, a moral realm. And despite the counsel of Jesus to love one's neighbor, his parable of the Good Samaritan (Luke 10:25–37) makes it clear that the golden rule, as the precept of the best morality, does not illustrate love of another. It illustrates pity or compassion, generosity or empathy; love need not enter any of these feelings. The Samaritan does not know the wounded person whom he helps by means of effort, inconvenience, and money. Morality's central place is not in intimate relations, even though it often matters greatly in face-to-face but unintimate relations in everyday life. The golden rule is for strangers, and almost but not quite for enemies who are intent on doing us the fundamental injustice of dispossession. When we do not resist enemies because we try to love them enough not to use violence against them (Matthew 5:39, 44), we also go beyond the golden rule (and even beyond the moral heroism of complete self-sacrifice for strangers who are not enemies) in the direction of self-denial. However, the parable of the Good Samaritan does not illustrate self-denial, despite some kinship between the golden rule and self-denial. Although practitioners of the golden rule eschew violence not only for their own advantage but to advance any moral purpose, they do not go the length of self-denial by refusing violent self-defense and the defense of those they love or those nearby who are innocent. But any use of violence stretches the golden rule and pollutes anyone who uses it even for self-defense and close defense. It would seem, then, that the golden rule cannot be the precept of public morality. It is too delicate to play such a role. The golden rule applies to private or personal morality. Who can say how many people practice it, and how often?

The difference between the counsels of the golden rule and those of either moral heroism or self-denial comes out when we think about Peter Singer's justly famous essay "Famine, Affluence, and Morality" (1972), in which he maintains that just by a "moderate" reduction in one's standard of living, one could save a number of lives, even if one did not want to perform a "strong" version of moral duty and decide to live barely above the minimum in order to save yet more lives. (In general, Singer's moral teachings display extremes of sensitivity and insensitivity.) It seems to me that even the moderate duty, as Singer conceives it, denies people the chance to make their lives more worth living by spending money on the activities that enhance life by giving it greater depth and grace. Singer's plea is not only to give supremacy to morality over everything else in life, but to make moral conduct the only valuable thing in life. Yet I grant that if one were to pit a life that is better worth living by a great deal for oneself against the very possibility that others (who are strangers) will live at all, the question becomes gruesome. I think that Singer is asking for people not to live by the golden rule but rather to practice moral heroism or, in a different spirit, self-denial. After all, a person has only one life to live and turning oneself into a hero or martyr (or close to it) cannot be a matter of duty.

In the most curious sentence that J. S. Mill ever wrote, he says: "In the golden rule of Jesus of Nazareth, we read the complete spirit of the ethics of utility." The reason Mill gives for this disorienting claim is that utility requires the agent to be "strictly impartial as a disinterested and benevolent spectator" when he chooses between his own happiness and "that of all concerned" (*Utilitarianism,* p. 218). The Good Samaritan, however, is not a disinterested calculator, nor is he radically self-minimizing. However, a stranger in need is a real person to him, not an ethnic specimen or a nuisance in the way; the stranger is almost as real to him as the stranger is to himself. A stranger in need counts as much as a neighbor would. Such a sense of reality is the source of his moral refinement. But he is not heroic: to himself, when he makes his decisions, he is not merely one more person who counts equally with others and not more than equally. In his own desperate circumstances, he may rightly prefer himself to others—certainly those not tied to him by love or family duty. I suspect that most advocates of utility would not wish to recognize their beliefs in Mill's formulation or in Singer's radical humanitarianism.

As long as one lives, there will be terrible suffering in the world; if one is lucky, and knows that luck is arbitrary, one still cannot afford to be overwhelmed by the suffering that exists everywhere and expect to go on living in the world with an undamaged will to live. One cannot define one's life by reference to the suffering of others, certainly not remote and unknown others, unless one is a saint (perhaps a better word here than hero or martyr). No matter how much anyone does, the tide of suffering is always high. Of course we should do something; it would be immoral not to. Still, answering the claims of suffering can be so oppressive as to turn into fantasies of suicide and destruction. These fantasies are present in what Bernard Williams wrote in one of his last essays, "The Human Prejudice" (2002)—an essay of great relevance to the idea of human dignity (and in which he perhaps wisely, but I hope not, advises against basing human dignity on uniquely human traits and attributes). He asks, "What would it be like to take on every piece of suffering that at a given moment any creature is undergoing?" He answers that "if for a moment we got anything like an adequate idea of what that is, and we really guided our actions by it, then surely we would annihilate the planet, if we could" (pp. 146–147). Williams would annihilate other planets as well if we had an adequate idea of their suffering, and their suffering was like that on earth.

We cannot pretend that Williams's outcry is an answer to Singer's problem. The outcry is an evasion, which is a rather suitable response, because the duty that Singer enjoins is intolerable to think about with the seriousness it deserves. Another understandable evasion of Singer's pressure is to blame many of the poor for their own condition by either condemning their vices or their adherence to stupid beliefs and practices that impede the cooperative energies required for self-help. Pushed too hard by Singer's kind of moral earnestness, people will find ways of squaring their consciences with their refusal to help or help enough.

The moral heroism of individuals does occasionally insert itself into political life. An individual risks self-sacrifice not as a warrior but as a solitary person. Socrates, the first and most famous example, was asked as a citizen to be an agent of injustice, and as a citizen chose instead to act by a moral precept he thought equally applicable in personal and public life. The precept was "never harm an innocent person, regardless of how much it costs you to abstain or forebear." He refused to allow his role as citizen to be defined by his fellow citizens and therefore did not think that his citizenship was a license to suspend his radical moral precept. His stand is inspiring, but he knew that no one else, no matter how physically courageous they were as warriors, would have the physical courage to risk death in the name of a moral scruple or conviction, as distinct from a concern with personal honor. In any case, heroism cannot be a duty; the golden rule does not enjoin moral heroism. It is not merely remarkable, it is a fantastic aberration, that states expect ordinary persons to be heroic in war and that many comply. The aberration is thought normal even by ordinary persons because of the unarticulated belief that people in their profusion are useable and replaceable by useable others.

We could ask: don't nonviolent political movements follow the golden rule? They forsake violence where violence could have been expected; we are not dealing here with the peaceful rule-bound politics of partisan representative government. (Accepting procedural rules in the face of one's political passion has its own moral delicacy.) A major consideration is that the golden rule does not guide conduct when it is adversarial. The upshot is that the golden rule cannot in any strict sense apply to any kind of politics, not even nonviolence. What is more, these movements, admirable as they are, as often as not, are struggling for their own rights. The cause is not selfish, but it is in some sense self-regarding. The golden rule is in no sense self-regarding. But in their rejection of violence these movements show a respect for the human rights of others; they place severe limits on their methods and prefer at least temporary failure to success at any cost. Therefore, there is undeniably some affinity between nonviolent political activity and the best personal morality. The people who take part in such activity see not only themselves but their opponents as individual persons. The nonviolent participants aspire to act in a way that is mindful of the requirements of morality and the dignity of their opponents, and do so by not losing sight of the fact that the adversaries are human beings just like the people on one's own side, not nonhuman entities. Politics loses much of its terrible abstraction, at least in the minds of the nonviolent. The situation is even more admirable when a nonviolent movement struggles for the rights of others. Here the affinity with the golden rule is even closer. Perhaps, then, the best personal morality can be approached, if not fully enacted, in the sphere of politics, when violence is forsaken and dispute is conceived as taking place between persons, even though the aims of the nonviolent participants are not merely personal, but systemic.

The vexatious problem is that people who practice the golden rule in everyday life are sometimes willing to give their support to political policies that do not rise to the best political morality. They are uncommonly good persons who go out of their way to help others, but who think that they are good citizens when they allow or endorse state activities that regularly invade the rights of people abroad or at home. They implicitly accept the division between personal and public spheres of action, but in such a way as to confine morality to personal life and exclude it from public life. It is as if the only goodness that can be shown is to people to whom one can do it in one's own person. The irony is that those who try to follow the golden rule show imagination in dealing with the suffering of a few, but lose all imagination of suffering when events are distant or on a large scale. They have the imagination to see what is before them but not to see what isn't. Patriotism is one of the passions that help to bring about the public blindness of private goodness.

The Best Public Morality Is the Justice of Rights

When we turn away from nonviolent movements and examine constitutional governments, we can say that officials of a state that recognizes and respects rights are not following the golden rule. Let me now add that when people claim their rights on moral grounds, they are not following the golden rule. Claiming justice and granting it are not examples of the golden rule, even if violence is not part of the picture. Is justice inferior to the golden rule? A brief answer (made less brief later on) is that if we regard the moral disposition that the golden rule exemplifies, it is superior to that of claiming or doing justice, but that if we pretend that we can figure out the total amount of moral good done, it becomes harder to say. What achieves the greater amount: widespread samaritanism or the justice of rights? I cannot begin to answer the question, except to say that each does the most moral good in its own sphere. The system of rights prevents or reduces suffering in many spheres of life.

In contrast, samaritanism is centrally about helping those in physical need or danger when the state is unavailable or is the source of the suffering.

In our discussion of the state's justice, which is the best public morality, let us begin with the obvious fact that a state is not a movement in its essence; it is not transitory or episodic. The system of rights must be backed ultimately by the methods of coercion and violence that are in the hands of the state. No doubt, some state policies, like relieving poverty abroad, can be seen as impersonal forms of samaritanism and thus as the projection on a large scale of the best personal morality, whereas relieving it at home is closer to doing justice than following the golden rule. If the state is negligent, citizens who press officials to help the poor by raising taxes may be guided by the spirit of the golden rule. Often, however, public opinion inclines to follow the rule "Neglect misery." The constitutional state that is true to itself will not neglect misery.

The morality proper to the constitutional state is guided by the precept that it should reduce, avoid, or prevent the infliction of pain and suffering to the fullest extent possible that is compatible with its own constitutionalism, and to do so as a matter of justice. But the top officials of a state are not engaged in intimate or neighborly face-to-face relations with its people. However, its officials know what it's like to suffer; they shouldn't have literally to see the suffering in order to reduce it. They need imagination to reduce it, and to avoid or prevent it—not much imagination, but as it often turns out, more than they can summon. In truth, it is hard for anyone to imagine that masses and blocks of people, strangers to the state and to one another, are made up of individuals, actual persons. The numbers coalesce into an abstraction. That is one of the aggravated curses of modern political life.

Let us set up a general scheme to account for the original revolutionary success of the theory of human rights. The point is to emphasize the distinct qualities of the best public morality and thus to set it off from the best personal morality. The scheme is a version of Locke that is completed by Madison. We look at the subject from the perspective of those who claim their rights. The people's demand for human rights begins as a demand for better treatment at the hands of government. It begins with such feelings as a desire to stop the oppression, and to be recognized as human beings. Let us here concentrate on the oppression, on the suffering when it is perceived as cruel or unfair and far beyond any necessity. At last, people see their suffering as a cluster of problems to be dealt with, not as an ordinance of fate or divine purpose. Surely remedies and mitigations are in the realm of possibility; perhaps one day there could be a much better life, a life maintained by more decent arrangements in society. People also notice that other persons dear to them or close by and similarly situated are also suffering. They need explanations that do not quiet them by locating the source of their suffering in their sins, or in their innate inferiority, or in some transcendental design. The idea of rights, an idea of lawyers and philosophers, emerges; it crystallizes the determination to be taken seriously in a radically new way and to receive better treatment.

In some circumstances, people are awakened—often with the help of those magnanimous few who benefit from the established oppressive order—to the sense that their condition should not endure and must be changed, even if violence must be employed. After all, violence and the threat of violence have always been used against them. To be taken more seriously and receive better treatment becomes an irrepressible need. The unlovely fact that can't be denied or helped is that vengeance plays a role in some violent revolutions: much more in Europe and Asia than North America. Under the banner of rights, whether native, natural, or eventually human rights, we know that in the seventeenth century and after, insurrections against oppression ensued and spread and became revolutions.

The golden rule cannot possibly encompass the deeds of an insurgent people in violent revolution against the old order. The more terrible the oppression that instigated the revolution, and the keener the sense that bad treatment can stop and must be stopped, the less relevant the golden rule becomes. Violence, when necessary, is still evil; the moral hope is that its use produces less evil than the condition that the revolutionaries want to overturn. It may happen that during revolutionary times, there is no functioning state, at least no central state, and no revolutionary movement that has yet managed to gain political ascendance. This is the state of nature; its most important political meaning is a condition of lapsed political authority. (Its most important existential meaning is that by right everyone is born free—free of inherited political obligation. One must individually consent to recognize a government as one's own.)

The inhabitants of a condition of lapsed authority are persons who were brought up in a society and have never existed like scattered mushrooms or isolated monads. They are hence social creatures (certainly not presocial or primitive, as they are sometimes misconceived by tendentious readings of the Anglo-American social contract tradition), but they are in violent group contention—insurrectionary groups against the forces of the hitherto established order. The violence causes pervasive fear. Lives and possessions are precarious, and liberty for some is unbounded. In such disorder, individuals and groups put themselves or their groups first and are covered by the thought that they have a natural right to preserve themselves at any cost to their oppressors or even, most desperately, to anyone at all. If there is a semblance of morality toward others, it is actually prudence at best. But disorder also gives license for transgression and wickedness on both sides. There is a need for order to be restored so that personal morality can once again exist and public morality, newly conceptualized by reference to rights, can prevail. Fear must be dispelled, and the kind of license that grows into or out of an intoxicated feeling of impunity can be repressed. This picture fits European popular revolutions better than the American Revolution, but there is sufficient similarity.

Let us say that revolution against the oppressive order prevails, as it obviously did in more than a few places. Immediately after the victory, people are still in a state of nature: there is not yet a recognized political authority, even though there is much less organized violence than there was during the revolution. There are disputes, uncertainty, and suspicion about the intentions of others; there is pervasive anxiety. The situation of inadequate security calls for a remedy, which can only be a government. However, this remedy always carries with it new dangers to rights; at times it feels as if the dangers created by a government, even one that has the form and uses the methods of constitutionalism, are as great or greater than the dangers of lapsed authority. It sometimes seems as if any government is, by the necessity of its nature, at war with its people; any government almost defines power as the ability to use the people for purposes not their own. The only hope is that the new government will not inflict the old grievances that brought on the revolution. That is to say, the new government must be constitutional; it must recognize rights, respect them, and enforce them within the framework of law. The new structure of authority, shaped by past experience of violations of rights, must incorporate guarantees against future oppression. But there are no lasting guarantees. That is why Locke countenances revolution even against an ostensibly constitutional government that has worked against the spirit of the laws, and displayed a steady pattern of measures that are too close to tyranny or despotism (or that has endured usurpation).

In established constitutionalism, rights are under threat whenever there is a crisis—real, imagined, or manufactured. Nothing suits many states better than a near-permanent crisis. Randolph Bourne said, "War is the health of the state"; we might add that crisis is the food of the state. Hard times produce hard cases, and political and judicial decisions in hard cases often go against a claimed right. Undeniably some rights are enhanced with time, but others undergo recurrent erosion. A polity's global foreign policy (a euphemism for imperialism) is almost certain to promote an obdurate pattern of erosion of many constitutional rights at home and the human rights of people abroad whose countries are the targets of such a policy. Some erosion can be repaired, if only temporarily; some erosion lasts.

The psychology of rights is thus marked by fear in several forms all along the way: the originating fear that the overthrown order aroused in the oppressed population by the denial of its rights; the fear that inheres in the disorder of the revolutionary state of nature created among individuals and groups; and the anticipated fear that even a properly structured and limited constitutional government will provoke, just because such a government has coercive powers and tremendous discretionary authority within the law, and develops an overconfident sense of legitimacy in elected officials and their subordinates. Many forces work to cultivate a political mystique that seems inexorably to deepen itself through traditions, habits, indoctrination, and historical memories both true and false. All of these features enable a legitimate government to transgress or otherwise be corrupt. Still, the political aspiration of constitutionalism is morally great: it is for justice. When a state is formed as a constitutional state, when it is charged to recognize and respect rights, it will dispense justice, even if imperfectly. The justice of rights is the best morality of state. When the state recognizes and respects rights as fully and as dutifully as possible, it operates on the highest possible public moral level.

But besides the weakness of any state's constitutional will, there are other reasons for knowing that this public morality will always be unsteady and imperfect. The main reason is that justice is always morally diminished by its inherent association with coercion and violence. Justice in itself is not violent; indeed, it stands for purity of method when it emphasizes the state's abstention from abridgement of rights; but justice nevertheless sometimes has to rely on coercion and violence to enforce rights. Rights are justice, but the methods of coercion and violence are always and only the necessary and lesser evil, not justice. (The evil that we normally have in mind when we speak of the lesser evil is not evil in its full sense of atrocity or crime against humanity but is rather synonymous with some considerable wrong.) Justice is shadowed by evil, by the wrongdoing implicated in its administration. The enforcement of criminal law is the model of the necessary and lesser evil as an institutionalized feature of government. Others say that war is another model, but a war fought to do justice by protecting rights is too rare an occurrence to count as a model of the necessary and lesser evil. The purpose of enforcing the criminal law is single; the purposes of any war, when not narrowly defensive, are multiple and cannot bear much scrutiny, which states naturally try to evade.

In general, we can say that even when an agent thinks that a proposed or completed act or policy is the lesser and necessary evil, that judgment does not conclusively establish the imperative that the agent has no moral choice but to do it. More has to be said. The existential value of individual self-preservation may outweigh the claims of action; long-term prudence may counsel against the deed. It is clearly imperative to have a system like punishment, which is not only a necessary evil but a lesser one. But there is often some room for doubt whenever a particular policy or act, judged as a lesser and necessary evil, is or was imperative. Any such calculation is prone to inexactness or shifting appraisals. We must be on our guard against use of the word *necessary* and countenance only its sparing use. What moral purity can a state reach in practice after all, in comparison to that of a person who tries to act in the spirit of the golden rule as exigent circumstances require?

The other main reason for the incurable imperfection of the best public morality appears when we take the perspective of a law-abiding citizen who lives in a constitutional society that is functioning well. The law even there speaks in commands. If it is obeyed merely as a command, rather than because of its good content, and if the obedience is motivated by fear of punishment or penalty and hence indicates a reluctance to do the right thing or abstain from the wrong thing, then we leave the realm of morality and enter that of prudence. Not only officials but also citizens tend to live somewhat below the highest level available to public morality. We have to settle for imperfection, the normal condition of human life at its best. The public justice of rights is not as morally refined as the golden rule, and it is not theoretically sufficient to defend human rights.

Egocentrism: The First of Three Theoretical Problems in the Defense of Rights

There are quite a few theoretical troubles that may perplex the doctrine of human rights. I say this despite my belief that the case for human rights is self-evident. Three main theoretical troubles stand out, and they are found in critiques that come from different directions. The critical points have some merit, but surely none succeeds in showing that a system of rights, in spite of the claims made for it, is such a bad interpretation of the requirements of justice that it actually becomes, if only recurrently, a system of injustice, or is otherwise profoundly deficient existentially.

The first problem is that rights are egocentric in their inception, and not only because fear of oppression plays such a large role in engendering the discourse of rights. Egocentrism is both an existentially unfavorable character trait and a source of immorality. The second problem is that though rights are not *narrowly* egocentric, they do take the individual as the basic moral unit, rather than society (or the world) as a whole. The greater good, however defined, can be sacrificed in the name of individual rights, which can be construed as an insistence that the rights of individuals and minorities must be upheld, even when a different moral approach would permit or require the abridgement of rights. The third problem is that people can use their rights lawfully but still poorly, lamentably so. Discussion of the second problem will take us to the critique of rights present in the doctrine of utilitarianism, which is a solely moral critique, but which is not based on either the standard of the golden rule or the principle of justice-as-rights. My discussion of the third reason will deal with the position of virtue ethics, which combines moral elements and ethical (in some sense, existential, not moral) elements, and where the emphasis is not on the unique identity of the person but on the good character of the self.

Let me begin by saying something about the first theoretical problem in the theory of human rights, which is the egocentrism of rights-bearers. What I say comes from within the theory of human rights. The complaint about egocentrism registers a principal worry about rights. Do rights build on and encourage further egocentrism? It is a worry about the way people attach themselves to their rights, and is therefore a worry about the character of people who hold their rights sacred, and by doing so, can act unjustly and also injure the dignity of other human beings. The emphasis in this worry is moral. Coming from within the theory of human rights, the point is, I hope, more cautionary than anything else.

The worry has weight only if the meaning of egocentric or ego-centered is not egotistical in the usual sense. When people fear being dispossessed of what is rightly their own, they are neither selfish nor narrowly self-interested. Their fear is perfectly acceptable morally. No one is obliged to accept oppression at the hands of superior power. The conceptual point is, instead, that the best morality that an individual is capable of does not emerge out of fear for oneself, whether the cause of the fear is oppressive authority, lapsed authority in a state of nature, or a constitutional authority that is given to policies that erode rights under the pretext of confronting a crisis. The conditions of fear are the most suitable for thinking about public morality but cannot serve as a model for thinking about the best morality, which turns out to be personal morality. Indeed, even amid oppression, the golden rule may be practiced; but amid the anarchy of lapsed governance, it cannot be practiced without turning into heroic self-sacrifice.

When Locke and other theorists of rights suggest that in cases where two or more people are trying to preserve themselves, and there is not enough to go around, each may prefer himself, adherents to the golden rule should agree. Neither the theory of human rights nor the golden rule demands self-forgetfulness to the point of heroic self-sacrifice. In extreme cases, the golden rule is self-limiting; generosity cannot be self-ruinous. But only in extreme cases do the two moralities converge. The difference in emphasis, however, is pronounced: to stand up for one's own rights is not as morally (or existentially) commendable as either standing up for another person's rights when one is safe in one's own (here, personal morality and public morality intersect) or acting morally in everyday life. The best morality is personal because only there can one think first about others rather than oneself. The additional advantage is that in personal morality there is no sense of official responsibility for others that is allowed to license moral irresponsibility.

Kant said that there is something morally questionable about revolution because the revolutionary people are acting as judges in their own case, even when it is apparent that they are acting in the name of relief from oppression and injustice (*Metaphysics of Morals* [320], p. 131). One can support this view not by Kant's complex definitional strategy that has to do with the notion of sovereignty, but by admitting that a society at any time is so complex that competing interpretations of the level of its public morality are always present, and commitment to one cause or another may produce propagandist simplification and the biases of partisanship. In that respect, Burke's criticism of the French Revolution is more instructive in its delineation of the pathologies of ruthlessness, and the self-defeating qualities of violence, than Kant's scholastic approach, even though Kant is famous for having expressed untheoretical approval that bordered on enthusiasm for the early days of the Revolution. Kant's sympathies were on the side of the French revolutionaries, but his considered judgment wasn't. A more impartial observer of revolution, who is less encumbered by devotion to a rigorous intellectual system, and whether situated inside or outside a society in revolt, may finally conclude that the forces of dissidence and insurrection have more—perhaps much more—moral right on their side than the established order does.

Of course there are extreme situations of politically inflicted or supported suffering about which it could be said, as Lincoln said about slavery (in his letter to Albert Hodges, 1864) or as almost everyone says about Nazism, Stalinism, and Maoism, all of them totalitarian regimes, that if they are not wrong, nothing is wrong. Earlier, Emerson had said that if resistance to the recent Fugitive Slave Law "is not right, nothing is right." Systematic and sustained evil is its own category. It is incomparably worse, from the perspectives of both morality and dignity, than even the immorality of sustained oppression. But the modern democratic revolutions against the ancien regime were not revolutions against exterminationist evil or literal slavery, "only" against oppression or injustice of varying intensity from one society to another. Of course, a person needs no excuse for defending his life or that of a loved one or friend against arbitrary and even potentially homicidal attack. A rebellion to end unbearable misery or poverty is also morally allowable. The moral doubt concerning being a judge in one's own cause and the supposed egocentrism behind it must be lifted because suffering or dying in oppressive circumstances without resistance, even violent resistance, cannot be morally obligatory. In fact nonresistance is, odd to say, perhaps morally or existentially impermissible. When saints are martyrs to the principle of passive nonresistance and even cooperate with gross harm that is being done to them, the sphere of morality has been abandoned for perhaps a higher one, real or illusory.

There is a morally significant mitigation to the egocentrism apparently implicated in persons' attachment to their rights. Whether at the start or eventually, people realize that what they claim as a human or natural right is not a claim that assigns different privileges and responsibilities to each caste or class; or a special preference, exemption, or immunity for any group (say, racial or ethnocentric) but not others. It is a claim that speaks for everyone equally. If one first considers oneself and one's own, then, responsive to the meaning of what one is doing by claiming rights, one looks outward. One is not thinking only of oneself or one's own when one makes a claim for rights, even though one never stops thinking about oneself. Obviously if a person sees that many others around one are entertaining the same sort of egocentrism, a sense of equal entitlement to rights spreads. Isolated egocentrism must develop into a commitment to equality or one risks serious self-inconsistency. Or, some persons, who are driven at the start by a sense that rights must be equal from their very nature, instruct others in that truth. In any event, the thought is that what is certainly good for me is good for others, or in reverse sequence, what is for good for others is certainly good for me. I am not better, more deserving than others, and others are certainly not more deserving than I am. The egocentrism, such as it is, is always at least on the verge of the imaginative act of putting oneself in the place of the other. Thus, I imagine: I would not like to suffer as he is being made to, or she would like to be in my place because I am not oppressed and she is.

Perhaps at least a tinge of egocentrism must always be latent in the sentiments of people who are used to living in a society where their rights are recognized and respected. But a good part of that egocentrism or self-concern comes not from self-promotion but from fear of the overreaching, hyperactive, constitutionally impatient or reckless state. It is not possible for a constitutional system to remain in tolerable good health without the people's fear or at least suspicion of the state, even when its structures and procedures conform to constitutional requirements. Of course, the people of a constitutional society, like any society, will have many vices, and not all of them owed to the particular egocentrism sponsored by the protection of rights; many vices will be more serious in their effects than the egocentrism that a concern for one's rights might encourage.

There is another point about egocentrism, perhaps the most important that we can make, and once again, from within the theory of rights itself. Too many people who are adherents of human rights affirm that the sovereign will of the people is the source of the validity of rights. What is involved here is a collective egocentrism, much worse than individual egocentrism. People are in the wrong relation to their rights, and consequently misuse them in defiance of their meaning, when they act on the belief that human rights require popular consent or authorization. Let us take up this point before turning to the two external theories that tend toward skepticism concerning rights.

My view is that though the idea of consent is of the highest importance in political thought, it is out of place in moral thought. It is so important in political thought that we commonly say that a government's legitimacy rests on the consent of the people. The people must authorize its existence, originally and thereafter tacitly, and must sustain it, once established, by the continuous and active consent that they give in elections and various kinds of participation and pressure. Some human rights are political rights, including the right to vote and take part in politics, hold office, assemble and organize to exert political pressure, form parties and movements, publish and read political commentary, and so on. I have no wish to deny the political salience of consent. But I see the original political consent as applying only to the structure of government and the procedures for filling the various offices, and exclude it from the original or added establishment of the rights that are enumerated or implied in the fundamental law.

If we take the original US Constitution as our example, we find specifications for the branches of government and a specification of a few rights. The people, through the states, had to ratify the Constitution for it to come into effect. Their ratification indicated first of all that the people, organized in states, consented to change their confederation into a tighter system, "a more perfect union." The partway state of nature that existed before the new union was between thirteen states, loosely confederated but also substantially independent; their state of nature could have continued, conceivably in peace for a while, because it was not between desperate individuals or warring groups, but between friendly states that were recently allied in a common struggle. The choice after the successful revolution was not between anarchy and a wholly new government but between a confederation and a union. Common constitutional and political principles informed the confederation and the proposed union.

It is clear that as far as the structures and procedures were concerned, alternatives were proposed and rejected before the necessary compromises were reached that issued in the system that we know. But alternatives were considered; other models were known. The people by ratifying the Constitution consented to the particular structure and procedures that were finally recommended to them. The conceptual problem is that at least some people also thought they were, by their constitutive ratification, giving their consent to the rights contained in the original seven articles prohibiting Congress from enacting ex post facto laws and bills of attainder and preventing impairment of contractual obligations, among other restrictions placed on government action. But I do not see how those who thought or now think that rights need popular consent, just as governmental structures and procedures do, could possibly be right. Consent to rights is out of place; it cannot be reasonably withheld. Popular sovereignty does not extend that far. The people were never morally allowed to authorize slavery. When a bill of rights or a bill of a particular right is ratified by the people or their representatives, a declaration of recognition, not authorization, is being made. In its absence the rights still exist as moral rights, awaiting their recognition, which should come out of a people's consistent adherence to the spirit of the laws and to the specific rights that they have already recognized and ratified.

The phrasing of the Declaration of Independence indicates that "we" hold certain truths to be self-evident—that is, those who deny these truths simply do not understand what human beings are and how human beings should be treated. They deny the truth because it interferes with their passions and interests. Even if we today would not want necessarily to refer to moral ideas as truthful but rather as the outcome of right judgment, and if by "self-evident" we mean only that their denial of right judgment leaves opponents with an alternative position that automatically excites the suspicion that only ignorance and selfishness lie behind it, we still see the sense that Jefferson was conveying. A political proposition is self-evident if after a historical preparation people ask the rhetorical question: What other proposition could possibly take its place? The structure of a government rests on consent, because no structure of constitutional government is self-evidently correct. But rights have nothing to do with consent. People who want their rights should realize that rights do not come from their sovereign will, as a particular system of government does—within limits. The limits are set by a theory of legitimacy, which precedes the government's construction, and ordinarily prescribes the separation of political powers and an independent judiciary, and certainly commands the absence of tyranny and despotism. But rights are not optional; there is no room for popular choice and hence for consenting or not consenting to their establishment. There is only the duty to recognize and respect rights, and not harm others by denying them their rights. The Thirteenth Amendment of the US Constitution, which abolished slavery, should not be seen as the people's authorization of abolition but as a belated recognition that slavery should never have existed and, even more, that it should never have been constitutionally established, though not established in so many words, as part of the right of property.

The more comprehensive point is that people do not validate by their consent any moral precept, whether *to each his own* or the golden rule or the categorical imperative. Human rights derive, in part, from the morality of justice, a public version of the precept "To each his or her own." So too, morality in everyday life is not an option. People must recognize and respect moral precepts in everyday life—if not the golden rule then at least the principle of reciprocity or fairness; unlike the golden rule, both are compatible with prudence, if not always motivated by it—just as the state, acting on behalf of the people, must recognize and respect human rights. That means, in turn, that any choice of the people to abandon rights of their own or abridge those of a minority cannot bind a government or the judiciary. People are not allowed, from within the very idea of rights, to alienate their rights or cancel the rights of others. And just as the soul of government is its constitutional recognition of and respect for rights, so to begin with, the people must recognize the meaning of their rights and show the respect for rights that consists in repudiating the idea that their sovereign will gives to rights an authorization that is optional, and that just as allowably could have been withheld.

It is absurd that the people of Colorado, by majority vote in a referendum, voted to deny gays protection against discrimination. The people repudiated the equal protection clause of the Fourteenth Amendment. Similarly, it is absurd that the voters of California, by majority vote in a referendum, could have decided that a judicially recognized right that allows people of the same sex to marry could be voided by their will, or that the voters of Maine by majority vote in a referendum could have repealed a law enacted by the legislature to legalize same-sex marriage. Like the people of Colorado, the people of California explicitly repudiated the clause of the Fourteenth Amendment that mandates for all persons the equal protection of the laws. There is no right to deny rights to others because there is no right to harm others by immoral dispossession (or injure them in their equal status), even if all voters but the person whose rights are involved agreed to deny them, and even if that person did not complain. This is straightforward Lockean teaching, after all.

There are similar popular abridgements of rights, enacted or threatened, elsewhere than the United States. Swiss voters used a national referendum to ban the building of new minarets in Switzerland, while popular pressure in France promotes the banning of head scarves and women's veils. Religious intolerance reenters Europe because the consciousness of rights falls asleep.

The matter of undoing the right of same-sex marriage is all the more scandalous because marriage is a self-regarding relationship. It is of moral interest only if, depending on the wording of the ritual, it is a pledge of permanence but issues in divorce, which then is a broken promise—that is, a promise to the world or to religious solemnity to stick it out until death ends it. But, secularly speaking, the offense is venial. To think that marriage is a sacrament is strictly a religious interpretation that has a claim only on the adherence of religious people. The interests of the children are of course of fundamental moral importance, but, conceptually speaking, these interests are separate from the nature of the act of marriage. The well-being of children is of fundamental importance not because they issue from marriage or are thought to be the purpose of marriage but because they are human beings who share our world.

I go on the assumption that the proper forum for deciding disputes about rights is the judiciary. Yet, I must face the fact that two court cases test what I have just said. The first is the decision in *Dred Scott v. Sandford* (1857), which accepted the prevailing doctrine that the right to hold slaves was part of the more general right to own property, which could not be taken without compensation, but drew from that doctrine the most extreme consequence that a black slave was not a person and was only a piece of white-owned property and that as such had no rights. Indeed, Chief Justice Roger Taney's decision made the US Constitution a racial contract that excluded blacks, free or slave, from any rights whatever. That slaves (named in the Constitution only as "all other persons") counted as three-fifths of their number, for purposes of the census and hence for the allotment of representation in the House of Representatives, indicates that in the original Constitution, slaves were regarded as human beings (each slave was not three-fifths of a person, despite the three-fifths calculation for electoral purposes) and not merely as property. They were also called persons when the issue was the slave trade: the "importation" of these persons was prohibited after 1808 (art. 1, sec. 8). When, as in the *Dred Scott* decision, there is no distinction between a person of the black race and a piece of property, human dignity is completely effaced, just as it is when categories of human beings are treated as if they were subhuman—a thought not far from the *Dred Scott* decision—or noxious vermin. The extreme point of slave-holding ideology was nearly reached. The ultimate logic of the decision, as Lincoln saw in his brilliant "House Divided" speech of June 16, 1858, was that a slave owner could carry his slaves not only into a free territory but also a free state: the country would become all slave, not "half slave and half free" (p. 426). Perhaps the further logic is that freed slaves could be reenslaved; black people can never have rights in America. On legal grounds alone, to leave aside both justice and dignity, *Dred Scott* was wrongly decided. This decision comes close, by itself, to discrediting judicial review, but we should not allow it to succeed.

The second case is *Roe v. Wade* (1973), which declared an unrestricted right to abortion in the first three months, then a regulated right thereafter. If a fetus is regarded not as a person, which it isn't, but as a potential person that needs only to come to term to be a child, then abortion is a quasi other-regarding act, and therefore could appear to violate the fundamental right of life of a quasi human person. Yet, to prohibit abortion, even in the first three months of pregnancy, is to convert a pregnant woman into a mere instrument of a purpose not her own or to punish her stealthily for her sexual activity. Abortion is the rare right where, at the conceptual root, there is a strong tension between morality (the right of life of the potential person) and the dignity of the pregnant woman, which demands that she not be treated as a mere means. The tension does not emerge, as with other rights, when, say, free speech and press must be defended on existential grounds because these rights lead to morally harmful results over a long stretch of time, but need not have done so. From the start, the decision for or against the right of abortion can plausibly go in either of two opposed ways. But I don't find it possible to say in general what receives the greater offense: morality from abortion or dignity from the absence of the right of abortion. When the pregnancy is owing to rape, however, concern for morality is overwhelmed by concern for the woman's dignity; when the rape is incestuous, if the argument for abortion on grounds of the woman's dignity is not overwhelming, I still think that it is stronger than the moral argument against abortion. If *Roe* were ever flatly overturned by the Supreme Court, which would therefore have overturned a right that it once recognized as fundamental and not merely as an optional legal right, I'm not sure we would have a decision analogous to the political decision in California (still in litigation) that overturned the judicially recognized right of same-sex marriage, but it would nevertheless be a shock to constitutionalism.

If there is dispute as to whether a claimed right is in fact a right— and perhaps in a few cases like abortion that is just barely possible— referendums or other modes of voting are not reasonable methods of decision. Legislation that abridges rights is no better, though legislation that takes the initiative in recognizing a hitherto unrecognized right is admirable. Overall, judicial, not political, opinion is more likely to be delicate enough to protect unpopular exercises of rights or entitlements to rights despite colossal failures, like the *Dred Scott* opinion, which augmented the evil of slavery; and *Korematsu v. United States* (1944), which validated oppression by countenancing the internment of citizens and resident aliens of Japanese ethnicity. In those cases, the Supreme Court either fell below the level of some sectors of public opinion or failed to rise above preponderant public opinion. But the failures test, without overthrowing, the superiority of judicial over political decision-making, when fundamental rights are at stake. It is a scandal that the legislature, with or without the urging of the executive, tries to strip the judiciary of inconvenient appellate jurisdiction in any case where a fundamental right like habeas corpus is at issue. It is of the same sort of constitutional absurdity that judges are, in some places, popularly chosen in contested elections. In democracy, political life, by its very nature, is framed by partisanship; the pressure of partisanship often overwhelms the moral subtleties that go to the heart of deliberation about rights.

Judicial deliberation can be shortsighted or lack courage; it can be beholden to extrajudicial dogma. But even the pretense of impartiality, and the disingenuous readiness to explore the reasons for contending positions and then set down rationalizations rather than reasons for the decision, is still better than the partisan brawl in the legislature when the interpretation of this or that right is the subject. Of course, we hope for more from the judiciary than pretense; we hope for genuine open-mindedness, and get it often enough, disappointed as we may be by any particular decision. The give-and-take of politics suits matters of public policy where rights are not at stake; but when they are at stake, and a definitive official decision has to be made, judicial reasoning is the appropriate way to make it. (Not to overlook the consideration that judicial reasoning is also superior in quality to bureaucratic discretion, which is often exercised confidentially, unilaterally, and sometimes capriciously.) People have the wrong relation to their rights if they think that their consent (or the consent of their delegates) is necessary for the validity of rights. I am tempted to say that democracy is a branch of constitutionalism, not the other way around. But it would be better to say that democracy is one essential element of constitutionalism, but not its source or basis.

When officials and citizens act politically, their line of action does not always affect constitutionalism, but the possibility of injuring it should not be routinely disregarded. Constitutionalism is not only but mainly inhibition, a kind of inhibition that does not block action but seeks to make it as scrupulous as possible. The spirit of constitutionalism gives the benefit of the doubt not so much to inaction as to the avoidance of ruthless indifference to the ultimate constitutional purpose of a political system—a lesson that is hard to remember when government is involved in every aspect of life; but we should hope that this lesson wouldn't be forgotten so quickly, even automatically, on numerous occasions. The foundational political value is not democracy but human rights. Democracy is the best form of government only when constitutionalism, ideally reinforced by judicial review, limits it. Unlimited democracy—so-called radical democracy—may not be the worst form of government, but it is certainly illegitimate.

It could be asked whether we must forever assume the existence of separate nation-states. Why not work to promote the cause of world government or at least a world federation? Wouldn't human rights be truly universal and altogether safer if there were a world government that was constitutional? This is a question that is easily asked but not readily answered. The number and kinds of consideration that would have to be taken into account defies assimilation. I will just offer a few thoughts. Our starting point is the certainty that as long there are states, there will be wars. The status quo is pocked by the violations of human rights that every war brings in its train. Not only does the conduct of war destroy the rights of those who endure it or die because of it, at home and abroad, it provides a big opportunity for leaders on all sides to abridge the rights of their fellow citizens in the name of security against the enemy. Just for the sake of getting rid of the wars between nations, with all their destruction or abridgement of rights, it is therefore not reprehensible to imagine a world with one global state, constitutional and democratic, that replaced the plural sovereign states we now have, even though the practical obstacles are insuperable.

But suppose the obstacles were overcome and that for a time the global state functioned constitutionally and that it was everywhere accepted as legitimate. The imagined world is thus made up of federated and unsovereign societies that are armed only for police purposes and that retain a significant measure of discretion and initiative in public policy. One question is, would the global state be armed? Against what enemies? Is it possible that eventually national sentiments here and there would prove resurgent, fed as they might be by different languages, religions, and mores—to mention the problems Kant notices in "Perpetual Peace"? Would a particular government, its will inflamed and supported by an aroused people, seek to dominate its neighbors and other societies more distant, and to do so in the name of a claimed superiority in one dimension of life or another? War would return and spread, unless the arms of the global state were so strong as to prove a successful deterrent or adversary. But if the global state were so powerful, would its tendency be to move toward despotism? Perhaps it would have that tendency even without its armaments. Then the constitutional world state would be only the façade for a bureaucratic despotism that would be driven by the effort to make the world as homogeneous as possible—in language, religion, and mores—in order to facilitate unity and ease of administration. Joining these cultural differences is the problem of great economic inequalities among the societies of the world. Would a constitutional world government be obliged to administer some degree of redistribution of wealth among societies and institute the reorganization of social life that this would necessitate? Even if morally desirable, and even if the right to property could survive such an onslaught, the obstacles posed by economic interests and prejudices of elites and people would seem so difficult that only a bureaucratic despotism could overcome them. The despotism would concentrate economic initiative and distribution and make all the people its employees, parasites, wards, or tethered beneficiaries. Taking care of one another is suited for personal morality, but it isn't the same as the state taking care of all of us. Care is not a feature of the public morality of justice. The state is not a parent or friend.

Our status quo of perpetual war is appalling, but if perpetual peace is obtainable only by universal despotism, how could we settle for that bargain? The main issue is the fate of rights: under what condition do they sustain the greatest injury, both moral and existential? We cannot answer because we would be comparing our reality with a hypothetical condition of unforeseeable changes. All we can say is that a global constitutional state that remained constitutional and that managed as well to work democratically and thus resisted the despotic tendency as strenuously as possible would qualify as eminently desirable. The European Union is an inspiring achievement. It is a federation of states in which the Union's bill of individual rights can be applied to each member state by way of a Union court, or at least invoked by the court, while these states retain sovereignty that is constrained not only by constitutionalism but also by strong moral restrictions on the independent use of force. The trouble is that Europe shares enough commonality of experience and aspiration, enough of a certain sort of friendship, despite all its heterogeneousness, to go on as a union. The world as a whole is not like that; the European Union cannot serve as a universal model.

Another question arises. Is anything psychologically or culturally valuable lost when there is a world government that is a federated constitutional democracy in the fullest sense and replaces all other sovereignties? Is there something inherently valuable in living under a territorially delimited sovereignty when the alternative is a constitutional world government? I doubt there is. If in certain nontrivial respects local autonomy continued to exist with plural government structures that were unarmed except for police functions, and where popular participation in politics counted for something, and where the variety of languages, religions, and mores continued to prosper, then perhaps nothing valuable would be lost. Perpetual peace without a political and cultural desert would be an inconceivably great good. But the ideal is utopian. As long as it remains so, we must begin and then continue to think about rights within the framework of separate nation-states.

The Critique of Rights Found in Utilitarianism: The Second Theoretical Problem in the Defense of Rights

Now that we have examined, from within the theory of human rights, some questions concerning people's relation to their rights, let us look at the second and third problems, actually sets of problems, posed to the theory of human rights by external critiques. One set of problems is contained in utilitarianism, which is a moral theory, and its critique of human rights is made in the name of morality. This critique can be answered by a moral counterargument, but the answer is incomplete and needs the assistance of the idea of human dignity. Utility pays little explicit attention to the idea of human dignity, but its views are deeply, if implicitly, hostile to it. The second set of problems is articulated in a number of versions of virtue ethics, which combines a moral theory and a theory of the best character. Advocates of virtue ethics have another idea of dignity and direct their critique of absolute rights especially at the idea of human dignity that is part of the foundation of such rights. I hope to rebut the alternative conception of dignity.

Under the pressure of the utilitarian critique of human rights, we must further elaborate the view, already discussed, that the defense of human rights cannot be confined to the moral argument that absolute rights look to the prevention or reduction of those kinds of human suffering that rights-denying governments, in their injustice, oppression, and evil, inflict or aggravate. The moral defense of rights has to be aided by the idea of human dignity—in particular, the concept of equal individual status, if the effort to prevent or reduce suffering is not to diminish or degrade human beings. Utility is inattentive to diminishment and degradation. Any version of the moral attack on totalitarianism does not take the full measure of its evil; the human degradation endured under it must figure in the reckoning, in order to see that totalitarianism does evil, not merely immorality. But the utilitarian conception of morality is deficient in itself. It fosters human diminishment in the name of happiness or pleasure; it also offers a theoretical justification for inflicting suffering on the lesser number in the name of the well-being of the greater number.

There is an enormous philosophical literature on the moral grounds of the tension or conflict between utility and rights. It goes back at least as early as Jeremy Bentham's *Fragment on Government* (1776). I will not explore this literature in any detail. I just want to isolate a few main points of controversy. I do not deny that there are complexities that defy any neat resolution. Nor do I deny that utility offers a bracing challenge, in both its skewed conception of morality and its usually latent but unmistakable hostility to the idea of human dignity.

One key to the controversy is the tendency of utilitarian thinkers to see pain and pleasure on a continuum, a tendency owing to their philosophical assimilation of human beings to animals and to their assumption that all pains and all pleasures are only sensations, which are comparable and potentially measurable. That means that pleasure (or happiness) not only counts morally but counts morally as much as pain and suffering do. Actually, in its Benthamite origins, the doctrine of utility sought to advance the cause of pleasure against ascetic disapproval; but there has never been any doubt that utilitarian thinkers think seriously about pain. They not only rely on the threat of the pain of punishment to deter crime, they are also fully aware of the sufferings that sinister or antiquated practices, laws, and institutions needlessly inflict on the population. However, utilitarian thinkers put pain and pleasure on the same continuum: for example, they tell people, after their laws have been sensibly reformed, to ask themselves the question: Is the pleasure gained from the spoils of a crime worth the pain you will endure if the state catches you in your crime and proceeds to punish you? Would-be criminals are asked to balance so much pain against so much pleasure. Whatever one may think of conceiving of the law-abiding citizen not as a person of moral disposition but as a calculator or a gamesman who is committed to rational choice, and is indifferent to the fact that a contemplated pleasurable act is immoral, the matter here is whether pleasure and pain are inseparable moral concepts, and fully comparable morally.

The continuum of pain and pleasure goes back to Plato. In the *Republic*, he claims that "nothing is more pleasurable than the cessation of . . . suffering" (583d) and that most of the pleasures that reach the soul through the body, and the most intense ones, are "some kind of relief from pain" (584c, pp. 254–255). Notice it is not the absence of, but the relief from, pain that is intense pleasure. (Pure pleasure, no matter how intense, is not yoked to pain.) Plato's view would seem to justify the continuum of pain and pleasure. But I would rather say that the cessation of suffering matters morally not for the pleasure it may or may not produce but for the amount and intensity of pain that the person no longer endures. Relieved of pain, the person can then go on to find whatever pleasures are congenial, or pursue an end other than pleasure. The extreme inference from Plato's defense of the continuum would be the foolish belief that a great suffering can be inflicted on a person so that he or she can feel a great or greater pleasure when the suffering ends.

The pursuit of pleasure or happiness is often the primary source of causing pain and suffering to others, and not only in criminal behavior but even more importantly in establishing and perpetuating social systems and cultural practices that institutionalize oppression and injustice. Oppression and injustice cannot possibly be justified by any reference to the happiness of those who benefit from them, no matter how happy and fulfilled the beneficiaries are. There are some utilitarian philosophers who go so far as to give moral weight to desires to act immorally. In his reading of R. M. Hare's utilitarianism, Peter Singer writes with apparent approval of Hare's conclusion that the Nazi wish to exterminate Jews is wrong only because it must be less intense than the wish of the Jews not to be exterminated. The side with the greater intensity of "preference" has right on its side. The idea that something called preference decides issues of right and wrong, and that consequently the preference for inflicting millions of deaths must count in the comparative reckoning that issues in the moral judgment that this preference is wrong, belongs in black comedy, not in serious philosophy. And the comedy would exceed Swift's or Terry Southern's inventive capacities. Such comedy can only be unconscious. I do not deny that the sufferings inflicted on wrongdoers and evildoers by those who resist them have moral weight, but neither the pain of their frustrated preferences nor the pleasure of their satisfied preferences has any. The world is made much worse just from the mere fact that perpetrators of evil and lesser wrongdoing are happy, flourishing, and fulfilled when they succeed or at least are happy with themselves because they tried.

From another angle: the moral excellence of a condition where rights prevail, and evil, oppression, and injustice are therefore avoided or reduced, does not stem from the supposed imperative that every person is owed as many pleasurable things as possible, to the fullest degree possible. It stems rather from the avoidance or reduction of preventable morally cognizable suffering for all. It is an individual's or group's resistance to pleasure and happiness that helps to account for the ability to avoid inflicting wrong on those they dominate. To be sure, there is another principal kind of praiseworthy resistance: when a person of conscience refuses to give priority to the duty to conform to the expectations of one's role or function or refuses to conform to one's dramatically idealized self-conception, when in either case serious harm to others would result. We are responsible in particular for the roles we choose; and in regard to the roles handed to us by prescription, inheritance, or conscription we are responsible for knowing that they are roles, not natural identities, and that any particular role is merely one role in a system of roles, and grants us no compartmentalized innocence.

Perhaps as great a source as any of evildoing and wrongdoing is the sense of responsibility that leaders and high officials of any powerful organization—a state, a church, and a corporation, especially—feel to preserve the organization at just about any moral cost. This sense of responsibility is related to but not the same thing as that for the well-being of the citizen body or church membership or the satisfaction of customers. Perhaps the preservation of the organization is perceived as the highest end. The organization as a means to the end of serving others turns into the end in itself. Many crimes are committed by those who feel that their roles at the top or near it permit any action or policy that saves the organization. Max Weber's "ethic of responsibility" rests on a deep but often unanalyzed commitment to the organization that can have perverse results.

There are a few roles, however, where conformity does moral good; role-morality can exist. A lawyer can defend a person who is accused of serious crime and thus protects the rights of that person, or a doctor can try to save the life of a universally hated person. Role-morality in these instances befriends conscience or is a form of conscience, as one's instincts are overridden. But much of the time, fidelity to role or function isolates the person from moral sense. And resistance to a grandly dramatic self-conception has to come from the outside.

The pursuit of pleasure or happiness, then, is not the sole culprit in the production of wickedness, but its contribution is a major one. At the same time, in everyday life, making someone extremely happy does not count morally, however much it counts in the life of the affections, in love and friendship. What counts morally is to avoid harming a person when one anticipates much pleasure in doing so, and could perhaps get away with it, and yet checks oneself. What counts even more is preventing or reducing someone's suffering with some cost to oneself.

In Mill's opaque formulation (in *Utilitarianism*), "pain is always heterogeneous with pleasure" (p. 213). They are not opposite kinds of sensation but incomparable kinds of experience. A person, thinking only about his preferences, can as it were weigh pains against pleasures, as long as the so-called calculation is made within moral limits, which are not set by utility, to begin with, and as long as a person alone endures the effects of the choice. But there is no genuine commensurability. One can choose to suffer an amount of pain for the sake of some great pleasure: an honor or prize, a victory in a lawful competition, exhilaration in taking part in an activity, gratification in overcoming self-indulgence, and so on. Pain and pleasure seem in these cases to be in a continuum, measurable by one standard, but only a pseudo-calculation is involved in the matching of means with ends.

What is not morally allowed by either everyday morality (even short of the golden rule) or the public morality of rights, however, is for an individual or the state to pretend to be able to inflict pains with the same untroubled will that is shown when facilitating pleasure, and then weigh the pains of some people against the pleasures of others, and then calculate that the pleasures outweigh the pains. Even to say that the pains outweigh the pleasures, if the supposed calculation comes out that way, is mistaken. The pains count morally, the pleasures do not, certainly when the pains involve the abridgement of rights, and the pleasures are, say, incremental material advantages.

Naturally, there is no life without pleasure. We are all attached to life in large part by the experience of various pleasures. To think, however, that we exist to be happy is unworthy, or that we exist to experience as many pleasurable sensations as possible is childish or senescent, or fairly decadent. Harsh words about pleasure or happiness are necessary when we see that enjoyment or the prospect of enjoyment of some people makes life bad, or worse than bad, for others.

I have already said that moral agents should put the pain and suffering of others at the center of their thinking and acting. Although a regime of pleasure, like Huxley's brave new world, can degrade its population, it does not violate morality: in that imaginary society, there is no deliberately inflicted pain, or any remediable pain or suffering that is neglected by the authorities. It is human dignity that is violated. I doubt that a utilitarian could criticize the brave new world when pleasure is either the paramount value or held to be commensurate with pain. But Huxley's false utopia is an extreme case, an imaginary reductio ad absurdum of utility. So let us stay with a utilitarian position that thinkers who do not always call themselves utilitarian, but rather progressives or pragmatists, have also supported. The case I have in mind is the willingness to compare the undeniable increase in the ordinary satisfactions of everyday life that hundreds of millions of people experienced in the twentieth century in the Western world and elsewhere (one the one hand) with the record of such atrocities as crimes against humanity; bloody, aggressive, and imperialist wars; bloody defenses against aggressive and imperialist wars; and war crimes in the twentieth century (on the other). The result of the comparison is that some utilitarian thinkers (consequentialists, as they now call themselves)— Peter Singer, for one—rather calmly say that the twentieth century is the *morally* greatest so far in human history; I would wish to say that it is the morally worst century so far. (I know Singer's view from two conversations with him.)

The complication is that when Singer makes his case about the twentieth century, he does not begin with society's increase of pleasure but with the relief of poverty and the advances in medicine—the overall relief of suffering and the prolongation of life expectancy. But he doesn't stop there; he thinks he strengthens his case by reference to the rise in the standard of living for tens of millions of people in the world and to the incredible new pleasures that every class enjoyed thanks to technological advances that facilitated unprecedented ease of communication and travel and thus the creation of a wide-open world with all its past and present riches accumulated for our benefit and delight. The total amount of pleasure supposedly far exceeds all the pain and premature death deliberately inflicted in the world wars, smaller wars, labor camps and death camps, induced famines, and constant everyday cruelty in life. If pain and pleasure are commensurable, I suppose that Singer is right in his calculation. Many more millions saw their economic lot improved in the twentieth century than endured evil, systematic oppression, and serious injustice, all over the world, on all sides in all struggles. But this calculation refuses to take the perspective of those people who were the worst off. That perspective should figure with an unusual importance when we attempt to make a general moral assessment of a whole condition or situation. Rawls has memorably advocated this perspective, and so have some Catholics.

We must not ignore the immense number of improved lives in the twentieth century, but the moral claims of those who suffer the most are prior; their suffering had no compensation; there are no scales that can measure it, and a fortiori no scales that can measure it while balancing against it, at the same time, the good of the much greater number, which falsely shows the much greater weight. Will the establishment of Japanese democracy ever *justify* in our retrospective analysis the US firebombing of Japanese cities and use of two atom bombs? In a review essay, Joshua Kurantzlick writes about the Khmer Rouge's massacres and barbarities, "'You must not cry out,' prisoners were told, 'while getting lashes or electric shocks'" ("In Pol Pot Time," *London Review of Books,* August 6, 2009, p. 10). How many new refrigerators is that equivalent to?

There is a modest-seeming utilitarian ruthlessness comparable to that of grandiose utopian, tyrannical, despotic, and totalitarian leaders. Singer is at his strongest when he intermittently practices "negative utilitarianism" and compares the reduction of pain and the prolongation of life expectancy with the humanly inflicted suffering of wars, camps, induced or neglected famine, routine cruelty, and premature deaths, and finds that the former phenomena far outweigh the latter, rather than taking the greatly increased pleasure distributed over many more people into account. When he compares the greater *number* of people who experienced relief from suffering with the smaller number who experienced evil and the worst oppression, his case for the superiority of the twentieth century at least retains the form, though not the substance, of a correct moral argument. Singer's calculation appears to be sensible, if of course such a calculation could possibly be made empirically. But it is possible that the moral calculation fails when we consider the intensity of pain of the worst off as well as the deliberate ending of lives prematurely. There are certain degrees of pain that seem to make other kinds less morally salient in comparison, ugly though it may be to say so. Perhaps the wars, camps, induced famine, and routine cruelty of twentieth-century politics—totalitarian, tyrannical, despotic, and democratic—are all, taken together, quite similar to the intensity of literal torture, are indeed kinds of slow torture, while the poverty relieved and the premature deaths prevented by advances in medicine, sanitation, and diet fall short of equivalence to release from massive torture and treatment like torture.

I leave aside, for the moment, the way in which twentieth-century atrocities degraded human beings and hence assaulted and often destroyed human dignity; our concern here is with immorality and the evil of imposed premature death. I just wish to say that the assault on human dignity in the twentieth century, the deliberate or incidental dehumanization of millions of people, would reinforce the indictment of the twentieth century. But solely on moral grounds, it is defensible to believe that humanly inflicted suffering in its intensity for any victim and the extent of intensity over many victims were worse in the twentieth century than ever before. If we cannot add up pains to produce one great pain that a single human being can experience because one person's pain is experienced by only that person, we can still say that there are depths of a given person's suffering that defeat the ability of the unsuffering, despite their anguished sympathy, to imagine, or the ability of the suffering person, except in rare cases, to articulate. This is not to deny that millions more suffered just from knowing about the suffering of others.

But we must return to the utilitarian view that pain and pleasure are morally comparable in order to notice a further deficiency in the utilitarian critique of human rights. Another way of challenging standard utilitarianism is to ask those thinkers who praise the moral glory of the twentieth century on the grounds that the increased pleasure available to ever more people far outweighed the pains of atrocities, whether they would have allowed, in advance, the infliction of these pains as a deliberate policy, so that the greater amount of pleasure could result. It is one thing, though misconceived, to compare pains and pleasures in the abstract and independently of any causal link between them, and then form a judgment of the totality of moral phenomena, which comes out in favor of the greater amount of pleasure, on the grounds that the amount of pleasure exceeds the amount of pain. That calculation is morally bad enough. But are utilitarian thinkers prepared to see atrocities deliberately inflicted as means to the end of achieving, in a set of circumstances, a greater amount of pleasure or well-being? I do not see how the criterion can be the greatest possible amount of net pleasure in the world, irrespective of how the pleasure is secured and how it is distributed. Do proponents of utility reason, for example, that without the Holocaust, there could have been no Israel, and that therefore it is better that there was a Holocaust? No one says so, but many people feel it and keep it to themselves, I daresay. Then too, a sense of the brute causes and a feeling for the astounding costs of valued things fade away.

Are utilitarian thinkers ready to accept atrocities—torture in the literal and extended senses—if they are the necessary preconditions for the production of the larger sum of pleasures over the lesser sum of pains? Other examples include accepting the slavery of some for the enhanced prosperity and culture of the majority; and hoping for war so that, after it is over, social progress can be made at home much more quickly than uninterrupted peace would have allowed. I mean to say that, in general, to make pleasure and pain morally comparable is to say that great pain for some persons is justified by greater pleasure for more persons, and that therefore to do great inconceivable wrong is justified by the production of an unprecedented greater good.

In moral thought, pain must be primary. Although human rights are defensible for more reasons than our concern with pain and suffering, such concern must block the assumption that pain and pleasure are morally comparable. The continuum notion strengthens the willingness to use some people for the benefit of other people, whether to favor a majority over a minority or a special kind of minority over a majority. Utility is on the side only of favoring a majority. But the theory of human rights disallows that calculation and does so in the name of preserving every individual in his or her rights, absolutely and inviolately. That is what justice demands; that is what each person is owed.

The nagging question, pointedly raised by negative (not standard) utility with its emphasis on the moral priority of pain over pleasure, is why shouldn't a minority be sacrificed for a majority, when the calculation is between a greater and a smaller amount of pain, and the intensity of pain is equal for individuals in the majority and minority? From that nagging question comes another: must not the public morality of justice favor, say, the right of life of the majority over the same right in the minority? If the answer is yes to either question, then it seems to me that the very idea of human rights is at serious risk or worse. If many of the most important rights of minorities are abridged or abolished for the sake of preserving the same rights in a majority, then rights for all cease to exist as rights, and turn into privileges. But no person or group exists to have its rights sacrificed in the name of morality.

The rights of each individual hang together: they form a whole of mutually supporting and enhancing entitlements, and are meant to be absolute, the absolute possession of every individual equally. Let us remind ourselves of what the important rights are: the right of life, understood to exclude almost all wars, and all massacres, induced famine, and neglected but correctable misery and poverty; the right of liberty, understood to exclude slavery, and arbitrary imprisonment; the rights of mind (free speech and press, and association); the right of religion, understood to exclude religious persecution; the right of property, understood to include the right of ownership and exclude arbitrary confiscation or uncompensated taking; and the right to due process of law. If any of these rights ceased to exist, there would eventually be almost nothing left in the charter of rights. Without all these guaranteed rights, a person is left exposed to unnecessary pain and suffering, or the danger one day, not far in the future, of being exposed to them.

By the moral reasoning of utilitarianism, the greater number must prevail at whatever cost to the smaller number. When any concession is made to this practice of supposedly moral calculation, it must be made with full awareness of the evil involved. Yes, "the numbers count"; yes, a few may be allowed to die (but not killed?) so that a larger number may survive when otherwise no one will survive; but that perspective is suitable only for those who have to choose, and when they so choose, they should not redescribe their act in any way that omits or disguises the evil. On the other hand, we should not expect individuals whose right to life, say, is about to be sacrificed, to go along heroically with their dictated fate in such circumstances; they are morally justified in trying to run away from death or resist its imposition. There are two incompatible perspectives; only superior might, not the public morality of justice, can decide between them, with the proviso that might never makes right. If we accept calculations that abridge or deny the rights of some people for the sake of the same rights of others, when people in both categories are equally innocent, we leave the realm of rights, but do so ostensibly in the name of some version of utilitarianism. The public morality of justice is betrayed because justice to be justice must be accorded to every individual absolutely. Although an imperfectly legitimate government retains its title to govern, the same government, in contrast, has no authority to dispense the compromised justice of utility or even to call it justice.

There is another disturbing aspect to the utilitarian critique of human rights. It asks us to regard individual rights as solely instrumental for the common purposes of society, with not even a prima facie case for the absolutness of rights. In utilitarianism, a so-called right is merely an optional tool or device that in some circumstances facilitates the pursuit and retention of pleasures and the avoidance and reduction of pains. Any right, thus conceived as a revocable privilege, may be abridged or cancelled if the state or the society sees that it is getting in the way of the common good. A people can decisively abolish democracy and grant power to an oligarchy or dictator, or return to power a party that has already demonstrated its hostility to constitutionalism, and do any of these things out of fear for security and hope for a newly effective state. The people are aware or strongly suspect that the new arrangement will keep a society under close state surveillance, or establish a powerful mechanism of censorship, or adopt secret legal procedures and withhold evidence at will in the name of state secrets, or substitute military justice for due process of law in the administration of civilian justice, or abolish habeas corpus and install indefinite preventive detention, or institute torture of suspects, witnesses, and convicts, or selectively abolish such counterintuitive features of criminal law (where they already exist) as guarantees against self-incrimination and against the state's ability to appeal acquittals in criminal trials. These are just plausible examples of the utilitarian suspension of rights, and what rights advocates would call alienated rights if the people accept the suspension.

Utilitarianism is a doctrine that not only endorses emergency rule without compunction but also generally tends to perceive great advantages to be within reach if only what people call rights are put on continuous probation, and where desirable, not merely plausibly necessary, suspended. All the while, utilitarian apologists can claim that rights get in the way of the defensible public purpose of either reducing suffering or increasing well-being. The utilitarian grievance against rights is they promote immoral outcomes while pretending to stand for justice.

The terrible truth is that utilitarian thinkers may be right. But if they are right, they are right only in the short term. In circumstances of desperate emergency, the public morality of justice is easily shaken up and will be surrendered, at least in some of its parts. But utilitarianism is not basically a moral theory of desperation but a theory of the nearly normal, and therefore argues, at its most consistent, that we should dispense with the concept of rights altogether and become pragmatic in our acceptance of the idea that rights are temporary privileges that can be diluted or abolished in ways that do not cause panic or constant apprehension in the population at large. The continuum of pain and pleasure is not the sole reason why utilitarianism is hostile to rights; but in nearly normal and normal conditions, the continuum plays an important part in disposing utilitarian thinkers to depreciate human rights.

The theory of rights has this great advantage (among others) over utilitarianism; it has a commitment to the right of life that utilitarianism, with its exclusive programmatic attention to pain and pleasure, cannot have from within its own theory. On the matter of life and death, utilitarianism is without theoretical resources. The value of a human life is not calculable by reference to the sum of pleasures and pains that a given person has or can expect to have. In contrast, when a theorist of rights takes up life and death, by means of an inalienable right to life, there is footing for discussion and further theoretical exploration.

If utilitarianism has some resources to employ in a debate on moral issues in public and private life, the theory of rights can answer, as I have tried to show. But a conclusion seems inescapable: the idea of human dignity does invaluable work in collaboration with the moral case for rights. Utilitarianism is not known for concerning itself with human dignity, any more than it cares about the moral case for rights. But to those who hold that the public morality of justice is embodied in a system of human rights, the idea of human dignity, as an existential principle, plays an indispensable role in helping to sustain the moral case. A major consideration is that by making rights optional instruments, utility turns the minority on any divided issue when rights are involved into the instrument of the majority. People take turns in being instruments; everyone is actually or potentially an instrument of society, a means merely, not an end. This unequal status is existentially unacceptable, no matter what may be said morally in its behalf. Utilitarianism is a terrible assault on human dignity.

Virtue Ethics: The Third Theoretical Problem in the Defense of Rights

Another theory (the second that I will take up) that is critical of human rights is virtue ethics. I use the phrase to designate a general outlook. The key point in this theory is that some rights are wasted unless persons take advantage of them to improve themselves. Rights matter for the most part as guaranteed opportunities for self-development. If they are not exercised by most people, or, in contrast, if they are often used to harm oneself, or to harm others within the allowance of the law, or tend to add to a demoralized or delinquent condition of society, the case for them is precarious and perhaps fatal. Furthermore, recourse to the idea of human dignity for the sake of defending the theory of human rights is in principle impossible to make because persons have to earn their dignity by showing that they have lives worth living. The only worthwhile life is that which is lived by a virtuous person. Human dignity is not to be imputed to every human being just because he or she is a member of the human species. It is also a mistake to attribute a unique identity to a person, apart from the cultivation of a manifestly unique and commendable self. A person, just as he or she is as given, can be pathetically incomplete or unfulfilled, and therefore counts for little from the perspective of dignity. Uniqueness of given individuals can be substantively trivial, and becomes better than trivial only when persons work to develop themselves, and become more fully realized.

There are some obvious affinities between the utilitarian case against rights and the virtue-ethics theory of the proper use of rights. But where the utilitarian critique is solely moral overtly, the virtue critique, at its most famous in the Aristotelian theory (formulated when there was democracy but not human rights), is both moral and nonmoral. For Aristotle, happiness is attained when every person of suitable rank is reared, from his earliest days, to acquire and display the full range of human virtues. The good society trains the virtues, gives them scope for their exercise, and rewards their bearers with honor and leisure. Many of these virtues are shown in moral relations with one's fellows, but some virtues show themselves only in the manner and comportment suitable to a person of virtue, and account for his aura. To be virtuous is to be happy self-evidently. A person's happiness is his highest end; it is an end in itself, and not a means to something beyond itself. The implication is, to use anachronistic language, that a virtuous person is an end in himself.

Yet one needs others on whom one expends one's virtues and who provide the audience for them. The society as a whole benefits from one's moral virtues, but Aristotle makes it clear that being of use is a secondary consideration. The Aristotelian virtues are colored by a self-pleasing and self-fulfilling quality. The highest virtue—contemplative wisdom—is solely for oneself. Thus, the virtues exist for my happiness; society exists for my virtues. Of course, I am unthinkable outside my relations with others, but only with a friend do I lose my sense of self-priority. However, Aristotle does not typically want instrumental calculations to infect the way in which one thinks about virtue and its place in society, though he sounds the instrumental note about virtue toward the end of the *Nicomachean Ethics*. Ideally, the cultivated person loses sight of means and ends; he displays his virtues as a happy person should. Performing virtuous acts is what the best human beings do; they make evident what it truly means to be human. There is no room in Aristotelian virtue for resistance to oneself or one's society, for Socratic self-examination and self-doubt.

Aristotle's ethics tries to provide the knowledge that Socrates said he did not possess—namely, how to train people "to excel in their proper qualities" (Plato, *Apology* 20a–b, p. 24). What a contrast there is between them. Morality for Socrates was the supreme consideration. He knew what injustice was, and he knew what harm was, but not what completion and fulfillment were. His concern was to try to cajole people into doing less harm to one another by learning that in the course of harming (unjustly treating) others, they were also harming themselves (damaging their moral disposition). Socrates wanted to help make people morally better, but never presumed that he or anyone else could possibly know what the best life is. You would have to know what being dead means, if you were to know how to lead the best life. Before death, the only life worth living was the self-examined life, the life that submitted everything to doubt except the truth that doing injustice was to be avoided, at whatever cost to oneself. Yet, even though almost no one leads an examined life, and if therefore their lives (in one formulation) are not worth living, the moral person will do nothing to deprive them of their lives, but in fact risk death rather than kill. A moral person does not treat people badly even though they treat others badly, and though they would not hesitate to treat the moral person badly, if they thought they could do so with impunity. At least on critical occasions, which one hopes are infrequent, a moral person has to try to be better than the world around him, and for the sake of the world. Socrates was a moral hero, but an unheroic version of his outlook conforms far better than Aristotle's virtue ethics to a culture of human rights.

I believe that the idea of human rights presupposes no commitment to the notion of an ideally best human life, and certainly does not hold that unless people lived the best life, they no longer deserved to have their rights recognized and respected, but rather should be placed under tutelage. We could extend Socrates' teaching and suggest that aspiration to the best life will usually mean that only a few can lead it, and that they can lead it only because others are doing the productive labor for them that makes it possible. In contrast, raising the average level of morality might be possible. The obstacles are formidable: every one of us, even the best, is at various times a slob, a sadist, and a moron; at our worst, we have hard hearts and jelly-like minds. The basic situation cannot be helped. But a little improvement is possible.

The Aristotelian vision is aristocratic, perhaps the best aristocratic vision there is; and like all actual or ideal aristocracies, it rests on the subordination and exploitation of a majority of the people. Unlike other aristocracies, Aristotle's construction makes rather less of war as the defining social institution and the core of breeding, training, and display. Sparta is not his model. All aristocracies are either unaware of the idea of equal human dignity, or as in Christian examples, relegate human dignity to immortal souls, not to living persons, and defer the question of equality of status to the afterlife. There is much to say about the contribution of aristocracies to the human record, but since aristocracy denies the equal status of human beings, its critique of rights (imputed or actual) is not moral. It is existential and finally aesthetic. But it does confront the question of what it means to be human. Aristocracies do not usually go the length of totalitarian extremism of evil, but they oppress systematically and inflict injustice rather casually. The ideal of aristocracy is one form of virtue ethics, where virtue is certainly not exclusively moral; the morality it adheres to in public life is not the morality of equal rights, and its morality of everyday life is a code that blends mores and manners that are suitable to a hierarchical society.

There are, however, versions of virtue ethics that are not aristocratic, that are partly or wholly moral, and that hold that rights should be considered subject to authoritative regulation. The use of rights should be monitored continuously; authority should intervene in order to curb the people when they waste their lives in self-indulgence, practice more vices than virtues, neglect their responsibilities, and create pressures for a culture in which high standards constantly yield to lower ones. The aim of authority, according to virtue ethics, is to raise the moral, cultural, and, if possible, the intellectual level of the people.

It is not the case that the typical virtue ethics critique of rights aims to spread aristocratic virtues and traits to the whole population. Aristocracy, from its nature, practices exclusion, selectivity, and sharp difference from the mass. Like anything high and intricate, aristocratic values are denatured or contaminated or diluted by being disseminated beyond a small caste. Aristocratic values cannot be democratized, even if people are well educated. Aristocrats must be at the top and feel their position in comparison to those beneath them and also feel that their position is costly to others. They want to be expensive and precious. Many virtue critics are democratic, however, and think that rights still exist when restrictively tied to their virtuous exercise.

The society that human rights need is a democratic society. In defending human rights, we must take democracy as the given. That is true not only because some rights are equal political rights for all citizens but also because, by definition, democracy is devoted to equality of individual status to an extent and with an intensity that no other kind of society is. Yet a defender of human rights must face Plato's contention that the most serious democratic vice is incontinence (as the most serious aristocratic vice is insolence; there's something of each in the other, however; they attract and encourage each other). Nothing can ever eliminate democratic incontinence. A democratic people will always dwell in impurity, the impurity that comes from holding nothing sacred that is social. Strict boundaries, rigid prohibitions, awe before tradition, are all incompatible with a democratic culture. The taste for change, for novelty and experimentation, and for leveling upward is ineradicable. To be sure, halfheartedness marks many democratic endeavors, a certain readiness to retreat from excess or definition.

All these ingredients demonstrate what one might call distaste for virtue in an Aristotelian sense, and equally in the old European aristocratic sense as well. The person's aim in a democracy, as succinctly and memorably pictured in book 8 of Plato's *Republic,* is to try one thing after another, one role after another, to have one experience after another, to dart out of one's place before nervously returning to it or to some place slightly better. This mobility does not show an aspiration to self-realization, but a desire to be relieved from oppressive discipline, from drudgery and boredom, and to enjoy moments and episodes of exhilaration and ecstasy. If we then add to this mobility another element of a contrary sort, yet consistent with democracy—namely, doing a worthy job well—we have not virtue, not the good life in the exalted meaning of the phrase, but the kind of life that is not ignoble, a life on which the protection guaranteed by rights is in no sense wasted.

Capitalism and its consumerism exaggerate democratic incontinence. But there is nothing surprising in the democratic appetite for the goods of capitalism. When capitalism succeeds, it succeeds because it feeds the popular craving for greater ease in the drudgery of life, less friction or impediment in the transactions of life, and for change, novelty, and experimentation. As long as we have the combination of democracy and capitalism we will not have virtue; in fact, each system is a powerful deterrent of virtue; we will have only moral goodness and some check on incontinence when we have it. Such goodness is joined, however, to numerous unadmirable and unattractive traits of character. People will seem to use their rights, especially those of speech, press, association, and religion, to immerse themselves in base activities. Reality TV and internet personal interaction are the next steps in democratic incontinence. It would take an iron paternalist moral dictatorship and a return to scarcity to purge a democratic people of these features, but then democracy would be left behind.

The Allure of Paternalism

Where the full range of rights is recognized and respected by the state, there will be a democracy, and only there. With time, the culture where rights take hold will become ever more democratic. It is also likely that the society, if originally oligarchic, will be strongly property-minded, from the start, and then democracy, though not by itself of course, will generate capitalism. I think that we must face the fact that the virtue-ethics critique of rights, whether or not aristocratic, is paternalist. But democracy must be inhospitable to paternalism, even when it comes in bits and pieces. Theoretical acceptance of the combination of democracy and consumerist capitalism makes the virtue critique yet more unpalatable to defenders of rights, just as it makes many of the critics of rights ever more unhappy; and though a capitalist democracy is bound to have more than traces of paternalism, the paternalism will go not in the direction of virtue, but rather of welfare.

If we define paternalism as driven by the idea that in any society, people often don't know what is good for them and must be corrected by those few who do know better—it must be a minority who know better, because majority paternalism, as with the legal prohibition of alcohol, is likely to be a rare and temporary blunder—the inference must be that paternalism is antithetical to the foundation of human rights. In a democracy, paternalists believe that some people are entitled to moral authority, and if possible, should throw their weight behind efforts to pass legislation and make policies that coerce, "nudge," or otherwise influence people into doing what is good for them. The solution for the failure of many citizens to use rights properly must be centralized and administered to the whole population.

No one would wish to deny that an adult person's relatives, friends, neighbors, and fellow workers—all of whom have a personal knowledge of or acquaintance with the person—can counsel, caution, and criticize him or her, and do so with good results. Every adult needs occasional correction. But the paternalist idea that a state apparatus should govern the habits and practices of the adult population indicates that people are seen as constantly in need of correction and must be kept under surveillance in order to ensure that the average level of conduct justifies giving them rights. Rights must be earned, especially the right to as much freedom as possible.

There are defensible standards of good conduct, but the source of correction should not be the state that takes on itself the power to improve people. By definition, paternalism is treating adults as if they were children; of course, children shouldn't have the full range of rights that adults do. But if adults in the mass tend to need to be treated like children, then the idea of human rights has no place. Rights rest on the view that the law's regulation of everyday conduct should appear only when people are acting criminally, by the usual standards of criminality; or are clearly unable to take care of themselves because of incapacitating illness or poverty.

On the issue of paternalism, too, we can distinguish between two perspectives: one perspective is the individual's and the other is the state's impersonal perspective. But the state's perspective, in this case, is scarcely compelling and verges on the fanatical. A rights-minded individual will rightly resent being told what to do and how to govern oneself by a cluster of official agencies that regulate large sectors of everyday conduct and proceed on the assumption that they know better. The state is unforgivably presumptuous. Individuals, however, face another obstacle in using their rights as they wish within the limits of regard for the rights of others. From the state's impersonal perspective, which is a bureaucratic perspective, not the judiciary's, the population at large is a force to be disciplined and put to work for society as whole. The society is understood as one among others, fit to be compared with others, and often in competition with them. A whole population is a kind of army that runs not on martial but on social discipline. No personal activity is without significance, potential or actual, for the country's standing in relation to other countries. No innocent activity is actually innocent. No activity is "self-regarding," to use a term introduced by Bentham and made philosophically rich by J. S. Mill.

It seems to me that the general conceptual understanding of freedom that underlies the specification of rights in a document like the US Bill of Rights is that the more freedom the people have, the better; freedom includes but goes beyond free speech, press, religion, and association. One must be free to live as one likes in an atmosphere of freedom that sustains daily life; it is mostly to the good when the common outlook favors limited government. If a large part of living as one likes means exercising First Amendment rights, there is nevertheless more to living a free life. A free life means making all sorts of choices from the most intimate to the most associative, and doing so without an anticipated penalty of one sort or another. A free life cannot bear being looked at too closely, especially (but of course not only) by an official eye, and it cannot be lived in a condition of tutelage. In American jurisprudence, judges use substantive due process—a clumsy name—to defend the greatest possible amount of free choice in one's life, and this idea is aided by the doctrine of privacy in an expanded sense. However, if the very possibility of self-regarding activity is rejected, the scope of the right to as much rightful freedom as possible is shrunk. Paternalist regulation becomes too tempting when the prevailing attitude is that people are a swarm, in which they constantly impinge on one another and affect one another helplessly. The case against paternalism is mostly existential, not moral, and certainly not utilitarian.

The greatest critic of paternalism is J. S. Mill; his influence shows itself even when he is not named. He is a terror to those who believe in moral authority, whether the state or mobilized public opinion claims it and exercises it. Although he did not overtly subscribe to a doctrine of human rights, his own language suggests an affinity to it; and he explicitly talks about dignity. A brief look at his arguments is useful. Of particular importance are the last two chapters (4 and 5) of *On Liberty*. In these chapters, especially, Mill argues for the proposition that freedom has nothing to do with the virtuous capacity to exercise it, provided people do not harm one another when they do as they like. In matters of self-regarding activity, freedom is absolute (or nearly absolute); the individual's unobstructed sovereignty should rule the individual. Unless self-regarding activity is practically possible, there can be no living as one likes; all of one's activities would be potentially subject to scrutiny with an eye to legal regulation. The individual's perspective, Mill thinks, must defend itself against the ever-ambitious state-bureaucratic perspective that is abetted by puritanical and censorious public opinion.

Mill defines a self-regarding act or practice as one that affects only the person doing it or does not affect others "unless they like" (*Liberty*, p. 276); if it affects others, it is with their "free, voluntary, and undeceived consent" (p. 225). By definition, other-regarding acts or practices—Mill calls them "social"—affect others without their consent. He is especially interested in social activity that not merely affects others, but harms them in their rightful entitlements. Mill is perfectly aware that people affect one another in countless ways in everyday life; often these ways are hard to identify or trace to identifiable sources and assess in their full impact in the longer run. Life is affecting and being affected, influencing and being influenced. A free person somehow manages, however, to be receptive and yet not merely porous, or too easily intimidated or seduced. Resistance is as important as reception. If there were no resistance, no real distance between the person and the person's immediate experience, social life would be like an endless and unremediable contagion. Freedom is not tenable in such a condition.

With these hopes in place, Mill proceeds to defend the freedom to misspend one's life, to waste it in low-grade self-indulgence, and to brush away the possibility of making one's life a project that enlists one's faculties and enables one to make a difference to others and to achieve a fully developed self. A lot of habits and practices that Mill himself and most of his audience dislike and find unworthy of admiration are defended in the last two chapters of *On Liberty* as exercises of freedom that the state or other powerful forces like punitive public opinion should not interfere with. He wants law and public opinion to tolerate gambling, drugs, alcohol, and use of prostitutes. All these activities concern only the agent until they create dereliction of duty to others, at which time the activities may become punishable, but only then, and the purpose of punishment should be not to improve the person, or express public disapproval in a manner that puts everyone on notice, but to deter others from similar wrongdoing.

It is important to emphasize the fact that Mill admires nothing more than a self-developed individual who seeks to cultivate and exercise his or her mental, moral, and practical faculties, and chooses a life-defining commitment that brings out one's best and may very well have beneficial consequences, intended or not, for one's society and the world. However, the third chapter of *On Liberty* makes clear that Mill does not expect a whole population ever to be made up of self-realized individuals. His commitment to high standards precludes such an aspiration. The rare self-developed individual becomes "a noble and beautiful object of contemplation"; a number of such individuals do deeds and works that bear their imprint, and at the same time enrich life for everyone, and strengthen, he says, "the tie which binds every individual to the race by making the race infinitely better worth belonging to" (p. 266). In recent times, Foucault has sponsored the idea that the worthiest goal for a person is to be self-disciplined by a style or to become finished like a work of art. Such ideas obviously do not fit the great majority of us, as Mill knew. The self-developed individual is not a model for us but one who merits our toleration, not our resentment or wish to penalize him or her as anomalous. No doubt many kinds of groups and organizations can discipline their members into a collective or corporate style that aims to be distinctive among groups and tell the world how special the particular group is. But from an individualist perspective, manifesting a group style is like wearing borrowed clothing, or more deeply, living on a borrowed identity. At best, one self-consciously accepts and obeys without reservation a set of rules that fully constitute one's identity.

Mill is passionately for *self*-development, whether it attains a praiseworthy individuality or a condition of self that is more ordinary but unmistakably one's own. He wants the state to get out of the way of the self-developing individual once the person is an adult, and confine its contribution to self-development by guaranteeing sufficient early education for everyone. And just as he is passionately for self-development, he is equally passionate for not forcing it on people through paternalist legislation (or coercive public opinion). What Mill admires most must come freely; otherwise it is not genuine; ostensibly helpful interference would be ignorantly presumptuous, or wise but still impermissibly presumptuous. *On Liberty* is devoted to praising developed individuality, but it is equally devoted to a pained but unrelenting defense of activities that, by Mill's standard, block self-development.

One argument that Mill makes in defense of individual sovereignty is that a person knows better what gives him pleasure than the people close to him do, and certainly better than either an official bureaucracy or an anonymous public opinion does. A general prohibition is ignorant of particular cases. I have suggested that the appeal to pleasure is often a poor argument and should not be a major consideration when we discuss human rights and their foundation. "Life, liberty, and the pursuit of happiness" is a hallowed phrase but it strikes a false note. Pain, however, is always relevant to the idea of human rights. Is this even true of the pain of frustration at failing to get a self-regarding pleasure that one can procure on one's own, when there is no obstacle in one's way except the state's ill-judged interference or punitive public opinion? Is it therefore consistent to exclude pleasure from moral reckoning? Yes, I suppose so, because what matters morally in such a case is not the reduction of a person's possible pleasure but the needless reduction of a person's freedom. The moral aim is to provide not as much pleasure as possible but as much freedom, and freedom matters for much more than the avoidance of frustration and the pursuit of pleasure.

Pleasure and its vicissitudes cannot be given the last word or even many words in moral discourse. Mill tries to save the honor of pleasure by having recourse to Plato's idea of higher pleasures (*Republic* 9.582–583, pp. 252–253) and does so for the sake of associating pleasure with a greater complexity of experience and with a more serious engagement with the purpose of giving some shape to one's life and some definition to one's identity (*Utilitarianism,* chapter 2). But if pleasure or happiness is posited as the end, rights turn into mere instruments, and instruments are always open to being replaced by better instruments. When rights are seen as instruments, however, so are persons.

Fortunately, pleasure, base or higher, is not Mill's only consideration. He suggests that it is an insult to the dignity of persons to try to save them against their will, to save them from themselves by means of state coercion. A population becomes collectively wards of the state, with or without the support of a censorious society, which typically feels prejudiced shock or inarticulate disgust when confronted with activities it wants to prohibit. Such shock and disgust play into the hands of a paternalist state that can go after now one group and now against another. Even if it can be shown that nearly absolute self-regarding freedom harms some people when they are left alone to live as they like, Mill is adamantly opposed to interference with them. In some cases, the value Mill invokes is autonomy, though he uses the word only once, in French, and in a letter to Emile Accolas, written in 1871, well after *On Liberty* was published (p. 1832). But the word doesn't matter; the thought is there. One must choose for oneself how one is to live, even though the choice is unpopular and many others may even find it unclean or repulsive, provided one does not harm others. If it is a group life, as lived by the Mormons, which includes polygamy, it would be tyrannical not to tolerate it as long as all the members of the group have consented to it. In this case, Mill does not take up the effects on Mormon children who must live in an otherwise monogamous society, though he was ordinarily highly sensitive to the well-being of children.

What about being free to practice such habits as drinking, gambling, and taking drugs? Often these habits are not only self-indulgent but life-wasting and even self-destructive. Mill defends the freedom to engage in them as well. The grounds here could not be defense of a person's autonomy, because a person addicted or thoughtlessly habituated to one or another of these practices has lost control of himself and his life, or stands the chance of losing control. Mill remains steadfast; but on these matters, his defense is based on freedom or individual sovereignty, rather than autonomy. Autonomy implies that one gives direction to the course of one's life to the fullest extent possible because one has the ability to resist impulses and break habits. Autonomy is the perfection of individual sovereignty; such achieved perfection, however, is not necessary for anyone to claim the fundamental right to be left alone to live as an adult who is not admirable or virtuous, but harms only himself. In many cases, persons may not even believe that they are harming themselves.

Mill was aware of what might be said against him. He made many of the most important points against himself before his numerous critics did. Self-regarding habits and practices can radiate a bad influence on others, and can work unwanted effects on "those nearly connected with him and, in a minor degree, society at large" (*Liberty*, p. 281). But society must learn that many bad actions are self-regarding, despite their unwanted effects, which are in the class "of the merely contingent, or, as it may be called, constructive injury" (p. 282), in contrast to the direct and palpable harm to the person who performs the actions. Society has only itself to blame if it lets "any considerable number of its members grow up mere children" who are incapable of rational consideration of "distant motives" (p. 282). He goes so far as to admit that some habits constitute a "defect . . . of personal dignity" or show a "want" of it (p. 279). But society should not try to treat an adult as a child, when it did not make proper efforts to treat the child as a child who needed guidance and education. The reason for noninterference with adults is what Mill calls "the greater good of human freedom" (p. 282). From the perspective of human dignity, being as free as possible within moral limits is what human beings are entitled to.

Mill could not have possibly accepted an assertion made by T. H. Green (1836–1882), who is perhaps for us the most valuable of his critics, contemporary or posthumous, and a great moral and political philosopher in his own right. In his "Lecture on Liberal Legislation and Freedom of Contract" (1881; Mill died in 1876), Green says, in a presentation full of excellent formulations: "Thus, though of course there can be no freedom among men who act not willingly but under compulsion, yet on the other hand the mere removal of compulsion, the mere enabling a man to do as he likes, is in itself no contribution to true freedom" (p. 371). What is true freedom? Green holds that it is "a positive power or capacity of doing or enjoying something worth doing or enjoying, and that, too, something that we do or enjoy in common with others" (p. 371). Notice that Green intentionally redefines freedom as power; he is not merely content to say that without enough power to attain some of one's purposes, freedom becomes hollow. The ideal of true freedom is "the maximum of power" for everyone to "make the best of themselves" (p. 372). What is worth doing? All that is done shows "the full exercise of the faculties with which man is endowed" (p. 371). These faculties realize and express themselves in moral and nonmoral activities. The developed social individual is Green's aspiration; but it must be the development of all persons, not just the few, even though, Green concedes, the highest human development privileged classes ever reached was in the ancient cities that rested on slavery (p. 371).

We must acknowledge that it is in the name of a conception of human dignity that Green is restricting the exercise of some rights to free activity. Indeed, the burden of his lecture is to permit government to regulate the use of private property in order to improve the condition of the poor, and make the poor, together with all other citizens, full and equal participants in a cooperative self-developing life. The incurable trouble is that Green is making instruments of all rights, and encouraging their regular abridgement in the name of self-development, in the name of virtue as a moral and ethical ideal. Every liberty can be "rightly allowed" only if it is not "as a rule, and on the whole, an impediment to social good" (p. 384). Green's "true" freedom is not freedom; it is the directed and constantly superintended power or capacity of persons to achieve a nominally commendable ideal, perhaps, but an ideal that, to be realized, must treat a large portion of the adult population as if they were children (through no fault of their own), when they actually are adults who live foolishly. For Mill, the ideal of self-development is lost when the self, hedged around by restrictions of many sorts, is developed but does not develop itself. In part, self-development proceeds by one's resistance to self-injuring temptations. But temptations should not be multiplied to test the ability to resist; to the contrary, if Paul is right, prohibition increases the temptation to transgress (Romans 7).

Green advocates prohibition of alcohol, not worrying that prohibition punishes the great majority who use alcohol innocently. "Every injury to the health of the individual is, so far as it goes, a public injury" because it is a "deduction from our power . . . to make the best of ourselves" (p. 373). We are meant to be tied together tightly. If I don't matter to myself as you want me to, I will be made to act as if I did. He also claims that there is no moral degradation in a law that makes compulsory what a given person would, without the law, have done freely. Yes, perhaps the insult is not always felt. But surely the mentality of congenial obedience to the law is not the same as the mentality of free choice. (We are not talking here about following the rules that frame or constitute an activity or practice.) A prohibition that is handed down by a law changes the nature of—contaminates—the act that I would have otherwise done freely. That a person relieved of the responsibility of making a good choice for himself on one matter can redirect his attention to another matter that is left to free choice is a possibility that consoles Green, but should not console us. Green says, "When all temptations are removed which law can remove, there will still be room enough, nay, much more room for the play of our moral energies" (p. 386). To remove all the temptations that law can remove? Surely this is a recipe for despotism. There is no doubt that Green was an exceptionally sensitive and humane man, oppressed by the suffering he saw around him. He thought he was delineating a new conception of human dignity with its source in a radically revised view of rights. But his theory threatens human dignity by its virtuous excesses.

Before Green wrote his lecture and other more fully developed works, Mill saw arguments that resembled Green's and battled them. Mill's passion for freedom rises to a climax in his condemnation of what others call their "social rights" (*Liberty*, p. 288). The temperance association was campaigning for the total prohibition of sale and consumption of alcohol for the whole population. Their position was that everyone's social rights are violated when available alcohol turns an appreciable portion of the population into drunks who cannot function properly. The association claims, in Mill's quotation, that allowing alcohol impedes "my right to free moral and intellectual development by surrounding my path with dangers, and by weakening and demoralizing society, from which I have the right to claim mutual aid and intercourse" (p. 288). For Mill, the advocates of this view desire a society in which every individual "shall act in every respect exactly as he ought; that whosoever fails thereof in the smallest particular violates my social right, and entitles me to demand from the legislature the removal of the grievance" (p. 288). This principle Mill calls "monstrous" precisely because it can justify any violation of liberty. He says, "The doctrine ascribes to all mankind a vested interest in each other's moral, intellectual, and even physical perfection, to be defined by each claimant according to his own standard" (p. 196). We live to become one another's instruments; or if that is an impolite way of putting it, we exist to be of use or to serve one another. We exist to instruct and be instructed in how to live. But in a large society of strangers and fellow citizens, who benefits by this mutual submission?

In Mill's eyes, the quest for a virtuous society must end in state despotism. The quest for social rights must end in the enfeeblement of all rights or, what is closer to the mark, the abandonment of the idea of those absolute (or nearly absolute) guarantees we now call human rights. Human rights cannot bear to be looked at as if they were always on probation. They also cannot bear the burden of high expectations, the utopian desire to see all human beings gorgeously developed and leading beautiful lives. This desire can lead only to perpetual disappointment followed by ever more intensive efforts to raise the average level by manipulation and the force of coercive regulations. That people may come to regard the continuously interventionist regulation of everyday life as normal is Mill's fear, which he learned to feel in part by reading Tocqueville on democratic despotism in the second volume of *Democracy in America.*

A more ruthless way of reading Mill is simply to say he really did not think that the great majority of any population would ever want and hence ever be capable of leading autonomous lives, whether or not these lives depended on the exploitation of others. For instance, Mill did not believe that the English aristocracy, with every privilege in the world, led truly aristocratic lives, even if one could overlook the exploitation by which this nominal aristocracy supported itself. They seemed interested only in staying rich or becoming as rich as possible, and by the strength of their prestige corrupted the whole population into striving for money to the neglect of all other human possibilities. No, the direction to look is not upward at the top stratum of any European society, but rather at isolated individuals here and there. The unwelcome truth suggested by Mill is that only a small minority of any population will ever lead nonexploitative autonomous lives, no matter how favorable social circumstances are. A scattered minority's independent experiments in living benefit society, despite society's own immediate resistance and intolerance; but for Mill the true justification for tolerating individuality is the benefit to the developed individual, whose experiments often arouse dislike. To be tolerated as an exceptional individual is a benefit that such a person is not likely to claim as such, but that must be claimed on his or her behalf. In Mill's view, the example of developed individuality can be influential only in inspiring weak or awkward, temporary or superficial, imitation, not (as Emerson hoped) in helping to encourage others to become independently self-developed in divergent directions.

Obviously it is easier for Mill to favor the freedom to live as one likes over the ideal of personal autonomy. He sees the basic dignity of the person just in being free; yet he admires most of all those persons who develop themselves splendidly. Pericles, not Alcibiades or Calvin, is exemplary, even though Mill says, perhaps with defective sincerity to conciliate his audience, Calvin is preferable to Alcibiades (*Liberty*, p. 266). But for an adult to be assisted by the state to become developed, when such assistance takes the form of the state's steady surveillance and its numerous and detailed regulations, to which it adds carefully engineered opportunities for enhancement, is to be neither autonomous nor free. The largest point is that human dignity cannot depend on autonomy as its ultimate justification because most people, no matter how favorable the circumstances to individuality, will never break out of conformity to the extent that autonomy demands. Nevertheless, there is dignity in a human being who has no noteworthy demonstrated virtue or excellence. No human being, autonomous or not, is a thing or a machine or an animal or a child that cannot manage to grow up. A human being, as such, as a member of the human species, as included in a common humanity, is entitled to human rights; most relevantly here, the right to as much freedom as possible to live as he likes and do as he pleases. Rights cannot be apportioned according to how well they are exercised, because human dignity cannot be denied any human being. I think we must side with Mill's view of dignity at its most difficult against Green's at its most humane.

Even conformists, who spend so little of their freedom and who are often enough averse to the expressive freedom of others, have a claim to human dignity and hence to human rights. Those people who conform too well, too dutifully, do not lead autonomous lives, but looked at with the kind of care they often enough deny others, they, too, can be seen as unique persons. Not only are they members of the human race equally with all others, they are also unique persons. Although they try too hard to be like others, they must fail just because in important respects they are not like others. Perhaps in their lives of affection they show, if not developed individuality, then uniqueness expressed in how and what they like and love. Or, let us say, uniqueness in some of the sentences they think or say or write, or even barely form, in going out to meet their experience. Every person is unknowable and therefore unpredictable. To think otherwise is to be falsely knowing.

A Few Other Moral Questions about Human Rights

At the start I said that some thinkers dislike the idea of equal human dignity of all persons because they think that people have to earn their dignity by being moral and may forfeit their dignity by being immoral. Only human beings can be moral or immoral: that is a unique human trait. But being immoral is an awful kind of uniqueness; only being moral is praiseworthy uniqueness. My answer is that even wicked persons are entitled to be treated, if caught and punished, with awareness of their human status. Limits must be set on the way they are treated, and those limits are specified in the overall notion of due process as given in the US Constitution and further spelled out in the provisions and amendments of the US Constitution and whatever other provisions, American or foreign, that accord with the US Constitution. The dignity component of the defense of human rights weighs in strongly on the side of limits, where the morality component by itself, in some interpretations, could allow capital punishment and sees no perplexity in the fact that there is no single theory of punishment that has won universal acceptance and that the various theories—retribution, neutralization of the criminal, deterrence, expression of society's sentiments, and the will to honor human dignity by holding a person accountable for his criminal actions—can issue in divergent degrees of harshness.

The US Constitution simply takes for granted punishment as an established practice, but we should notice that the protections it gives suspects, defendants, and prisoners evince a determination that the state should manifest reluctance to punish and a consequent leniency in administering punishment. In its fullness, due process of law is meant to create obstacles, in the form of certain procedural rights, between prosecution and a guilty verdict, and between a guilty verdict and punishment. If punishment is mandated, it should not be cruel or unusual. Advantages are given to all those caught up in the criminal law that honor their dignity as human beings, whatever any version of morality says, and whatever the idea of punishment that seems to prevail, if any does. I have already mentioned the bar against self-incrimination: no one can be compelled to harm himself; and the bar against a state appeal of acquittal: no one should be compelled to live with the constant possibility of being charged with the same crime and tried until he is found guilty.

A much harder moral problem arises when we realize that the protected rights of mind—speech, press, and religion—injure people at home and abroad by mobilizing populations for aggressive or imperialist policies, or for racist practices, or for subtle forms of religious persecution that avoid violating the explicit guarantees of religious freedom. In Mill's scheme, these rights of mind and conscience protect self-regarding activities, but the notion of self-regarding acts suffers its greatest strain when we see how potent is the effect of uncensored thought in a given society in affecting minorities at home and people abroad without their consent and in actually harming them. Aroused citizens are gullible, ill-informed, and seem almost eager to be mobilized. In an imperial democracy, the freedoms enumerated in the First Amendment are always creating clear and present dangers, especially for foreign populations, as Marcuse said in "Repressive Toleration." What a large fraction of utterance is harmful. The corrective capacities of good speech, press, and religion are often weak or belated.

Yet censorship is to be condemned, despite its occasional good moral or cultural tendency, on the grounds of human dignity. The injury done to the dignity of obnoxious and offensive or thoughtless users of free speech and press by punishing them through a system of censorship is great, while the injury to the dignity of a whole population that lives under a system of censorship, even contentedly, is almost as grave as any injury can be. Censorship violates the negative aspects of human dignity—dignity based on what human beings are not—by treating people as if they were children that can never grow up, as if they must not be allowed to say and write or hear or read what they wish. If my answer gives cold comfort, then all I can say is that censorship would never be in the right hands and would become another potent weapon for the infliction of suffering at the disposal of the state and its elites. In defending the rights of mind and conscience, dignity intermittently outweighs morality in the short run, but then eventually they cooperate in defending these rights.

In sum, my attempted answer to both the utilitarian and virtue critiques of rights turns on the point that the existential idea of equal human status of every person does work for the defense of human rights that morality by itself cannot do or that it may, in certain cases, inadvertently or not, block. Yes, morality is the supreme value; pain and suffering are the prior considerations. But morality should sometimes make concessions, especially when the kind of morality at issue is one of majoritarian calculation and dominance. My specific answer to the virtue critique is that the idea of human dignity that helps to defend the theory of rights cannot be the idea of dignity that sustains notions of paternalistically assisted self-development.

There is one other problem, and it will not go away. How can we defend the idea of equal human dignity when the historical record is so full of wickedness? Why give human beings such a title of honor when they regularly harm one another? The heavens rock with laughter. We deal here not only with the wrongs that are done when the human rights of some people are used to produce injustice, oppression, and evil for others, but with the record of wrongs that were done long before the theory of human rights was sent around the world. The obvious truth is that we cannot undo the past. To say, as I wish, that if people took to heart both the morality and the dignity components of the theory of human rights, they would then do less wickedness is not to say much. I grant that bills of rights can easily turn out to be mere parchment barriers or cynically used rhetorical devices.

But should people now feel free to inflict pain and suffering and assault the human dignity of anyone they please because the historical record is full of such treatment by human beings of other human beings, and the contemporary record, even in societies that claim to recognize and respect rights, is mixed or worse? Is no one worthy of rights because some have denied them to others, and many have acquiesced in the denial? Should the struggle for rights be abandoned?

Although no balance can be struck between the humanly inflicted suffering and atrocities that fill the human record and the amount of decency in the world, much of it unrecorded but manifest in the persistence of human life, and although nothing should be allowed to cover over the record of human wrongdoing with obliviousness, there is no desecration in affirming that all people are owed human rights, on grounds of both morality and human dignity. There is no moral justification of the human record, only allowance—let it continue. Even without moral justification, we must unequivocally want human life to go on. But perhaps there is an existential justification; if there is, it is a justification based on the stature of the species rather than a justification based on the moral goodness of countless individuals, which is often overwhelmed by politically organized crimes and atrocities made possible by the docility and energy of countless individuals.

3

Human Uniqueness: Traits and Attributes

⌘

There is a nonmoral perspective that lets it be said that humanity can be justified in its own eyes, not merely allowed to go on as a matter of course without an effort to ask whether it deserves to exist. If we are willing to say after taking thought that humanity has dignity, that statement would appear to be sufficient justification by itself. From this perspective, there is no species like humanity. It is capable of doing not just a few remarkable things that no other species can—the same is true of many other species—but an indefinitely large number of remarkable things that no other species can. It can also imitate some of the best natural activities of other species, on land and sea and in the air, and surpass them through technique and technology. But there is one thing that only humanity can do that would count as its justification in the eyes of some external judge, if there were one that was appropriately designed in accordance with the highest human standards. (Of course there is circularity in such a thought-experiment.) The activity that would justify humanity in the mind of this judge, which perceives with the most complete understanding, cannot be self-interested (or not only so), and must devote itself to what is real and not itself, and do so with the high intellectual and aesthetic virtues of magnanimity, wonder, and gratitude. If perhaps we can indicate that nature, understood as distinct from humanity, would be worse off without it because humanity can do for nature in the comprehensive sense—the earth and the universe—what must be done, but cannot be done otherwise than by humanity, we have arrived at the best justification of the human species. Such devotion removes the taint of self-worship from the stature component of human dignity and thus enhances the whole idea of human dignity.

Only humanity can perform the three indispensable functions: keep the record of nature, understand nature, and appreciate it. The human species, alone among species on earth, can perform these services to nature on earth and beyond, and do so in part not for its own sake but for the sake of what is not itself. These services constitute the stewardship of nature. Indeed, the wager should be that humanity has the only mind in the universe and allow its obligations to nature to flow from its nobility. A fine sentence by Edward O. Wilson catches a good part of the inspiration: "The most wonderful mystery of life may well be the means by which it created so much diversity from so little physical matter" (p. 35).

I borrow the concept of stewardship from Heidegger, but not the word. He says that "Man is the shepherd [der Hirt] of Being" and that "Ecstatic dwelling [Ek-sistenz] is the guardianship [die Wachterschaft], that is, the care [die Sorge] for Being" ("Letter on Humanism," pp. 221–222). I prefer the word *stewardship* because the word *shepherd* tends to imply guarding the flock for the purpose of slaughter; the sense of protective watchfulness is good, but still too passive for the human stewardship of nature. I depart from Heidegger in seeing the accumulation of objective knowledge of nature and its record as essential to stewardship and also refusing to see objective knowledge as a barrier to either preservation of nature or appreciation and admiration of it. Given that I have nature in mind, not Being, I know that what I call departure might actually be abandonment and even betrayal of Heidegger's teaching, or incomprehension of it. My departure would be even greater if Being is not a certain perspective on beings but is instead independent of beings. The idea of stewardship would be irrelevant, despite many passages in Heidegger in which particular phenomena are contemplated so that their reality can be established.

Given the human record of atrocities, which show humanity at its most inhuman—obviously, being inhuman is also quite human—and the told and untold accumulation of many kinds of pain and suffering (on the one hand) and the diminishment and degradation imposed by one system or another (on the other hand), the justification—if that is what we seek—of human life must be sought in the praiseworthy treatment that humanity is capable of giving to what is not itself and apart from its self-interest. The standard would be met if humanity is selfless enough to be able to treat the nonhuman disinterestedly or reverently, in distinction from the brutality that human beings inflict on one another. This move seems to be a leap, so I will try to give an account of my reasons as we go along. There are many steps before the leap.

Yet it is also the case that aside from its service to nature, the human species can receive another nonmoral justification—justification by great achievements—that does not depend on the ability to be selfless, as toward nature. Rather the justification is human-centered and still rests on what is unique and commendable. Great achievements are the central manifestation of the partway separation of the human species from nature and thus help to substantiate the special kind of human uniqueness and hence human dignity. We are now dealing with the existential concept of human stature, which can be and is displayed not only in the stewardship of nature and which can be explored and defended for the sake of rebutting naturalist reductions of humanity.

Humanity in the Service of Nature

Humanity rises above itself by putting its break with nature, its partway nonnaturalness, in the service of nature. It would repay nature for human existence and try to compensate for the damage it has inflicted on nature. To be sure, uniquely human traits and attributes, when applied to nature, serve humanity as well; but they can also and do sometimes serve nature for the sake of nature. The irony is that only by nonnatural traits and attributes, which are uniquely human, is the human race able to serve nature: to record its history, to know it, and to appreciate and admire it. But also by these same traits and attributes, the human species has given repeated praiseworthy demonstrations of its nonnatural stature apart from its service to nature.

The question of the commendable uniqueness of the human species is made more pointed by the assertion that the earth would be better off without it, or with a drastically reduced human population. There is a genocidal tendency in those thinkers who teach the undesirability of the human race and the superiority of all other species to the species that thinks of itself as superior to them. John Gray's *Straw Dogs* (2002) gives an invaluable statement of this idea, which he appears to endorse. The principal reason is that the human species has destroyed parts of nature and is threatening other parts with desolation. The destructive capacity of the human race far exceeds that of all other species put together. I think that it is therefore urgently true that the most important service that humanity can do is to save endangered animal and plant species from extinction, when possible, by attending to the preservation of the environment that species require. We must abandon the human prejudice that animals and the rest of nature exist solely for human use. The only theoretically tolerable method of preservation is not wishing the human species extinct but rather drastically controlling the growth in human population, and practicing radically new forms of human abstemiousness. That is to say, the abstemiousness that feels intolerable when it is advocated for the sake of saving other human beings must come to feel tolerable for the sake of saving nature to the extent that is feasible.

I am unable to add anything to an already large literature on the practical steps human beings must take to save as much of nature as it can. But my interest here is to say that there are other services to nature, the ones that I have just mentioned above, that only humanity can perform, and to suggest that if we are looking to justify humanity in the face of its terrible moral record, its continuous assaults on its own dignity, and its terrible ecological record, then perhaps we can make a reckoning that comes out in humanity's favor. The reckoning is vis-à-vis nature, and if it continues to be carried through it would be a sufficient justification of the human species. I also think that humanity's possession and demonstration of commendable and unique traits and attributes, its partway nonnaturalness, just by itself, is a sufficient justification, though this justification is more nearly self-flattering, a quality that we should avoid when we can in a discussion of human worth.

The intellectual and aesthetic powers of the human species that have been and will be put in the service of nature would not outweigh the harm that humanity has done and continues to do to nature. Much of the harm may be irreversible by now. Rather, the uniquely human powers constitute a service that is incommensurably great. The service to nature is not a moral enterprise; it does not refer to the dealings of human beings with one another. I grant, however, this much to a utilitarian point of view: the infliction of cruel pains on animals is, if not immoral, nevertheless violation of a duty that is quasi-moral. Killing animals for sport also violates a duty, from a more conventional moral point of view. Animals shun death, feel pain, and have a certain dignity. We could even speak of animal rights, made up of two components: the quasi-moral and the quasi-existential, in analogy with human rights.

The service to nature I have in mind consists in the impossible task of making nature be *to* itself. All things and species exist *for* themselves: they are what they are and do what they do, and exist and move with something like the will to be and persist of the sort that Schopenhauer powerfully theorized in *The World as Will and Representation*. The will to be and persist is manifest, not hidden. The point is that unlike humanity, nature does not exist *to* itself; it is not self-conscious; animals, conscious creatures of purposive behavior, know how to exist but do not know that they exist, or what they are and where in the realm of nature they have their place. Language is what nature lacks and what humanity has; where language is lacking, a thing or creature cannot exist to itself. Only a mind can say, I exist, can describe itself, try to understand itself, describe and try to understand and appreciate what exists around it. Only humanity can speak about the rest of nature and for it. (Many species know what they do when they kill, but whether some species sense what it means for themselves to be dead is not relevant here.) The human mind cannot pretend to be nature's mind, as if nature is a ventriloquist's dummy. No, nature cannot know that it is being served by uniquely human powers of mind and aesthetic sense. Rather, it must be treated as if it deserved to know, if only it could. Only unique human capacities make it possible for human beings to speak about nature, as if we were speaking to it, as if it became a *you* to whom we spoke.

The temptation to epistemological idealism is strong, but it cannot be the case that without humanity to know and admire it, nature might as well not exist. There is always the chance that some other species will emerge on earth or elsewhere with a mind able to know and admire. But if the universe is unknowing and unknown and also unadmired, can it even be said to exist? Who could say that it exists?

The purpose is not to exult in uniquely human powers, but to know and admire nature for its own sake: to treat it not as what can be used or wasted but as if it had incomparable value just by being what is not human and what humanity did not create. Despite the human power to make hybrids, grafts, clones, and now "chimeras," and new forms of life, the original substance, even of man the maker, is not man-made. Is there futility, however, in knowing and admiring what cannot ever know that it is being known and admired? (We know and admire the dead of generations back, who cannot know what later generations think of them, but they were entirely capable of understanding that one day they could be known and admired; they knew and admired the generations before theirs.) If nothing in nature can be aware that its history is being recorded and that knowledge of it is being continuously advanced and that its intricacy, interdependence, and beauty are appreciated and admired, then is the disinterested and reverent service to nature futile?

What can I say? To know and admire nature is a form of gratitude for existence, if not for one's own life, then for the rest. We could not feel gratitude to a creator, if there were one, whom we hold ultimately responsible for evil, whatever the good. It is precisely the absence of a creator that makes wonder truly possible, and therefore makes possible gratitude for the wonder, inhibited but not checked by moral or even existential horror at the guiltless nature of things.

Then imagine the greater horror of nature stripped bare of most of its charismatic species and many of the marvels of plant life, landscape, and seascape. That there have been mass extinctions of animal species over the millennia, most often not the fault of humanity, and that indeed the record indicates that 99 percent of all species that have ever existed are now extinct, cannot assuage the loss of species we know and admire (Elizabeth Kolbert). Cloning could save samples of these species, but they would be fit only for captivity in zoos, if their natural habitats are desolate. We must work to preserve the objects of our gratitude, for our sake, and theirs.

I will soon turn to the commendably unique human traits and attributes that account for human stature and that are a necessary part of the study of human dignity, and that can serve nature, though futilely. There are many difficulties in our way, and quite a few conceptual issues that we must face; and I am sure that I cannot be as persuasive as I would like.

In being partly nonnatural, humanity inherits some of the traits and attributes formerly conferred by humanity on divinity. Humanity alone can look at nature and call it good, and has the advantage of not praising it as its own creation, as God praised his, but as the sole species or entity able to find it good and worthy of praise—if not only praise. Humanity inherits for itself the role that it has generally preferred to entrust to God, who is wholly nonnatural. But human beings will always be too given to evil and other wrongdoing toward one another, and terrible destructiveness toward nature, to deserve the efforts at humanity's self-divination and self-worship that some thinkers have promoted. The idea of human dignity must coexist with the knowledge that human beings have never lived up to their moral and existential standards, whether personal or public, with much consistency, let alone a determination to do so through thick and thin. The works of humanity are better than its days.

Against the Philosophical Reduction of Human Stature

We now deal directly with the element of the stature of the species in the two-part idea of human dignity. Could we speak of either element if we dropped the other? Isn't affirmation of the equal individual status of every person sufficient to maintain the idea of human dignity? Why trouble ourselves about the human species? Isn't it true that the defense of human rights will generally go unaccompanied by speculation about the stature of the human race (just as earlier glorying in the stature of the human race went unaccompanied by thought about the equal secular status of individuals)?

We see that the uniqueness of humanity and its superiority over the rest of creation, but subordinated to divinity, was for the most part just assumed in the period when the theory of human (or natural) rights was first put forth, despite a stream of philosophy that reduced humanity to matter or machines or a purely animal nature. I doubt, however, that thinking about rights could have got started if that reduction held sway over the sentiments of many people. Hobbes, a powerful reductive theorist in one strand of his intellectual design, subscribed to materialism; yet he held a theory of individual rights, which is a strange thing to do if you really believe that human beings are just bodies in motion following impulses and impressions when they move about so energetically. Does Hobbes actually manage to persuade even himself that we need not accord the human species a special stature among types of beings if we are to grant that human beings have standing to claim their rights? Why should human animals have rights that other animals don't? Regardless, let us stay with him for a while as a consummate genius and a representative case.

When we explore Hobbes's political philosophy we see that his description of passions, emotions, sentiments, and susceptibilities is dependent on a more complex understanding of human beings than any reductive account—certainly his own account—provides. He wants to reduce human pride by likening human beings to machines by way of likening them to a mere animal species that is not nearly as sensible, in its untrained condition, as the social insects. Humanity is not spontaneously cooperative, but always given to dispute and suspicion. He knows that his deflationary enterprise will offend the pride of a self-admiring species. But his theory in its fullness, while pessimistic, is not despairing, and not at all consistently deflationary.

Hobbes says that the troubles people create for one another come about much more from the possibilities opened up by language than from any purely bodily imperative. Language is uniquely human, and by being used in the natural course of things to form diverse judgments and opinions, it creates the complexity of the human psyche. Strife of many kinds is the inevitable result of psychic complexity. Constant strife is traceable to the human proclivity to prefer many pursuits to self-preservation; to prefer, for example, the risk of death to unavenged insult or offended conscience. People are constantly frightening one another by what they say or write, and by their gestures as much as by their activities. Owing to the complexity of the human psyche, which is the real foundation of Hobbes's political theory, his materialist reduction could not possibly account for the turmoil of political life. Language is not an animal function, as he is too well aware. No other species has language and the proliferation of opinions and judgments that language brings with it, and therefore no other species seems to survive in order to struggle rather than struggle in order to survive. (I shall soon return to the unique human ability to use language in my inventory of human traits and attributes.)

Hobbes sees perversity everywhere; no other creature in nature is perverse. The complexity of the psyche, and its distance from natural appetites in many respects, accounts for Hobbes's passion for peace and his effort to justify absolute monarchy so that speech and press may be regulated, and opinions and judgments, which are the roots of ultimately self-destructive strife, might be turned away from dissidence and tumult by various methods of social discipline. Any opinion that is likely to engender strife is, just for that reason, false: honest thinking always converges on the good of peace. Most opinions are false, but must be rendered harmless by forcing them out of the public sphere. There would be no need for the absolute powers of Leviathan if people were only bent, as a simply animal species would be, on survival: any reasonably strong state would do.

Hobbes's passion for peace, joined to his conviction that the diverse religious and political opinions and judgments that are at the source of strife in society and between societies are based on either illusion or self-interest, leads him to make of self-preservation the right that should condemn to absurdity the claims to all other rights, such as freedom of speech and press, of religious conscience, and of political participation. Hobbes was overpowered by his sense of human folly; he refused to try to accommodate it by granting it more freedom to think, believe, and act. Once the claim for rights is part of the atmosphere of society, as it was in Britain in his time, he should have known that its people would not forever relinquish rights they thought would lead to a fuller life; a bargain for prosperous docility was unacceptable. The people would not again be, if ever they were, the "blank paper" on which the sovereign could inscribe the opinions and judgments that would reform human nature. Human beings could not be made as animally simple as he would have us think that he wished. His materialist and mechanical reduction of human beings would never be believed, especially when it was quite clear that his whole political philosophy did not believe it. The political philosophy was actually built on the premise that humanity is radically different from all other species in possessing language and hence a psyche that no other species possesses. Opinion and judgment would tend to break out of any confinement. A new Leviathan, closer to the French system of absolutism, could not stand for long. Hobbes thought that the proclivity to strife could be eliminated by Leviathan. Spinoza knew better: strife can be moderated and placated only by at least the rudiments of a constitutional state of guaranteed freedoms.

I think that the defense of human rights needs a philosophical anthropology that explores human uniqueness, and that means, among other things, that it must avoid material or mechanical reduction. It is plausible that such an exploration not only will add more weight to the dignity or equal status component in the defense of rights but also will move in the direction of the notion of human stature. The word *stature* implies elevation. Obviously, for human beings to raise the estimation of the human species in its own eyes is to praise themselves. Self-love is always unattractive. But there are no other judges than human beings. If humanity can serve nature, at least its self-praise would be less gross. However, if only for the sake of truth, the reduction of the human species to a merely natural and animal species must be fought. There are many scientific or would-be scientific reductions extant in the world. They all tend to reject human uniqueness or give an impoverished account of it. They do not ring true, no matter how many factual details they get right.

One need not use the term *stature* if one is embarrassed by our species' self-praise, but perhaps that is being overscrupulous. At the same time, we should not be content to conceptualize stature solely by a comparison of humanity to nature, whether we say it is superior to all other species, partly discontinuous with nature, or uniquely capable of serving as nature's steward. There is another element that helps to fill out the concept, which depends on the will to acknowledge that human beings are capable of great achievements. Stature pertains to greatness. Great achievements matter because they make humanity a cause for wonder in its own eyes, a feeling that can arise from the barely credible and not fully explainable display of great achievements. More species self-praise, to be sure; but there are extenuations. We need a general account of human stature. Just as in the discussion of equal individual status, so in the discussion of human stature, the theme of uniquely nonnatural human characteristics is all the while in the background when not overtly present.

Human Stature and Great Achievements

In what follows, I will concentrate on great human-centered achievements, and then return to humanity's service to nature. In this context, when I invoke human stature, I apply the standard of great achievements to the human species but not to the individual. There are of course great individual achievements. But of the millions and millions who have ever lived, how many have attained greatness in any sphere of activity? Individual self-expression rarely attains greatness, but that fact does not affect the dignity, the equal status, of every individual. If human ordinariness, however, were the highest level that humanity reached, it is not certain that the idea of human dignity (or ideas like it) would have arisen. Not to deny that uniquely human traits and attributes are shown in human ordinariness; leading an everyday life, no matter how apparently routine, a person is constantly demonstrating the uniqueness (commendable or not) of humanity among the species of the earth. But moral and dignified ordinariness, which is the special object of the equal concern for human beings that the theory of human rights exists to preserve, does not exhaust human potentiality. This disjunction between the individual and the species is, I think, what best suits the idea of human dignity. Human potentiality is a major human trait, but to appreciate its extent, we need a view of the species' historical record. Kant says that "those natural capacities which are directed towards the use of his reason are such that they could be fully developed only in the species, but not in the individual" ("Idea for a Universal History," Second Proposition, p. 42). Kant emphasizes the capacities for moral improvement guided by reason, "which corresponds to nature's original intention" (p. 43), but he also indicates a more general sense of human potentiality that time does not providentially terminate and that realizes itself in more ways than serve morality or reason. His remark is powerfully suggestive, but we should not be bound by his teleology. We are closer to the mark in Emerson's view that "Man is explicable by nothing less than all his history" ("History," p. 237). As long as there is humanity, there will be history; and if humanity ends, its history ends, and then there will be no mind left to give a full explication of humanity. Even then, no full explication would be possible because of all the potentialities that went unrealized and all the realizations that went unrecorded.

The attempt to understand the complexity of the human psyche, the only psyche in the world, must depend on some appreciation of the human record, including of course all the periods of history when human rights were not recognized. Historical understanding is required to make vivid our sense of human potentiality, which first and last depends on the human mind or psyche. As Rousseau says, humanity's unique capacity for general ideas makes its perfectibility, its realization of potentialities, possible. Mind is a summary term for those unique traits and attributes that are especially relevant to a discussion of human dignity. (Mortality, for example, is a human trait, but it is not unique and does not in itself contribute to human stature, though what people make of it does.) The human record, as much of it as possible, is needed to demonstrate the tremendous range of realized human potentiality, to demonstrate what humanity has been uniquely capable of all along, and all of it unpredictable before the fact, and to signal unforeseeable future achievements that will flow from inexhaustible potentiality. One connection between individual status and human stature is that both rest on the same traits and attributes. But no individual can possibly demonstrate the full range of human of potentiality; we need the human record for that. And then we must add that at any time human potentiality makes the record radically incomplete. I refer not only to the unrecorded: much more in the past is unrecorded than recorded; much more is unknown than known. Rather, I refer especially to what lies ahead and what therefore in principle no generation can ever know even about its immediate future, much less about successor generations. Potentiality and unpredictability are linked.

There is no human end to history and therefore no way of saying what humanity is capable of in the future. In addition, given the same biological endowment but somewhat different conditions in the total natural environment, and different contingencies of all kinds, humanity would have realized different potentialities in the past. If more people had lived longer or had more advantages, who can say what further achievements would have been forthcoming? As it is, given the same biological endowment, human beings have produced remarkably diverse cultures, not only in different natural environments but, much more important, in roughly the same. Analogously, no human being can be fully known, because everyone is unpredictable, and what is more, if by some chance a person had been transported to a different society at birth from where he or she in fact grew up, that person would have in important ways turned out differently and have displayed potentialities that went unrealized in the actual life the person lived. The human species is an indefinite species in a qualitatively different manner from all other species. So, too, every human individual is an indefinite being, possessing "infinitude," in Emerson's term ("Address at the Harvard Divinity School"). And just as every culture is a complex and sometimes internally inconsistent response to life, so "the least of its rational children, the most dedicated to his private affair, works out, though as it were under a disguise, the universal problem" ("Nominalist and Realist," p. 586). Although it is dangerous to think that the state is a superperson, it is benign to think, as Emerson does, that the individual is a ministate or even a world in miniature.

I am not saying that when we regard any particular individual we should see in him or her an embodiment or personification of the whole human record, and by that conceit inflate the person into the species, or even allow the full range of demonstrated human capacity to bestow its aura on any given human being or on all human beings equally. No, we deal here with the stature of the species, carrying with it a past that grew out of other species and will be extended indefinitely into the future. But the fact remains that every individual has all the uniquely human traits and attributes that the human record shows. The human record shows and will show, however, a cumulative display of these traits and attributes that surpasses any individual and any particular group or society.

Human stature is shown in achievements that deserve to be called great. The study of stature is the study of greatness. There are great individual achievements, but great also are cooperative achievements that require groups for realization. The human species as a whole has a stature, but as I have said it is not a collective agent. Its stature is the work of individuals and groups, and it needs thinkers to register it. There are always great individuals, but above all, the human species has always been and must always be broken up into groups that not only nurture individuals but work in conscious and unconscious ways to create cultures. Diverse cultures are put together from different languages, religions, philosophies, ideologies, codes of conduct, practices and habits, rituals and procedures. A complete explanation of why in a given culture, this rather than that language, religion, and so on originally emerged can never be given. There is no believable cultural determinism: a culture is not entirely determined by natural conditions, as distinct from the generational transmission of culture as affected by natural conditions. Only from a human perspective that strained to be non-human but not divine does the diversity of cultures appear as trivial in comparison to the biological uniformities of all human beings. Such a perspective would throw out any discussion of human dignity, but it also throws out interest in animals and plants in their phenomenal variety.

The sources of any major human phenomenon can be traced only so far, and then it disappears into the unknowable—unknowable not only because there are no records but also because the beginnings of most human phenomena stem from intrinsically inaccessible regions of human feelings, buried thoughts, and imagination. Every culture is opaque to those who inhabit it or try to understand it not only from the outside, but also from within. If a culture is a response to life, the response can be internally various or even confused; and certainly it changes over time through revision, abandonment, and crisis, but also owing to causes hard or impossible to decipher. Every culture is an achievement because it is never a mere adaptation to the natural environment. Its complexity is in excess of natural imperatives and creates its own artificial imperatives that override or transform natural ones. The very idea of adaptation to the enclosure of environment does not capture humanity's place in the world. Exploration of outer space is an apt symbol of that fact. The achievement of culture and the particular achievements in every sphere of a culture are made possible by unique human traits and attributes, with the human psyche in the lead and master.

Who shall judge that the human species has an incomparable stature, and that its achievements deserve to be called great? Just as there is no source outside human awareness and self-awareness for the precepts of morality, whether the golden rule or the public morality of justice and with it, the acceptance of the equal human status of every human being, so there is no external audience to confirm the praise given by human observers to the human species as a whole for the achievements that lead us to confer an incomparable stature on it. Nature, on earth or in the universe, has no consciousness on which humanity's knowledge and appreciation of it can register; similarly, there is no nonhuman consciousness on which human greatness can register. I have said that it would be nice—*nice* isn't quite the right word—if a more-than-human or other-than-human entity or entities could set the standards and judge. But there are none; there are no second opinions from outside humanity. We crave an entity greater than ourselves that is able to know the truth about us and also determine moral rules for us infallibly—a divinity to dissolve all intellectual perplexities. But belief in such an entity creates philosophical problems that are even more intractable than all the other ones combined. God is only another way of saying that we cannot dissolve certain perplexities, some of which are probably the fault of our tiredness, confusion, or longing. We end up attributing to divinity the standards we wish invested with sacredness, and then fool ourselves into thinking that the divinity has pronounced and authorized them.

Just as the only enemies to individual status are human beings, so the only deriders of human stature are human beings who try to take away human pride in itself by deflationary reductions of the human species. Their strategy is to picture humanity as just another animal species among other animal species, with some particularities, even uniqueness, but none so commendable as to elevate humanity above the rest, and some traits and attributes that tend to sink humanity below other species. Hobbes was not the first derider or will be the last. More recently, approaches to understanding human consciousness such as evolutionary psychology (all our conduct emanates from what is "hard-wired" in us thanks to natural selection; we are, like any animal species, essentially creatures of instinct, impulse, and reflex, or at best our more complex conduct is always traceable to instinct, impulse or reflex) and neuroscience (the mind or psyche is only the brain) are also naturalist reductions that misrepresent the human species, and unnecessarily tarnish human dignity by taking away commendable uniqueness from it. These days, the notion of human stature is directed in part against these reductions, in the name of human dignity, but also in the name of truth. If not truthful, despite all the difficulties and doubts, the notion wouldn't be part of the idea of human dignity.

Against evolutionary psychology, in particular, we can say first that it is a category mistake, indeed a serious blunder, to say that on any given occasion, a person's motive, mediated as it is by mind, is unconsciously determined by evolutionary inheritance. No human motive is reducible to a natural cause. Human self-description in ordinary language is not a superstructure of superstition. A conscious motive is based on an interpretation of reality; an unconscious motive is an inchoate interpretation. Science should not interfere with phenomenology by telling us that when we act we think we are doing one thing but are actually doing another that cannot be described in the ordinary language we use to describe ourselves.

Furthermore, humanity cannot be counted on to follow the path of least resistance to its aims, or pursue only those aims that offer the least resistance. Indeed aims are frequently defined in such a way as to create or welcome obstacles in order to overcome them, or even to imperil survival. Self-mastery is shown through the mastery of self-created obstacles. We can even hazard the notion that at its greatest, the mind is what has managed to survive the imperatives of survival, as defined by natural selection, and that it is always turning its attention to making survival only the precondition for something artificial and worthwhile. That the mind is the great engine of survival does not preclude us from saying that its forgetfulness of or indifference to the imperatives of survival, or even defiance of them, is as great or greater yet. When concern for survival is held at a distance, and greatness is sought, human freedom is evinced and human stature thereby more purely exemplified. Even if all that human beings ever did was merely adapt to their natural environment, they show a remarkable ability to adjust to changing circumstances. Natural change calls forth from an indefinitely large repertory of responses with now these, now those admirable characteristics. Human beings also deliberately change the circumstances to which they must adjust. But human life is more than adaptation; it is also transformation. The creation of diverse and changing cultures is not a continuation of the process of biological evolution, nor is any culture continuous with the conditions that the first human beings faced. Of course, change is not always for the better, by a rational standard. The more general point is that not all traits and attributes of creatures are advantageous for adaptation; some are even disadvantageous but still endure. Nature is imperfect. There is secular truth in Emerson's remark, "There is a crack in every thing God has made" ("Compensation," p. 292). An undisappointed way of putting the point is that there is a swerve in nature; all nature shows a surplus beyond the requirements of adaptation, an excess, an extravagance, but above all the fact of humanity's emergence. The point is not teleological: humanity did not have to emerge from nature because nature wanted to be known.

Against neuroscience, I just want to say that when a section of the brain lights up on a scanning device as, say, the person is listening to music, we learn nothing interesting about the person's experience of the music or the music itself. And the same consideration holds for thinking, speaking and listening, writing and reading, and engaging in the countless other employments of the mind. Neuroscience is no substitute for phenomenology; that the reverse is true matters only to natural scientists, which is all well and good, provided boundaries are respected.

No attention to human stature, in the face of attempted naturalistic reductions, however, should obscure the other part of human dignity, the equal status of every human being. The necessary precondition of great achievements is the mobilized and largely anonymous collective labor of the mass of the population. We cannot be allowed to forget the prodigious effort of the mass or many to sustain the great number of cultures the world has seen and to facilitate their changes through time, not through personal creative genius but through the daily work of embodiment and the slight but cumulatively great revision of the culture's response to life.

Having no collective mind, the species nevertheless lends itself to generalizations. As observers we can try to think about the human species as if from an external perspective. In contrast, all individuals experience themselves from the inside (so to speak); each is unique to, and has a unique relation to, himself or herself, whatever the judgment of others is. One has unique access to one's inwardness: one's stream of consciousness and dream life; one's sentiment of being alive rather than being nothing, and being the individual who one is. A human clone would not have access to the inwardness of the original or even have a substantively identical inwardness.

The concept of equal status, equal individual human dignity, can be carried internally by a person, in varying degrees of steadfastness, while the concept of human stature must be imputed by human observers to the human species as a whole. Who can say how many persons have internalized it, thought about it, and acted on it?

All the evidence a person needs to claim human rights is contained in a minimal self-knowledge that is found by looking inside oneself combined with a self-awareness of one's conduct in the midst of other people. All the uniquely human traits and attributes can be found by self-inspection. Individual rights depend on possession on them. Pride in the achievements that constitute human stature, however, is not required to accept the validity of any individual's claim to equal status as a human being. Just as for a long time, the concept of human stature perforce sufficed for human dignity, so now the concept of individual status appears to suffice for human dignity. But we should not do without both concepts. In a democratic age, when human rights are central, we must nevertheless insist that the stature of the species is the other component of human dignity.

A Selective List of Uniquely Human Traits and Attributes

It would be foolish to attempt a comprehensive philosophical anthropology. Even more, it would be foolish to try to present a view of human nature, if by that phrase we mean a detailed description of everything a human being or the human species is capable of, together with a complete repertory of their characteristic behaviors. A catalogue of innate instincts and drives is another matter, but not easily given because it is often not clear as to what is innate and what is socially acquired. A detailed description of, say, the nature of a bear or wolf cannot serve as a model for a view of human nature. Perhaps the very notion of human nature is mistaken: the human species is not only natural. Being not only natural, the human species is boundless, obviously not because its technologically unaided physical feats are boundless—they clearly are not, and in this or that respect, we are inferior, even when technologically assisted, to one species or another—but rather because human cultural activity is indefinitely various, just as human creativity is so to speak infinite. Therefore, even the most comprehensive philosophical anthropology can give only a selective inventory of human traits and attributes, even as we remember that they all tend to make the human species unpredictable; the species is characterized by immeasurable potentiality—the species cannot measure itself.

I will give quite a selective list of traits and attributes common to all human beings. But the emphasis must be on the word *selective*. The field to be covered by philosophical anthropology is too large, and invites many interpretations, which derive from many perspectives (religious and metaphysical) and compete with one another by providing various emphases and ingredients or different clusters of inclusions and omissions. There must be a purposive selectivity. All the items on the list are uniquely human and commendable, and differentiate humanity from the merely natural; they all point to what all other species are not and what they cannot do.

In what I say I leave aside possible efforts to enhance human capacities by genetic manipulation. How such efforts would affect the idea of human dignity I do not know. Whether the work would enhance the whole species or just some members or groups of it is purely speculative. Many of the efforts could well be incompatible with human dignity, as Heidegger thinks in his "Memorial Address." His barely sketched nightmare is even more dire than Aldous Huxley's. His fear is that the old rootedness of human works in nature would give way to a transformed relationship between humanity and nature, in which human mastery is horrifyingly total and has no roots except in human will and technological capacity. The success of these efforts is far more likely and hence represents a "far greater danger" than "complete human annihilation and the destruction of the earth" by means of atomic weapons (*Discourse on Thinking* [*Gelassenheit*], pp. 55–56). A similar line of thinking is resourcefully amplified and defended by Francis Fukuyama in *Our Post-Human Future* (2002). My discussion, however, takes us as we are and also rejects any appeal to the need for roots (Heidegger's word is *Bodenständigkeit,* durable adherence) as a sentimentally archaic gesture unworthy of the thinkers—Heidegger, Simone Weil, and others—who make it. The alleged need for roots is in the same class as the alleged need for enchantment or reenchantment. Both are examples of bathos. In contrast, the need for meaning must be respected, provided it does not become a source of intolerance and persecution, as it easily does, or represent an inflamed will-to-believe that nourishes a degrading self-deception.

We come now to gather together some main uniquely human traits and attributes. In their uniqueness they make possible those human achievements that testify to the human stature; they lead us to say that human dignity belongs to the species as well as to individuals. The question is that since every individual has all the traits and attributes, should that lead us to enlarge the basis for the defense of human rights by enlarging the dignity component in that defense? Does the idea of the equal status of every individual need a more elaborated philosophical anthropology than I have already given? I will delay attention to this question until I take up the subject of free agency as one of the uniquely human attributes.

Let me now list the uniquely human characteristics, traits and attributes, abilities and capacities that I think should figure in a discussion of human dignity. The listing must be made up of what we should think are obvious items, yet challenges must be expected to the existence or the human uniqueness or praiseworthiness of one or another of them. All the traits and attributes are based in the body, but none is reducible to a merely biological phenomenon with an exclusively biological explanation. They all establish that humanity is partly nonnatural. These are the traits and attributes: the use of spoken language; the use of written language, and other notational systems; from language comes the ability to think (including memory, the glue of thinking); from thinking, the ability both to accumulate knowledge and become self-conscious; from all these comes the capacity for agency; from agency comes what Rousseau calls "perfectibility," a synonym for which is "potentiality"; from potentiality comes unpredictability and creativity; necessary to unpredictability and creativity is imagination, which is interwoven with language but conceptually separate from it. Imagination shows itself in many ways, but one that deserves mention here is the ability to represent or reproduce the world, through verisimilitude or consciously repudiated verisimilitude, as in drawing and stories.

Just a word about *potentiality*, a word that I have frequently used. I do not here have in mind natural growth as, for example, when a child (a potential adult) becomes an adult. Rather, I mean a latent ability to achieve some work or deed that is not only a surprising move in an established activity or game, which therefore shows unusual skill within the framework of established rules or conventions but is also, more important, a breakthrough. The latent ability to produce a breakthrough reposes in the unconscious and the semiconsciousness of persons and sometimes pushes successfully for realization; it can be favored by outside events or conditions, or it can go unrealized. The latent ability can be unsuspected; the realization is therefore a thoroughly unpredictable work or deed—a new style or practice, or a revolutionary invention or discovery. We retrospectively call the breakthrough creative. More personally, one can turn on oneself and change one's life.

Of enormous interest is the fact that the human species existed for tens of thousands of years without writing (and other notational systems) and hence without many kinds of complex mental operations. Writing came in only afterward, ten or six thousand years ago. It is worth pondering the fact that tens of thousands of years passed in the life of humanity before the invention of writing, and it appeared independently in only a few societies. If there were a catastrophic end to civilization all over the world, who knows how long it would take to recreate civilization, or even whether the condition most advanced in the development of human uniqueness would be like what we now know? I do not intend to tarnish human dignity, but it is not a stretch to say that contingency, the contingent invention of writing—speech was perhaps inevitable—has made almost all the difference between the last few thousand years and the much larger amount of human time that came before. Even so, the common and protracted life of hunting and gathering, as still may be observed here and there, demonstrates uniquely human capacities for speech and what is made possible by it, including the beginnings of technology. Even a way of life that is close to nature is partly not natural, but characterized by freedom from strict natural determination in some aspects of life. The unpredictable and creative transition to written language and novel sorts of psychological, social, and technological complexity, while the biological endowment remained constant, is another fact of enormous interest. This fact is finally inexplicable except to say with Rousseau that without general ideas, without some capacity to symbolize and abstract, and to see sameness in difference, the undestined transition to greater complexity could not have taken place.

In brief, Sartre's doctrine that human beings are always able to become different through an upsurge of free creativity and hence can never be conclusively defined or delimited captures, as well as any other doctrine, the philosophical anthropology that underlies human dignity as I conceive it in its two components of individual status and human stature. Human beings are more than they think they are at any given time; if they choose to deny it, they are guilty of bad faith. If persons choose a fixed definition for themselves, they cannot choose for the whole species.

Implicit where not explicit in my discussion of the theory of human rights so far is the centrality of two uniquely human capacities, free agency and moral agency. But the other mentioned traits and attributes make both kinds of agency possible, and I wish to discuss them before returning to agency. As I proceed, I will look at unique human traits and attributes not only as presuppositions of free agency and moral agency but also as an elaboration of human stature, and beyond that to the purest and also most urgent expression of human stature, the stewardship of nature.

I am guided in what I say by one of the greatest philosophical anthropologies, Rousseau's *Discourse on the Origins and Foundations of Inequality among Men* (1755). He speculated richly about human uniqueness, commendable or not. He also gives in *The Social Contract* (1762) a description of a society in which human uniqueness can become mostly or only morally virtuous. Rousseau starts in the *Discourse* with the supposition that the natural endowment of the human species is free of any innate tendency to wickedness. Even so, human history is a long story of mostly wickedness, of the social perversion of that natural endowment. Too much of what we read about humanity or observe honestly shows a disposition to wickedness; yet everything Rousseau surmises on the basis of imagining what a child well brought up by a single tutor in a secluded setting would turn out to be ratifies the wished-for inference that humanity was good at the beginning because it was not social but existed in primitive individual isolation. The good society that Rousseau theorizes is the highest turn of the spiral: his aim is not to go back to nature but forward, no matter how unlikely the prospect is, to a political and social condition where law-bound freedom replaces primitive independence and becomes the condition most appropriate to the perfection of humanity's natural endowment. To be politically equal and participatory, the new condition must be a small and homogeneous society that is culturally simple and static and economically austere and not too unequal. In this condition only, natural pity can be transformed into a reliable sense of justice in the body of citizens. Here alone moral liberty in its fullness can exist: the convergence of a good will, a sense of duty, and an enlightened understanding of self-interest.

The *Discourse* offers a conjectural history of how primitivity was lost and replaced, in stages, by one kind of regrettable grouping or society after another, from not so bad to bad to worse and then even worse than what preceded it. The worst of all awaits humanity. For Rousseau, the movement, driven as much by accident as by human desire and will, is always toward advances in human skill, each of which softens the human body and blunts the senses but enlarges the mind, and deepens dependence on others. Rousseau makes much less of creativity, daring, and initiative than of resilient adaptability. Primitive freedom is solitary independence. The engine of decadence was the combined pressure of increased population, and with it and because of it, growth in the human ability to master and exploit nature by technical means. The pressure and the growth worked to intensify each other. The exploitation of nature is tantamount to the denaturing of humanity. Pervading the process is the growth of inequality that derives from naturally unequal skills, which are inexorably and artificially developed to become the foundation for established hierarchy. The good society reduces inequality rather than diversifying and fortifying it.

Rousseau wants to defend the idea of human dignity; in its defense of rights it seems like the idea that, as I have suggested, ideally supports the theory of human rights, but the stature of the species counts for nothing. Although Rousseau is carefully attentive to human uniqueness, his ideal society is a war on human stature and on the dignity of the species. He wants no trace of the achievements of the ancien regime to remain. In the culture of the good society, the emphasis on social equality, simplicity, and stability purges the society of the capacity to accomplish great achievements. The social arrangements block the growth of mind, deny the resources and atmosphere for individual and social experiment, and stifle every energy but patriotism. Rousseau makes the attainment of justice exorbitant. We go to Rousseau to learn from what he says about human uniqueness, not human excellence. For all that can be said against him, however, it is to our advantage that he is for the most part secular in his philosophical anthropology.

Language Is the Key to Human Uniqueness

The key to human uniqueness for Rousseau is language. And this is where I would like to begin my discussion of specific traits and attributes that are uniquely human. He offers two accounts of language of special interest to the theory of human dignity. Both were written in the 1750s. The published reflections are in the *Discourse* of 1755, but there are equally compelling reflections in the posthumously published *Essay on the Origin of Languages*. In both works Rousseau insists that language is a uniquely human phenomenon. In what follows, I deal with some of his thoughts and add some other ones, too. I begin close to where Rousseau begins, with the observation that no other species has the ability to use language, even though other species can communicate their biological imperatives in various ways, including sound, and do so complexly. In contrast, human language opens up infinite possibilities of meaning. Meaning is not an event in nature. A sentence is usually more than a simple communication of needs. Metaphysical or speculative modalities like the past and the future, the possible and the necessary, the hypothetical and the conditional, the contingent and the accidental all refer to the invisible. The actual gains clarity from the other modalities, and only language makes all of them possible.

Rousseau emphasizes that language makes general ideas or concepts possible, and ideas or concepts help make possible everything else that is uniquely human. A language is an intricate artifice that is constructed of parts of speech, cases, tenses, and other features that are not instinctive or reflexive natural occurrences. Nouns are not the only kind of words, and not even nouns originally appeared one or a few at a time out of thin air. There are also notational systems, like written language, music, and mathematics. Language (spoken and written) helps to establish and develop the latter two, which are of course nonverbal manifestations of mind; but instruction in them cannot be mutely mimetic. Music and mathematics develop indefinitely and autonomously (so to speak) out of their own systemic possibilities; but they still need the aid of language. Given a structure by rules, notational systems are forever open to novelty of occurrence. Some of the rules may change over time, but the incidence of novel occurrences does not depend on innovations in the rules. The coming of literacy amplifies, if it does not initiate, the indefinite or infinite power of language to make new meaning as the most important existential fact.

Let us say that by making language possible, the human brain makes possible the mind, from which speech and notational systems come. Language not only makes thinking possible, it is the medium of most thinking. I do not say *all* thinking because we should allow for unconscious, preconscious, and inchoate thinking, in all of which images and words are mingled. Dreams would be one example of unconscious thinking. A child's growth is measured in a significant degree by increased mastery of language. Language by itself is enough evidence for saying why brain and mind are not interchangeable terms. The brain is indispensable for something greater than itself and not reducible to itself; it prepares the way for the mind. The brain does not program the mind to study the brain. Perhaps in all species the brain prepares the way for something greater than itself, even though we wish to reserve the word *mind* for human beings. Only the human brain prepares the way for humanity's unique departure from nature. The mind enables the human species, alone among species, to move against nature's direction and avoid eternal recurrence of the same.

There are quite a few striking formulations about language in the historical sketch of language that Rousseau offers in the *Essay on Language* (in some respects similar to Vico's earlier reflections) and that are relevant to the claim that no reduction of human beings to mere animals can account for the occurrence of speech. Animals do not have conventions: "Conventional language is characteristic of man alone" (p. 10). Grunts and gestures could have been enough to convey needs; passions, not needs, account for the urgency of language, the urgency to use words. He says, "It is neither hunger nor thirst but love, hatred, pity, anger, which drew from them the first words" (p. 12). Passions speak in tropes: "at first only poetry was spoken; there was no hint of reasoning until much later" (p. 12). Only human beings have passions and hence only they have virtues and vices.

Leaving aside the temporal sequences that derive from Rousseau's commitment to an original individual isolation in nature, we can distill, but also revise, Rousseau's teaching for the subject of human dignity, especially the stature of the species. Material or animal necessities, or what we call imperatives of survival, could not sufficiently account for the human use of language. Language arises from the urge to change the imperatives of survival, from the overflow of human energy, a refusal to remain stationary, a will to excess, a fascination with the apparently impossible. Rousseau also takes up the origin of writing, but that is so obviously humanly unique and so obviously owing to an inexplicable leap in human creativity that we need not dwell on it. No other species speaks, much less writes. And if many groupings and societies got on without writing, we could still say that it is indispensable to the indefinite proliferation of meaning. With a particular intensity, written language defines the world by giving it meaning and coherence; and also creates a parallel world that seems to detach itself from direct reference to the given world and either re-presents it or abandons it altogether. As a matter of course language also distorts or covers over; it is not only a reliable lens, window, prism, mirror, magnifying glass, microscope, or telescope, it is also a poor reflection or representation of reality, a film of opacity, even a funhouse mirror. Undeniably, language is inadequate to convey many sensory experiences, the effects of some other kinds of experience, and the texture of dreams. As Conrad's Marlow says in *The Heart of Darkness,* "no relation of a dream can convey the dream-sensation . . . being captured by the incredible" (pp. 27–28). But language is needed to express its own inadequacy. That language fails mystics who take refuge in the notion of the inexpressible, however, may indicate a problem with the notion. Literature exists to give us the feeling that experience we thought too elusive for articulation can find its words.

Then when we add such other notational systems as music and mathematics, both of them more systemically self-enclosed than speech or written language, but still indefinitely expansive, we find the uniquely human so commendable that we can wonder how it is that many intellectuals can persist in denying that humanity removes itself from the merely natural and manages a break with nature. There is nothing theological or transcendental in saying as much. Reference to transcendental divinity as the causal explanation of the break with nature introduces magic, which simply restates the problem without solving it. Nature blindly produced the species that has broken with it, just as the species was impelled it knew not why to break with nature.

Marx says in his "Critique of the Hegelian Dialectic and Philosophy as a Whole" (1844) that "man is not merely a natural being" (p. 116).

He speaks in his own voice what Hegel could have said. The formulation is in itself correct, it seems to me. Marx may take it back, however, when he immediately adds, "he is a *human* natural being." (He wrote this piece before Darwin, and never published it. It is doubtful that after he read Darwin he still agreed with his formulation that man is not merely a natural being, even though Marx's moral psychology is not always naturalistically reductive and remains often subtle and unbiological, as when he discusses the theatricality of revolutionaries and the fetishism of commodities.) After Darwin, though it is hard for anyone who is not religious to accept the formulation, the uneasy truth should have its way. The truth requires us to accept, on nonreligious grounds, Marx's early formulation, while we also accept the truth of Darwin's theory of evolution through natural selection and random mutation. The trouble is that the theory of evolution is made to yield a questionable conclusion—namely, that there can be nothing animate in nature that is not completely natural and amenable to an exclusively naturalist explanation. I think that evidence of human uniqueness rebuts this claim.

Marx also says that the good society is "the consummated oneness in substance of man and nature—the true resurrection of nature—the naturalism of man and the humanism of nature both brought to fulfillment ("Private Property and Communism," p. 85). This sentiment seems to reincorporate humanity entirely into nature but make humanity its telos. Rousseau is the sounder guide. Humanity is not like any other species; it breaks with nature. Nature has no telos that drives humanity to reach the point where it is able at last to consummate nature while remaining entirely natural, and to do so for the sake of nature. (In Marx's work after 1844, the idea of progress figures, but the historical process has no telos; that is, there is no end that from its very nature had to be reached, and when reached, represents a consummation.) Since nature has no telos, the human species is at its greatest when it breaks out of nature. Humanity does not resurrect nature or humanize nature, when it becomes more human or humane. The process by which the break with nature comes about is mysterious, but invocation of the magical powers of an unknown divinity is no help in making it less mysterious. There are mysteries in nature but none are intentional. Nor is there any warrant to claim that what allows humanity to break out of nature is soul, a supposedly nonmaterial, nonnatural element infused in all human beings by their maker. Fictions don't help solve mysteries, though they may certainly alert our attention. There is nothing like speech in nature. Also, there are no notational systems in the world that are not human; these are only human creations. Stalin's letters on linguistics contain a surprising and resonant formulation: "Briefly, language cannot be ranked among bases or superstructures" ("Marxism and Linguistics," p. 431). Language floats free of being a mere instrument of production or a mere epiphenomenon that plays on the surface of a brutally wordless and all-potent substratum of productive energy. Stalin almost says what we can say bluntly and without hesitation or his ideological discomfort: spoken language is the medium of human life in every historical and social form, and written language marks a tremendous further advance into the nonnatural. There is no human life without language.

Rousseau thinks that there is an unresolvable paradox in the leap from human beings without spoken language to human beings with it. The paradox is forced on him because he posits an initial isolation of individuals as the original human condition, before they came together for one or another pleasure, cooperative or isolated. His paradox is that society is needed to create language and language is needed to create society. But there has always been some kind of grouping, never human isolation. The grouping was held together by spoken language, no matter how simple. At first sight, Locke is the better teacher in the canon of political theory in his conjectures about the early ages of man, because the state of nature—apart from its primary meaning as a condition of either illegitimate or revolutionarily suspended authority—refers rather to the earliest condition of the human species, which is in Locke's account always made up of families and extended families, not of solitary individuals. Rousseau's analysis eventually gets around to saying that "one catches a better glimpse of how the use of speech was established or perfected imperceptibly in the bosom of each family" (*Discourse,* p. 147), but he thinks that for an immensely long time human individuals lived alone except for occasional sex. It might be safer to say that human beings are always together, and together, they cannot help but speak. Speech is a break with nature, the most important testimony that the human species is partly discontinuous with nature, and for that reason perhaps more than any other, the highest species. That God spoke the world into existence is a parable on the transformative powers of human language.

If, however, Rousseau's paradox is changed into another paradox—language is needed to create language—then the paradox is insoluble. Language did not evolve one word at a time, any more than mathematics did one number at a time, or music one note at a time. There is a system or nothing. Languages grew piecemeal, but how could they have arisen from nonlanguage? Once in existence, languages could spread by imitation and adaptation. But how did any of them start? Is there an answer? There must have been a leap. By a genius? But that is no answer. We slap the questions down but they slap back. We endure the puzzle, but also turn it into a source of wonder at the uniqueness of the human species. It is the only source of the miraculous, though it did not create itself and was not created at all, but evolved; the miracle is not that out of nothing humanity produced something, but that out of nature, it can produce nonnatural phenomena. These phenomena show its partial discontinuity with nature; that too is evidence of its stature, though it certainly cannot take credit for its natural endowment, which makes the break with nature possible.

Of course many thinkers deny the inference that humanity is partly discontinuous with nature, even if they are willing to see something special in language. They dislike the inference, if it makes sense at all, because it can be construed as species self-praise; they worry that human hubris, which does not need encouragement, will justify the disregard of the interests of nature. I grant this much: such self-praise incurs a grave debt, but perhaps it can be paid if the human species becomes the steward of nature, no matter how well or badly human beings treat one another. By being the steward, the only possible steward, we would show magnanimity in caring about the nonhuman, provided we do so for the sake of what is not ourselves and also allow our use of nature to be constrained by magnanimity. Let us say that one principal virtue of human stature is magnanimity, which is never a virtue that is easy to practice. It is harder than courage, or at least much less common. Perhaps only being good in the spirit of the golden rule is harder—unless that spirit is by definition magnanimous.

Yet an old question reinserts itself. Is it a problem that only human beings can appreciate achievements like language, music, and mathematics? It seems as if humanity keeps encountering only itself in all its achievements. It can never shatter the human self-enclosure and reach some other form of life that is capable of rendering an independent judgment on those achievements that human beings cherish and identify as the reason for affirming the human stature. We crave an external vindication. But there is none. The rest of earthly nature cannot possibly supply it. At least, however, we can rebut the reasons for denying human stature that are based on reductive theories of the human species.

Language and Thinking

From language comes thinking, a trait that is essential to free agency and moral agency as well as to human stature in general and a prospective stewardship of nature, in particular. But the uses and purposes of thinking cannot be itemized and neatly circumscribed. Language is the medium of human life because thinking is. Thinking can be about anything and show itself in varying modes, and in degrees of intensity and rigor. For Rousseau, what differentiates human thinking is the capacity to form general ideas and concepts. For my purposes at this point, I would emphasize those ideas that could motivate human agency in the uniquely human project of serving as steward of nature. This is the most needed expression of human stature. All the processes of scientific thinking that go into studying the history of nature and into accumulating knowledge of it, and the philosophical thinking involved in speculation about cosmological questions, and the philosophical and aesthetic thinking that prepares the intellect for the contemplative appreciation of nature in its details and patterns—all these in combination emphasize the human distance from nature and the difference between the human species and the rest of nature, and can do so, ironically, for the sake of nature. We have already admitted the further irony that nature doesn't care whether its record is known and knowledge about it is accumulated, and whether its beauty and sublimity are apprehended. Nonetheless nature is not there so that human beings can project thoughts and feelings onto it; it is not as it were a statue waiting to become human and able to reciprocate the care and attention that humanity can give it. It is to be treated as if it were orphaned and left in human care but must always remain unresponsive. Robert Frost memorably renders the craving for a comprehensibly responsive nature in his fathomless poem "For Once, Then, Something." The something is close to nothing.

A little later I will emphasize the importance of thinking about oneself and the role played by such thinking in human agency. But first, let us look a bit more closely at the kinds of thinking that sustain the stewardship of nature.

Human stature can be shown in the selfless subordination of human interests where need be, and in impersonal appreciation when the stewardship of nature is made a central task of thinking. The palpable fact that human interests are served, especially by the accumulation of scientific knowledge, does not compromise the stewardship as long as all along some practitioners are mindful of the possibility that what they do can be done disinterestedly—that is, motivated by love of truth for the sake of the truth and also in admiration, where humanly possible, of what is studied. Often admiration grows with increased knowledge. In fact some scientists pursue their work disinterestedly and suggest that beautiful theories answer to the beauty of phenomena.

The obvious question is what good is the stewardship as I have just sketched it, if the human species, led by the technologically advanced countries, continues to despoil nature? What if, *per impossible,* humanity would suddenly reverse course and bend every effort to preserve endangered nature? It is already too late or nearly so for many species. These questions must be left to others to answer. Perhaps it is only when it is late, or too late, if even then, that the passion for stewardship can prevail over all the interests that carelessly or greedily, or out of desperate need, deny the will to human stewardship. I will continue exploring the idea of human dignity, even though some people hold that no exploration should ever begin, given what humanity has done to nature.

Thinking and Knowledge: Perspectivism

Let me stay with some of the expressions of thinking that go into stewardship. They raise certain questions that bear on human stature. I cannot answer these questions, either, with any thoroughness. The overarching question is whether human knowledge is actually knowledge. This question can be divided into two branches. The first branch of the question is whether human knowledge is only a species-wide perspective. Isn't it possible that some other species with traits and attributes different from those of the human species, with a different sort of mind and with different sorts of senses, and that lived on some other planet in a different natural environment, would know the earth and the universe differently from the way the human species does? In Nietzsche's summary judgment, there is only "a perspective seeing, a perspective 'knowing'" (*Genealogy of Morals*, 3.12, p. 119).

The second branch of the overarching question is whether any species anywhere in the universe can really know what it claims to know about nature, when no species anywhere made itself or the universe? It is said that beings can know only what they have made. They can manipulate nature but not know it as it is from the inside, as it is in itself; or why it exists, what the intention of the maker is, what the meaning of it is in the mind of its maker. The two branches of the question concerning human knowledge of nature are full of difficulties; the difficulties are so great as to make these questions appear intractable or unanswerable.

The claim that there is only perspective knowing is a judgment that applies in the first instance to the puzzle that results when we observe— ideally free of any perspective for a brief detached moment—that different human beings can perceive and assess the same phenomenon differently; that is, they pick out different features of the phenomenon to highlight, and they do so because they occupy different positions in social life or they have had different experiences in life; they have different preconceptions, beliefs, prejudices, interests, backgrounds, passions, levels of interest, and so on. Different individuals and groups make something rather different out of the purportedly same event, situation, or condition. It sometimes seems as if they are not talking about the same thing because their assessments are not only different but directly opposite.

A perspective is what happens to a person without the person knowing it, an unresisted result of background and temperament, until the person notices that other persons look at the world differently, whether in one's society or in other societies. Then the possibility arises of understanding that persons have only perspectives, and from such understanding comes the chance for self-correction, revision, and selective borrowing from other perspectives or compromise with them. Even more, one can develop an interest in perspectives one has no wish to share; one is interested in perspectives as such, in the phenomenon of perspectivism. Nietzsche is not only the theorist of perspectivism, he is the exemplar of overcoming some of his own perspectives and understanding those he rejects, while remaining faithful to the idea that there is only perspective seeing and knowing. He is especially perceptive about human perspectives he says he dislikes and wants to discredit; he actually enhances some of them and makes them more cogent—one splendid example is asceticism in book 4 of *Thus Spoke Zarathustra*.

The metaphor of individual and social perspectivism relies on the fact that a physical object looks a bit different depending on where you stand, what time of day or night it is, what the weather and atmosphere are, what mood you are in, and so on. Colors are changeable depending on the light, much to our epistemological unhappiness and to our aesthetic delight. It is impossible to see an object as it is in itself, or see an object in the round with one glance. Extend physical perspectivism to human phenomena. It seems impossible to perceive an event, situation, or condition as it is in itself. One has to put together impressions at one time or over time to consolidate one's perception of the same thing, only to have what one believed to be consolidated change again in one's impression of it. There is something partial about individual and group perception: partial in both senses: incomplete and biased.

Obsessed by the obvious fact that things taken in by the understanding and by senses that guide and are guided by the mind are not only perishable and hence deficient in reality but also unstable, even protean, over time, and prone to decay in stages, and are—perhaps most infuriating of all—amenable at any given time to competing and even contradictory perceptions and assessments, Plato proposed that only in the abstract, not in sensory reality, is any adequate perception and understanding possible. The true reality of a thing or quality or phenomenon cannot be instantiated materially on earth; in our human limitation, we perceive and understand only perspectivally, which means that we apprehend only shadows or simulacra. But through a painful but gradually pleasurable and eventually ecstatic discipline, a rare soul can reach knowledge of every thing or quality or phenomenon in itself, in its idea, its wholeness, its true being as it is in itself, which is never physical but is rather an abstract idea. Kant's alternative was to say that full knowledge of things in themselves was beyond the ability of human reason, though human (scientific) understanding could deal with natural phenomena quite adequately.

What drives someone who takes Plato's analysis seriously is the readiness to entertain the Idealist contention that if there is only perspective perceiving and judging, then there are no phenomena there, not even rough approximations, but only shadows and simulacra. Human beings are duped by illusions or, still worse, they take their own mental projections to be external reality. Or, the thought insinuates itself that any particular thing or quality or phenomenon is there, but unknowable; nothing can be said truthfully about it because the whole truth can never be said. A perspective is just a perspective, or angle of vision, or a slant. Or, at the least, we are forced to think that there can never be a complete description or interpretation of anything at all because a new perspective on it is always possible; but an accumulation of descriptions or interpretations from an indefinitely large number of perspectives cannot possibly add up to the whole truth, if only because they not only diverge from but contradict one another. Only another (mere) perspective can select from many perspectives the aspects that are found most compelling in order to produce a precarious synthesis that invites skepticism, even from the one who produced it. Then, too, of course, everything changes and will not sit still for anyone's perspective, no matter how self-aware and receptive to other perspectives one is.

The relevance of the problem of perspectivism for the aim of accumulating human knowledge of nature is that what we call natural science may be only our species-wide perspective. In regard to human phenomena, people can talk among themselves and try to correct the partiality and bias of any perception or interpretation. When the subject is human deeds and practices, human beings can correct and enlighten one another, and perhaps, as a result, reach agreement across initially contrasting perspectives. There are rather narrow limits, of course, to these processes of consensus. But in regard to natural phenomena, why think of science as a perspective, rather than be confident that it is knowledge? If human beings agree on the findings of the sciences, why deny that humanity has discovered the truth about nature? Just look at the tremendous technological achievements that scientific knowledge has made possible. How could a mere perspective account for the success of human activity in controlling and directing nature? The argument from successful applications of science to human needs, wants, and passions seems to settle the matter.

What holds us back is the thought that perhaps there are extraterrestrial perspectives on the universe and its natural constituent parts, which would make our knowledge into just one perspective, while these other perspectives are just perspectives, too. The solution to the problem of truth, when we believe that there is only perspective knowing, cannot be, as I have said, to multiply perspectives, to think that the more eyes and the more affects directed at the same thing, the better. We cannot literally see with the eyes of others; we can see as others see only with our own eyes. There is only a perspectival judgment of perspectival judgment. Nietzsche is deriding the very idea of objective truth. (But who would read him if we did not think he was telling the objective truth, or at least trying to be truthful?) The multiplication of perspectives on the ostensibly same phenomenon can be a fascinating spectacle; it can enrich our sense of human individual and group diversity, of the indefatigable resourcefulness of human interpretative powers; but its effect is to keep the word *knowing* in Nietzsche's quotation marks, where Nietzsche left it.

By extraterrestrial I do not mean transcendental. Suppose natural creatures exist elsewhere than on the earth? Words fail when we try to describe the difficulty of the matter, but we must try anyway. Would their science be ours? Could we even communicate with them to find out what their science amounts to? Suppose that they have evolved with utterly different minds and senses; suppose, as a result, that our and their concepts and categories are mutually untranslatable into anything either species could make sense of. How could there be mutual comprehension, or even one-way comprehension? What then? In relation to each other, we and they would be at most as earthly animals are to us and we are to them. We would lack another species' perspective on nature to go alongside ours. Perhaps, then, on earth or extraterrestrially, mental beings on planets cannot break out of the enclosures of their species-wide perspectives. We would also lack another desideratum; namely, the perspective on the human species that a nonhuman mind holds. That perspective, if it could be communicated to us, would really give us something to think about. It is hard to imagine any human triumph greater than discovering an extraterrestrial species with a mind. Perhaps the problems of communication could be surmounted, so that, in Scott Fitzgerald's words about the European discovery of the New World "something commensurate with his [man's] capacity for wonder" would be found (*The Great Gatsby,* p. 182). At last wonder would be exhausted—at least for a long while.

Pascal in a bemused tone says: how many kingdoms *(royaumes)* know us not (*Pensees,* 207, p. 61). Suppose we were to say what Pascal is close to saying: how many *worlds* know us not. Whether we are bemused or not, there may very well be no world that knows us not. That there may be no nonhuman beings with minds that know or can know the human species is complemented by the fact that the human mind does not know any nonhuman species with a mind; the one supposition and the one fact compose an epistemological tragedy. We cannot communicate with other earthly animals about their science; they have none. Their unlikeness to human beings—and each animal species is also unique—cannot count as relevant to our epistemological problem. We need to be in touch with other minds, which may not exist; but if they do, they may be closed to us as our minds are closed to other species with minds. How wonderful it would be if there had been a record of communication between hominid and other incipiently human predecessors of homo sapiens in the genus Homo, or perhaps a record of mutual observation; or, best of all, at least some definitive word about the comparative mental capacities of Homo sapiens and its Neanderthal contemporaries (thought to be an early incarnation of Homo sapiens). In his novel *The Inheritors* (1955), William Golding tries to render the mentality of Neanderthals and the experience of their encounter with humanity. The work's great value lies not so much in its unverifiable surmises as in the mere effort to contrast two kinds of adult mentality that are substantially different, but have a measure of commonality. If Golding's thought experiment were ever borne out, we would come much closer to having the species-wide perspective on humanity of a species that is not totally unlike humanity—if this other species had language. The simian primates that now exist, in all their cleverness, do not qualify as having perspectives; whatever other traits and attributes they might have, they do not have conceptual minds; they have no language, only communication.

Despite the advantages to human knowledge and self-understanding, however, it could be better for the other species in the genus Homo that only the human species has survived. It is hard to imagine how human beings could ever get on with species much more like itself than the primates and yet not itself, not nearly as capable as itself or as marked so powerfully by unique traits and attributes. The thought of near rivals to humanity among kindred species makes one queasy. Humanity would have enslaved or exterminated them, not caring what it could learn from them.

We are left with no choice but to assume that human science is objective knowledge of nature, always open to revision by the very canons of inquiry that assembled the knowledge in the first place, even though the assumption that we have knowledge must always be made with some unease because of the remote and possibly insubstantial extraterrestrial possibility of challenge. Yet even if our knowledge is in fact knowledge, humanity could still perish from its ignorance of nature and its inability to foresee nature; or from a combination of ignorance and self-destructive knowledge. Leaving that prospect aside, we say, in sum, humanity can carry forward the stewardship of nature (in part) because of the unique human ability to accumulate what we must believe to be real knowledge of nature and its history.

Thinking and Knowledge: Maker's Knowledge

I now turn to the second branch of the overall question concerning the kind of thinking that bears on stewardship of nature and hence on human stature.

Notice that scientific knowledge does not deal with nature as if nature had inwardness. Nature on earth and in the rest of the universe, as far as we now know, has no psychic depths. What other depths could there be? The pursuit of scientific knowledge operates on the assumption that things are just things, that animate and conscious matter is just matter. Animals of course have consciousness and some sense of what they must do in order to avoid destruction. But their awareness and self-preference do not extend to self-knowledge; they do not conceptualize what is around them and their place in it. Developed inwardness depends on language. Animals have no language and therefore no inwardness that makes a difference to what they do. If they have, in analogy with human infants, an inwardness that is, in a manner of speaking, made of images and dreams, we have no access to it. Can we even imagine what their images and dreams would be like? Some animals might have emotions, but the risk of anthropomorphizing is present, and what apparent similarities there are do not establish that the word *emotion* can be used in exactly the same way about animals and human beings, if for no other reason than that animals do not have language and do not have imagination, both of which are interwoven with human emotions. It would therefore seem that behavioral science, which gives sole attention to what is outward, when joined to biological science, is what the study of animals requires and nothing beyond it. Instincts, impulses, and reflexes together with appetites and drives seem to define exhaustively, at least for the purposes of study, all other creaturely species but humanity.

No, we do not know what it means to be a bat, in Thomas Nagel's formulation. But neither does a bat know; a bat is a bat and does what bats do; and what bats do is splendidly complex and would be amazingly virtuosic if human beings could do it naturally, as the activity of practically every species is or may be. Animals may or should strike us as mysterious just by being what is not human, even if we say that they have no inwardness. They are conscious and behave; they are not mere machines. So we study them; but we cannot be said to interpret them, as we interpret each other. Animals are not interpretable; interpretation would not be suitable to abate or dissolve their mystery, if anyone ever wanted out of human vanity or theological commitment to make their mystery vanish.

It is even impossible for one human being to know what it is like to be some other human being; one cannot experience the consciousness of another person by means of one's consciousness; one's consciousness is the only consciousness one can experience. One cannot be oneself while simultaneously being another person and thus compare two experiences: being who one is and being someone else; there is no one mind that can be two minds at once or serially. Empathic interpretation goes only so far, and often not very far. Looking back at oneself at various ages with a comparative eye is not analogous to trying to know what it is like to be someone else. Under the influence of mind-altering drugs, or other extreme experiences, one afterwards feels, when restored to oneself, as if one had become another person, perhaps; but that other person is not literally another human being who already exists, but an ephemeral person new to the world, an emanation from oneself, engendered by oneself alone, and connected to oneself by memory, like a dream. In any case, behavioral science does not explain much about human activity. I have no interest in disparaging animals; much of the point of redirecting the idea of human stature toward the stewardship of nature is to make us feel that our worth depends in significant part on our appreciation of the worth of animals and the need to save them from extinction. But reducing human beings entirely to animality is not the way to ask us to raise ourselves to a proper height so that we may serve as stewards of nature.

The idea of human dignity goes well with the thought that studying human beings is much harder than studying anything else. Human stature is thus affirmed by the unique human ability to gain knowledge of nature for the purpose of serving as its steward, and also by the human inability to know itself fully. I think that it is well to reverse the old view, associated with Bacon, Hobbes, and Vico among others, that the maker of something knows it better than anyone else can. This is the doctrine of *verum-factum*: maker's truth or maker's knowledge. The inference from this position has usually been that only God the creator can understand nature as it is in itself. He not only made it, he also intended it to be this way rather than that; he has a pattern in mind; he gave all his creation a telos; he invests all his creation with meaning, which human beings cannot fully or really decipher. God made humanity; his understanding of it far surpasses its own self-understanding, and so he can understand it as it cannot understand itself. An infinitely greater mind created the human mind and all the rest of nature. We see nature, which human beings did not make, and ourselves whom we did not make, as in a cloudy mirror, at best.

I think the teaching of "maker's truth" should be reversed. I wish to suggest that if we are right that only humanity has inwardness on earth, and that the inwardness of possible extraterrestrial species that have minds is likely to be altogether closed to us, then we can say that nature, which was not made, has no inside or psychic depths, and has no intended meaning, pattern, or telos, is easier to understand than human life is—human life as human beings "make" it, and give it meanings, patterns, and teloi. I do not refer primarily to the initial impenetrability of foreign customs and practices, beliefs and religions, not to mention the incomprehensibility of foreign languages. I mean mostly that, a fair amount of the time, human motivation is opaque or obscure. Understanding human beings is made still harder by subconscious and unconscious motivation.

Furthermore, mixed in with motivation—even in the largest sense when it includes a worked-out intention, purpose, or policy, rather than being an immediate response to a situation—are such uniquely human propulsive characteristics as spontaneity, eruptive creativity, and unpredictable upsurge or outpouring—the whole realm of uncharted freedom. These sources of action are all interwoven with language, but except for conscious motivation, they are not the result of deliberation or meditation. The uniquely human capacity of imagination, which is the crystallization of the invisible, figures energetically in all action but the most routine, habitual, or mimetically conformist. To take an instance: no one could have predicted Beethoven's third symphony from his first two, or if he lived to write it, predicted his tenth from his ninth. No effort to compose the tenth symphony by analysis of the first nine, and then claim that this is what Beethoven would have composed, can be warranted. Looking back we can say that his tenth is unlikely to have been atonal, but who predicted atonal music? We can never say with confidence what is possible to creativity at any given time. The evidence for what is possible is not what is actual: the evidence for the actual is always incomplete, and new knowledge usually provides quite a few surprises about human capacities. We should be especially hesitant in setting down for the past what could have been or must have been thought or said, or enclosing any period of time, including our own, in one of our procrustean epistemological categories.

Given that human beings have these capacities, these traits and attributes, they are partly or largely unknown to themselves; each person is unknown to himself or herself and to others. In addition to this significant ignorance about what moves human beings to act and live as they do in the present, the human species, as I have already said, could never know itself sufficiently to define, delimit, and measure itself because it can never know what it is capable of being and doing in the future. We cannot predict concepts, ideologies, and philosophies, or inventions and discoveries, all of which are sure to happen and help to shape future reality. If we could predict them we would already know them, which is absurd. Of course there are good hunches and speculative inferences that might be confirmed, but the general point of human unpredictability remains.

Much of fiction is about why human beings must search to find the elusive truth about, or the meaning of, the overt conduct of human beings and what the obstacles are. Its source is entirely different from the imperceptibility of the atomic and subatomic structure of matter by technologically unaided human senses. Conscious motives were successfully hidden from others if an overt act can have more than one explanation; subconscious motives can come to light, but often evade the person whose motives they are; and unconscious motives are often not brought to light but exercise an unmasterable domination in such forms as obsession and compulsion, which at the extreme can be called infinite passions. These are not merely inflated passions, which can be satisfied. In contrast, nothing can distract, deflect, or satisfy infinite passions; only a moment's gratification is possible because every gratification is entwined with a despair that can never be assuaged, but even that moment cannot be counted on to occur; these passions survive the body's infirmity, and die only when the human being dies or his or her mind dies first. They are like bleeding wounds that can never be staunched or appetites that can never be sated. Politically, the difference between inflated and infinite passions is the difference between the imperialism of Pericles and that of Alcibiades. An infinite passion does not arise from the fear of never having enough—say, wealth or power—even for an indefinitely open-ended purpose.

Let me stay for a little while with infinite passions because they account for a sizable portion of the elusiveness of human action, for the apparent lack, in T. S. Eliot's phrase about Hamlet, of an "objective correlative" to answer to the force of the emotions in a human being's response to an event or situation. Sanity means to have a sense of proportion and not to have an emotion "in excess of the facts." When there is excess, there is a passion that the person cannot understand because he cannot "objectify" it through some detachment from it; he cannot see through or beyond it, and it therefore remains to poison life ("Hamlet and His Problems," p. 125). One major passion is mourning that can never subside into acceptance. Another infinite passion is compulsion occasioned by early trauma, particularly punitive humiliation imposed for a misdemeanor; the effect is a repeated desire to transgress and be punished. Sartre explores it in his great book on Jean Genet, *Saint Genet* (1952).

Perhaps the worst infinite passion, or as bad as any, is the desire for inflicting excessive ("cruel and unusual") punishment, to respond even more savagely to what is perceived as a savage assault. The crime was so great that it can never be punished enough. O'Brien the inquisitor in *Nineteen Eighty-Four* imagines the desirable future as "a boot stamping on a human face—forever" (p. 271). Khalid Sheik Mohammed, an accused organizer of the 9/11 attacks, was waterboarded 183 times in March 2003: O'Brien's fantasy not realized but approximated. Captain Ahab must pursue the white whale that harmed him in order to destroy it, cost what it may; the cost turns out to be his own destruction and the destruction of his ship and its boats and all the crew on it but one; but the harpooned "stricken" whale is not yet dead when the book ends. If the guilty cannot be punished, then the innocent must be. Tashtego must nail a bird, a harmless sky-hawk, free and innocently there, to the mast of the sinking ship, which "like Satan would not sink to hell till she had dragged a living part of heaven along with her" (*Moby-Dick*, p. 565). There must be punishment inserted into the world that will reverberate through the world, through the universe. Vice President Dick Cheney's design for the response to the 9/11 attack was characterized by the same infinite passion, a surplus passion that reasons, even sinister reasons, cannot fully account for. Then, when inconsolable grief is added to an unquenchably angry appetite for revenge, the infinite passion becomes infinite in its reach; it desires the whole world to perish for having been the scene of a great crime, or being forever unable to compensate for it. What in general can begin to explain the excess?

The passion for excessive punishment is often the passion for vengeance, but not always known for what it is. But vengeance for what? I think that what must be avenged above all is some form of *lèse-majesté*. The avenger, when human, must have a hypertrophied sense of his own dignity, his stature. The model and sponsor is God's unending punishment of the human species for the first couple's disobedience: in all generations, the descendants are condemned to be mortal. Yet worse is the Christian doctrine of eternal hellfire after death for those who sinned terribly or were chosen by God for that fate. The real sin is disobedience, *lèse-majesté*, offense against the dignity of the divinity, not the harm done other human beings. Indeed, the offense need not harm other beings in its commission; eating the forbidden fruit harmed nothing but God, and harmed him by its sheer affront. God's anger at human disobedience also shows itself in genocidal slaughter by drowning in the time of Noah. Some of the eternal punishments that Dante imagines in Hell bear a relation to their respective sins that only Freud's concepts of overdetermination and the dreamwork can help us decipher.

Overdetermination is not the same as multiple causation but rather points to the fact that the causes of a phenomenon are not only multiple, but more numerous than is needed for the phenomenon to appear; and when the phenomenon does appear it misrepresents its causes, thanks to processes similar to the dreamwork. The manifest dream results from several factors: the unconscious mind's tendency to distort and condense the actual causes (thoughts and emotions) of the dream; to displace identities of persons and objects; and to revise content ruthlessly for the sake of what turns out to be a specious clarity. We cannot interpret our dreams with any conclusiveness. In imagining divine punishment in the Jewish and Christian traditions, poets give us an idea of unappeasable inhuman rage, which human beings often express in ways that seem incomprehensible unless one is willing to consider the possible use of the concept of overdetermination. Oddly, God's unappeasable rage is not sent to punish human beings for their own unappeasable rage. The story of infinite passions is a major part of human uniqueness, too, but the least happy part.

It is not only the Jewish and Christian religions that imagine the infinite passion of divine punishment. The stories of Tantalus, Sisyphus, and Prometheus are striking for the ingenuity, though perhaps less like that of the dreamwork, that the gods show in punishing those who have aroused their ire.

That truth about the sources and meaning of human conduct must be elusive is also indicated by the countless wishes and responses, inclinations, and purposes that were never realized and were known, if known at all, only to the persons themselves. If ever told by a superhuman observer and recorder, they would make an infinite story of what is for us, to use George Eliot's phrase from *Middlemarch,* forever "on the other side of silence." Only infinite sympathy would be adequate response to that story, but no one, not Buddha or Jesus, can feel it. And not only sympathy but also tireless patience.

The cause of our incomplete and imperfect understanding of the human psyche and hence of human life is not that humanity did not make itself, or even that, like the rest of earthly life, humanity has no maker, was not made, but evolved. Rather, all the psychological phenomena that I just mentioned come from within, come from inwardness, which is uniquely human. The only firm knowledge is behavioral knowledge—knowledge of what is outward where the only inside is physiological; and this is appropriate for animals, and for human beings only when they are newborns or when terrible suffering reduces their lives to an animal-like narrowness of concern in which self-preservation, in the literal and uninflated sense, is dominant. However, even with terrible suffering a few human beings demonstrate unpredictable and commendable altruistic courage and magnanimity; they retain their human complexity in having the courage to be able to think of something more than the next step to take to try to stay alive at whatever cost to others. (This is not to deny that some animals sacrifice themselves for their young or their group, when their biology prepares them.)

Human inwardness prevents firm or objective knowledge of human beings by human beings. They are hard to know even when they are visibly going about the activities that constitute human life, doing things that only human beings can do. The same activity can be motivated in the same person by more than one motive, or can be interpreted and explained in more than one way. Different observers can impute different motives to the same act by the same person and hence describe and interpret the same bodily activity in different and competing ways. They cannot agree on what a person's motive or purpose is, and thus put to rest doubt about what he or she meant to do and therefore did. A good deal of activity does not consist in following a recipe without deviation, no matter how important a framework of rules and conventions is in making the activity choice-worthy or even possible. And when activity is not like following a recipe, and most of the time it isn't, human conduct can be anything but transparent, though sometimes it is. Yes, we can be pretty sure about how a given act or steady activity *cannot* be described and interpreted. We can rule certain obvious things out.

There is no extraterrestrial mind that can supply help in either making good the deficiencies of human self-understanding—or validating it. There is no external view that can assist in the endeavor. No sense is made of human beings if a would-be scientific observer sees only "bodies in motion." Various and contending human perspectives from within the experience of human life must battle interminably over the correct descriptions and interpretations of human conduct.

Human beings all together are the authors of human life, but human understanding of human life often comes up short. There are countless explorations of it, and from countless perspectives enlightenment is achieved, only to fade, or appear in need of replenishment. The accumulation of works of great and good philosophy, literature, and history grows; we are or should be grateful for the accumulation. In these genres there is accumulation but not net progress. We nevertheless feel that there are not enough good and great books; we could always use more of them; they exist in order to incite their own proliferation, not to exhaust the possibilities of articulation or its need. Here is where Nietzsche's praise of numerous perspectives finds its home, because objective truth, which can be found only in behavioral science, is not at issue.

Human life at any time and all through time is ultimately incomprehensible. This incomprehensibility is testimony to human stature, perverse as that might sound. Human stature is not so great as to have the capacity to take the measure of human stature. Humanity is too much to be encompassed; it is indefinitely large in its actuality, past and present, and unpredictable in the future. In contrast, objective knowledge of nature, which has no inwardness, is easier on the talented mind, despite formidable obstacles, than understanding human life, which is governed by human inwardness. This is not to say, however, that large-scale natural processes on earth or in the universe and that stretch over long periods of time are predictable. But the reason may be incomplete knowledge that can in principle be made ever more complete; at least the retrospective explanation becomes ever more complete. The same consideration does not hold for knowledge of humanity. One major reason that inwardness is typically resistant to the understanding is that human beings are moved by a sense of possibility or potentiality, of the unrealized, of the not-yet. Without language, that sense could not exist, even though at the beginning of many human endeavors, whether individual or collaborative, people are not able to give a full account of what moves them to try, or what their purposes really are. Even leaders and initiators can be barely articulate at first; they may be gripped by they know not what.

Knowledge, Self-Consciousness, and Agency

I have been discussing the unique human capacity to think, which language, spoken and written, provides much of the medium for—makes possible in that sense. Some philosophers want to go further and say that language thinks through us; it has its own impersonal domination, to which we succumb without knowing that we are doing so, and believing instead that we are simply using language as we please. No doubt there is truth in the observation that much silent thinking comes unbidden; the mind is passive as well as active. Also, much expression is unrehearsed or spontaneous and seems to follow its own direction. Whatever we are, however, we are not merely ventriloquist dummies. Let us turn away from this matter. I wish to take up one's ability to think about oneself. I discuss thinking about oneself because it is implicated in human agency, which concentrates human uniqueness by enlisting all other distinctively human traits and attributes. Both the notion of equal individual status and the notion of human stature turn on agency. Another term for thinking about oneself is self-consciousness. Animals have consciousness; they shun what harms them and thus show some kind of awareness of themselves as separate beings; they constantly engage in purposive behavior; but they do not inspect themselves and try to figure themselves out with the aid of ideas and concepts. Although animals have consciousness, they have no inwardness in the usual sense; as far as we know, they are always looking outward.

Permit me a digression. Should we not make more of the fact that animals have consciousness? I mean that perhaps we should say that consciousness in any species represents a break with nature. Locke in *An Essay Concerning Human Understanding* (1689) says that consciousness could not emerge from matter, even if matter were of eternal duration. Isn't consciousness, which human beings share with all other animals, a greater wonder than the uniquely human capacity of self-consciousness? Isn't consciousness a greater wonder than inwardness, which is only a derivative from consciousness? By wonder here I mean the appropriate response to nature's apparent capacity to engender breaks from itself—breaks of such a quality as to seem not natural, and that are not merely metamorphoses within the realm of the natural. Perhaps in my eagerness to defend human uniqueness I overlook the commonality of consciousness shared by humanity with all animals. I certainly have no wish to deny that animals are wondrous or to brush aside Locke's perception that the appearance of consciousness from matter seems inconceivable. For Locke, matter can produce only matter, but consciousness, the immaterial (the not-natural), must be created by what is transcendent. Consciousness, especially human consciousness, is so extraordinarily distinct from and discontinuous with matter that it must have been created intentionally, and only a supremely great consciousness could have created it. Locke posits an omnipotent creator; but that is no explanation because the creator, he is not afraid to say, is incomprehensible. He replaces the incomprehensibility of consciousness with the incomprehensibility of the creator. Where's the advantage? Let us go directly to the hypothesis that some of the questions we ask are beyond our powers to answer and are therefore unanswerable, rather than saying that they are answerable by a superior mind that we cannot even begin to describe and for whose supposed activities we do not have even the beginnings of an explanation. One puzzle leads to another. But if one puzzle leads to another, it is better to stay with the first, which seems in principle to be solvable, especially if we hold on to the thought that given endless time, what retrospectively looks impossible turned out to be possible.

Where shall we locate the greatest wonder? The foundational wonder is that there is the world and that, since nothing can come from nothing, the world has always existed. The eternity of the world induces an uncanny feeling, which is then intensified by the multifariousness of nature on earth. To posit divinity domesticates the uncanniness; the divinity is personalized and given a mind or will and is therefore made personally relevant to human beings. The question is posed, Why is there the world (or a world)? The answer is a just-so story that is formed in a way that makes sense to human preconception. We want a defined universe, so we define it. But all this artful construction of teleology dissipates wonder. The why question—why is there something rather nothing?—deflects wonder. True wonder about the universe is not compatible with teleology. It is best just to try to isolate some of the main causes of wonder without asking why and then trying to make up purposive answers. On earth, what is the greatest wonder: is it the change from the inanimate to the animate or from the animate to the conscious or from the conscious to the self-conscious? Furthermore, is the animate also a break with nature, is the conscious also a break with nature, just as I say the presence of humanity's mind is a break with nature? Or are developed life itself and animal consciousness, especially if they are peculiar to the earth in the whole universe, anomalously not natural, like the human mind? It is perhaps impossible to decide. An answer would require a complete knowledge of the capacities of matter, but the transformations we can isolate preclude possessing knowledge that can never be surprised.

I must content myself with starting conceptually with language and self-consciousness, and arrive at the formulation that in engendering the human mind, nature can engender what is not natural. The science of nature cannot produce a sufficient explanation of mind. Divinity was made incomprehensible by philosophers because of an intuition, often not publicly stated, that the human mind, divinity's maker, is finally incomprehensible. Let it go at that. I also know that without consciousness there would no self-consciousness. But I believe that self-consciousness is not a mere derivative from consciousness. I would like to see it as a tremendous break with animal consciousness, as a tremendous break with nature altogether, perhaps the greatest one (if there are other ones), because only humanity can, in breaking with nature to the extent or in the way that it can and does, introduce free agency into the world. To be sure, people who are not ever conscious of themselves as selves can act; not all action is self-conscious, even among self-conscious people. A lot of anyone's action is impulsive, habitual, routine, scripted, or prescribed. A person tends to become thing-like or machine-like. It is still action, and all of it uniquely human. But agency seems conceptually to require the person to be self-aware, and thus to give an inside to action.

Self-consciousness is the basis for being an agent commendably, whether a free agent or a moral agent. (Of course, agents of wrongdoing can also be self-conscious.) A uniquely human trait, self-consciousness is potentially but not actually possessed by all human beings, whereas consciousness is actually possessed by all the living who function. To be a self-conscious person is to be conscious of oneself as a self, as a person who can think about many things, but also about himself or herself. A person can arrive at a self-conception. But the process is not automatic, and cultural conditions—say, tribal life or village life—may discourage it or be so rigorous in suppression of the sense of self that many people would find it strange to imagine what it means to have a self-conception. They know themselves through a group, and the group knows itself through its differences from other groups. Without a self-conception, *we are* tends to take the place of *I am*, in most of the transactions of life. Some choices might be left free, and particular members of a group might stand out because they perform exceptional deeds. In larger hierarchical societies where human rights are not recognized, self-consciousness is closely tied to membership in a class or caste; there, self-consciousness is actually consciousness of oneself as a member of this class or caste rather than that one. Such consciousness is quite compatible with individual egotism, but the ego is defined by reference to membership. One cannot imagine oneself separately from membership. But in a society in which the people have a sense of individual human rights and the state recognizes and respects those rights, a particular self-consciousness will develop; the ego will grow in a certain direction. One feels special not because one has what others lack, or has a rank higher than others, but because one has what everyone is entitled to have, just by being human.

To have rights, to have them with a presumption of their absoluteness, easily produces the idea that no one should be a mere means to some higher end; each is an end, and all are the end for which society and state exist. That is what human dignity demands. People must be disposed to think this way if rights are to take hold and withstand assaults on them that are bound to come, just as they have come in the past, even in supposedly constitutional societies. An attitude of dissent and civil resistance must be viewed as normal and be a recurrent force in public opinion.

I am not saying that every person should try to be a political theorist; just being an attentive citizen is good enough. Consciousness of rights can sink deep into people's minds even though they are not able, without effort, to give an account of why they hold their rights that satisfies the judge or thinker. Thinking about oneself can therefore include reflection on what rights mean, and why people are entitled to them. The practice of rights is meant to make a great difference in the culture; indeed the practice is meant decisively to differentiate the culture from all other cultures that did not or do not recognize and respect human rights. However, one is supposed to feel sympathy, not contempt, for people who have been denied their rights: that is the sense of difference that is suitable.

A rights-based self-conception can lead to self-possession. By that term I mean the awareness of oneself as susceptible to intimidation and mental capture. One must catch oneself if one is not to conform thoughtlessly to codes, customs, and practices; if one is not to yield to the self-imposed tyranny of compliant habit; if one is not to give in to the inevitable pleasures of simplifying ideologies and the agitation of shifting fashions. One's dignity rests on the ability to resist being too easily ensnared, and to avoid being a target of solicitations. One has to engage in self-examination in order not to succumb to false needs and wants; one must struggle hard and with only a modicum of hope to discover what one truly needs and wants and thus to approach somewhat more closely to being oneself rather than being a poor imitation of oneself and hence an unconscious parody of oneself.

Mill's idea is that one should have a "plan of life" that permits one to have a commitment that gives shape and coherence to one's life and makes one self-possessed. This counsel may not take into sufficient account the place of accidents in any life, the place of good and bad luck, or the desire to break off and change course, but it does encourage us to want to live our own lives. We cannot be sole authors of our lives, however; authenticity may come only in moments and episodes. But even if authenticity is only occasional, there is still a distinction between on the one hand tacitly consenting to one's whole life as either the adherence to an externally imposed discipline or the performance of a function in a system that one has in no sense authorized and on the other hand trying, if only fitfully, to lead a more self-examined life. To be trained to see an assigned social role as one's inescapable fate is a cruel inheritance. But suppose people are happier in such confinement?

One who tries to lead a self-examined life is not looking for the consolations of inner freedom in the Stoic sense: a condition in which one obeys without complaint the commands that are issued by those with power and that are intended to go unquestioned, while nevertheless exulting in one's self-ownership amid mental and even physical captivity. A person feels superior to any situation, even captivity, because of lucid awareness of it, while holding on to his or her ability to be detached from it. No matter what, one is free if one is reconciled to the situation through a process of controlling one's perception of it, and can detach oneself from it in perfect indifference. Stoic superiority, however, is too much for almost all of us; it is therefore not good enough advice; human rights exist to make it unnecessary, admirable as its courage in servility is. Trying to understand what is going on inside oneself and in the world gives inner freedom, in defiance of ideology, propaganda, clichés, and lies, and one's own confusion and gullibility; and this kind of inner freedom may very well be better than many things in the world; but it is not enough. It is good in itself, and yet it is also ideally only preliminary to an engagement with the world, mental or practical, in an atmosphere of freedom (in Mill's phrase) that is sustained by constitutional rights, if for no worthier reason than the enrichment of one's inwardness.

Socrates' counsel is more plausible than that of the late Stoics. The gist is found in his teaching that greater self-knowledge can lead to greater moderation. The hold of artificial needs and wants must be weakened and more self-knowledge can weaken it. This view may be true, especially if one has known love and patience in one's early years, and therefore has been given examples of parental and familial self-control, which have sunk in. One's deeper nature has been made milder perhaps, and the overlay of artificial needs and wants is somewhat less likely to become a second nature and then turn into the fanatical desire to dispossess others by crime or complacent acquiescence in an unjust social system from which one benefits. One is also less likely to support or embrace aggressive and predatory national projects in an unexamined conformity that damages one's dignity.

It is also possible that thinking about oneself and what one really wants can go alongside a cultivated disposition to reflect on how one has acted in the past and what one is now doing. This reflection can build up conscience on a foundation of decency acquired from childhood. As Thoreau taught, conscience tends to show itself in resistance, especially on behalf of the rights of others. The hard resistance is to one's normal desire to follow the path of least resistance, which often means overlooking the obvious fact or condition that begs for response and remedy. Too much of the time we go along as if nothing is happening, when what is happening affects not ourselves but others with whom we are implicated, but at a distance, and who are devastatingly affected. A livelier sense of what rights mean helps to quicken conscience. An altered self-conception can ensue when a person takes on more than superficially and is affected more than casually by the fact of living in a society where rights are recognized and respected. This is one of the most important results of the unique human capacity to think, when thinking is directed inward to the one who thinks. Thinking about oneself does not mean living for oneself. To the contrary, a certain self-enclosure, a certain care taken to know oneself better, is necessary if we are to be more sensitively receptive to what surrounds us than one's conformity, in its hard-shelled group enclosure, would permit. It is more than likely that a person of strong conscience will rarely have a good conscience. This dissatisfaction with oneself is not neurosis (or not only neurosis) but honesty.

The silent dialogue within oneself is the sponsor of conscience, as Thoreau and, more recently, Hannah Arendt memorably perceived. A person is inhabited by a continuous stream of images, words, phrases, unformed ideas, many voices, of recollections and anticipations, of wakeful moments that resemble hallucinations and dreams. All of this incessant accompaniment of one's life can be arrested by one's self-attentive intellect and submitted to examination, as if a person is not one but two at any given moment. Not two different persons, but one person capable of treating oneself as if one is two; one's flow of inwardness as it passes over one as one remains passive becomes an object confronting a subject who is self-consciously inward. But such "doubleness," as Thoreau calls it in *Walden*, is not literally having two personalities in one individual. Instead it is a kind of self-estrangement and strangeness to oneself, in which we can prepare ourselves to make other persons less estranged from us, less inhumanly strange to us.

One should pay special attention to one's fantasy-life and dream-life. Thinking about one's dreams, not necessarily with the intention of interpreting their disguised meaning, but with the wish to see how strange one is when sleep has released the self into mental anarchy, is preparation for a beneficial wakeful self-estrangement. Dreams also promote the feeling that each one of us harbors a creative capacity. In the dream, the dreamer creates a world as if from nothing, and that is suddenly there; in it, I am myself, but also other persons than myself; I see myself as if I were another person detached from myself when I act; I create other characters, too, and observe them as if I did not create them, but am only a witness to their emergence and action; the same identity passes among different persons, as the same activity does. Trying to understand that dreams are self-generated spectacles in which the dreamer is both omnipotent and helpless enables us to grasp that the wish to be fully empathic means to make others into oneself and to lose oneself in complete surrender to them. I am all selves; my self is nothing. Any dream is a dream of empathy. The dream must dissolve, but in its vanishing we appreciate empathy's limits, while our readiness to empathize can be made sharper.

As I have said, we cannot be another person, or know what it is to be another person from the inside, though we know (that is, we would be insane not to assume) that each person has an inside. We can try, however, to understand each other while also understanding that we can be only ourselves. High generosity is shown when we try to know others by seeing them as they see themselves and when we also try to know ourselves by learning from others how to see ourselves as they see us. One can try to imagine why a person has done a particular act by searching more thoroughly into oneself to remember whether one has ever acted in a comparable way and why one did so, or whether one has detected in oneself the beginnings of comparable temptations.

Empathy is based in part on self-knowledge, not only on observation. One could of course be mistaken about oneself, and, more important, about the other person one is trying to understand by means of one's self-knowledge. But human life could not go on if most of self-understanding and understanding others were regularly mistaken, no matter how hard we try to be right. At a certain level, though not at all of the deeper ones, we have enough to go on. Freud's knowledge of our self-ignorance can shake us: the irretrievable or only indirectly retrievable impact on us of the pile-up of the remains from early life of unfocused, unformulated, unrecognized, and never more than deficiently satisfied wishes and desires. But the world's activities in their rules and conventions, in their frequent disregard of empirical selves in favor of performing selves, break free of the hold of the unconscious and become at least partly, even quite adequately, legible. And even if one has not acted like the other person or initially imagines that one never could, one could have acted in an analogous fashion. I don't mean that in similar circumstances everybody feels the same thing and acts in the same way. That would be an awful reduction. But people couldn't know one another if they were utterly dissimilar. Each person is not a separate species, even though every person is, in a manner of speaking, a world. Knowing how people are alike is a preparation for appreciating their differences. Their individual differences arise from a common humanity and are comprehensible only on that basis. Thus, thinking about oneself is crucial to human agency when action is set in a society of equal human status. Thinking in general is the greatest manifestation of the uniquely human ability to use language; it is essential to the status of the individual and the stature of the species. There is no human action without thinking, only movement.

An account of the basis for rights cannot be devoid of some speculation about what it means to be a human being. In my discussion earlier of the defense of human rights, I made do with the unique human capacity to be free agents and moral agents. Obviously both kinds of agency are required to begin thinking about why it is necessary and good for people to have human rights. If we were not capable of free agency, the claim to rights of speech and action would not arise or would arise in an enfeebled condition; if we were not capable of moral agency, we could not be trusted to exercise our rights in ways that do not harm others routinely, by action or inaction. However, the concept of agency needs further attention.

The uniquely human characteristics I have so far singled out—ability to use language and from that ability, the further ability to think about the world and about oneself—sustain free agency and moral agency and make discussion of agency more complex than perhaps we would like it to be, especially when, say, a defense of free speech, press, and association is at issue. Why introduce consideration of uniquely human characteristics in a discussion of rights that are self-evidently valuable? The reason is that sooner or later, threatening issues arise, and I think that the defense of these rights might profit from an exploration of human characteristics, which reveal a depth to the person that exclusive attention to overt conduct could obscure. No defense of rights can exclude the need for a philosophical anthropology, no matter how selective. In any case, there is always one that is implicit in the defense when none is overt.

Thinking about the traits and attributes of the human species in relation to other species is the way to start constructing a philosophical anthropology. We cannot start with any particular individual in isolation: we need generalizations about the relationships among members of the species in its various societies to make sure our analysis is not anomalous. It is also the case that the ability to use language, the most basic kind of human uniqueness, is not a phenomenon that can be understood as an achievement by one individual or by scattered individuals. It is a group phenomenon, but it is also a species phenomenon: language is everywhere there are human beings, even though they have never spoken just one language all over the world. Reflection on the species assists reflection on the individual, just as reflection on the stature of the species can assist reflection on individual status.

Free Agency and Creative Unpredictability

A main point in regard to free agency is that we could never know what we would be missing if potentially creative uses of the opportunities afforded by rights of free speech, press, and association were suppressed; human beings are unpredictable because they are often moved to act by a sense of unrealized potentiality in themselves or a sense of latent possibilities in their situation; the sense in either case can be only incipient and half-formulated. An atmosphere of freedom conduces to personal experimentation and collaborative daring. I do not deny that both political suppression in some areas of endeavor and the anticipation of only partly predictable censorship and penalty can force creation into admirable achievements. Still, the constraints that work by means of prohibition, fear, and intimidation are not like the liberating constraints offered by the disciplines of form and style. Achievements under adverse conditions are a tribute not to repression but to the indefatigable human capacity to initiate and innovate under almost all circumstances and wrest a form or style from fear, caution, and the politically dictated exclusion of the invigorating elements that a freer life would have made available. The case for the rights of freedom of utterance and conduct—for free agency, in short—is even more compelling when we have the history of the species in mind; creations can come from unexpected sources, and the beginnings are often untraceable or anonymous or not assignable to named individuals, even in a literate society. We simply do not know where a valuable contribution to human life will originate. And of course the most general point is that only the human record, in as much fullness as possible, is adequate testimony to the display of creative free agency; the record teaches the reiterated lesson of human uniqueness and the height of human stature.

From inside the concept of human stature, I am not saying that it is perfectionism that most interestingly sets people in motion. To improve oneself or make the most of oneself, or to improve a situation or condition or make the most of it, is common enough, and certainly commendable. Common and commendable are such efforts as doing one's work while trying to improve one's skills, trying to set records, and trying to live up to the best expectations for one's most important roles in life. But human stature is more strikingly shown in such occurrences as the creation of new works of art, new styles in art, and new kinds of art; inventions in technology and discoveries in science; creation of new styles and fashions in appearance and manners and in experiments in living; creation of new media; and the initiation of political reforms and new public policies that redound to the enhancement of human life. The will to break with what has gone before, to try what has not been tried before, to turn aside from what is already good enough—in other words, the will not merely to carry a situation or condition along its own lines to a further point but to start on a different path altogether, out of boredom or a spirit of adventure or some other passion that is not easy to identify or name—is a tribute to the unknown potentialities that people suspect, if only dimly, lie hidden in them. The sources in the psyche of the will to embark for the unknown are obscure and not readily describable. Potentiality is a reservoir of capacity. We know that potentiality always exists, but we know the nature of the specific potentiality only when it is realized. The most general characterization of potentiality is the latent capacity to say or do or make or perceive or understand something new, and without being able to explain fully how it has happened or to have predicted that it would happen. The greatest adventure for the human species is no longer to conquer nature—that has always come naturally to a species that is only partly natural—but to save it from the human species. That adventure would be a radical departure from past practice and signify an admirable species self-overcoming.

A last word about free agency. In his *Discourse on Inequality,* Rousseau defines free agency as the awareness of being free, which sponsors the ability either to succumb to or resist nature's command, which a human being experiences as resistible pressure *(impression).* All other animals succumb without choice to whatever nature commands; they can resist no pressure, no urge that comes from within them in the course of coping with what is outside them. Augustine had earlier called this capacity by the name of will, unique to human beings and the orders of beings higher than humanity. Although Rousseau says he is eager to use nature as an inspiration for restoring human beings to health and sanity amid so much intricate and painful artificiality, his eagerness does not prevent him from insisting on the human difference from the rest of nature. He emphasizes free agency as uniquely human, and would not have it otherwise; though just to keep his readers off-balance, he says that reflection is unnatural and that a human being who meditates is a depraved animal; and that perhaps what we today call a lobotomy is needed to be happy—contented as distinct from exhilarated or ecstatic.

To leave aside external obstacles, there are of course internal limits on free agency. In Rousseau's account, perhaps the greatest obstacle to free agency is imitation of those around one, an unthinking conformity to prevailing customs, prejudices, and fashions. One enslaves oneself very easily because one doesn't know that one is doing it, but the spell can be broken, self-emancipation is always possible. But there are other psychological obstacles; an account of them can build on Rousseau but can benefit from later thinking to highlight obsession and self-compulsion, here understood not only as engendering infinite passions, as in our earlier discussion, but rather as engendering nearly unbreakable habits by which one loses oneself to repetition, to being lived by one's passions and tastes rather than living through them. Nevertheless, before time's accretions disfigure a human being, free agency is buried there, but not irretrievably.

Free agency is linked to free will, though they are separate concepts. Free will is the ability to do or abstain from doing what a society or other social grouping has conditioned or educated its members to do and not do, and to live up to what its rules of interaction expect of people. No social entity asks for the impossible, although deviation and transgression are common. Every human being has some capacity to resist internal pressures, but every human being also has weakness of will. Free will is a regular occurrence, and so is its failure. If free will is a question at all, a simple answer will have to do. Yes, free will seems to be necessary to free agency and hence dignity and rights. To the extent that free will remains a problem without a solution that is found universally persuasive, as Rousseau acknowledged, we have to say that our doubts, in the spirit of constitutional democracy, lead us to advocate, as I did earlier in our discussion, reluctance to punish weakness of will when it causes people to break the law, and lenience in the administration of punishment. We should mitigate our conception of human responsibility without abandoning it. The usual cause of lawbreaking is not a perverse determination to break the law for the pleasure of transgressing but temporary helplessness in the face of temptation or ungoverned passion. It is revelatory that the rationale for punishment, even apart from the question of free will, is still and always a matter of unresolved dispute. That is another reason for reluctance to inflict it, and for lenience in its administration. Harsh punishments, and incarceration, when some penal response other than incarceration is eligible, go against the spirit of constitutionalism and hence against both justice and dignity. A corrupt puritanism often lies behind harshness. When he writes to defend the justice of the death penalty, Rousseau says that his hand trembles; he should have followed its promptings. Capital punishment is death to the spirit of constitutionalism. Punishment of any kind, even when not deemed excessive, should be an uneasy establishment.

A selective list of commendable and uniquely human traits and attributes, characteristics, and capacities is now completed.

Summary

I have said that the purpose of this selective philosophical anthropology is to help provide a basis for the idea of human dignity, but also to look forward to highlighting the unique human capacity to serve as the steward of nature. We began with the proposal that the idea of human dignity has two components and both are existential, not moral: the equal status of every human being and the stature of the human species. We saw that the defense of human rights depends on both the existential notion of the equal status of every individual and the concept of the public morality of justice: typically, neither the existential component nor the moral claim is sufficient, but each is necessary, and together they are ordinarily necessary and sufficient, except when the moral claim seems to countenance, in the name of the reduction of suffering, the effacement of the existential or status consideration and thus mortally injures human dignity. Then, the concept of individual status must do its work and do it alone, and is necessary and sufficient. We also saw that since status is only part of the idea of human dignity, there may be tension between status and the other part, human stature.

4

Human Stature and Great Achievements

I turn now to a problem that I have occasionally touched on, but that should be given more than a glance. It is the problem of social inequality and how it looks from the perspective of the project of human stature. The heart of the problem is that societies that have not recognized and respected rights and have therefore been, by our lights, deficient in various degrees in both components of the basis for rights, the public morality of justice and the existential value of equal individual status, have achieved great things that strongly reinforce the uniqueness of the human species and therefore its claim for a stature incomparably greater than that of any other species. How does a defender of rights answer the charge that treating the great mass of people poorly was a necessary condition for the pursuit of great achievements? (There is no audience other than human beings on whom human achievements can register. I assume at this point that human beings can speak nonfoolishly about the greatness of humanity, foolish though it seems.)

Another part of the problem is that the innate ability of human beings to contribute to great achievements appears to be unequal. A perfect meritocracy would demonstrate this supposition quite clearly. And though no society is a perfect meritocracy, almost all societies in various degrees do encourage and reward talent. Thus, strictly hierarchical societies, which were not governed constitutionally, except with a prudent selectivity, did great deeds and accomplished great achievements; from another angle, human beings are unequal in their possession of those uniquely human characteristics that conduce to great achievements, even though all people possess these characteristics to some degree. I will fold the problem of innate unequal human endowment into the overall problem of the moral cost in suffering and the existential cost in equal status that the majority was made to pay so that the world could keep on teaching itself a certain lesson. The lesson was that humanity is vastly superior to all other species because, in relevant respects, some people were better than other people and deserved the surplus they got. The surplus paid for their endeavors. Even so, the higher ones had to use force and manipulation to attain and preserve their privileges.

We must remember the obvious: all constitutional societies are socially and economically unequal. The usual tendency, if not telos, of freedom is to create inequality, or permit inequality to manifest itself more easily. Rights are recognized and respected, and for that reason, socioeconomic inequality results and is preserved in the name of rights. People have different levels, partly innate, of talent, drive, and self-control; freedom allows this fact to register, though imperfectly. And of course constitutional governance perforce establishes the structural inequality of officials and citizens. Another obvious fact is that a democratic culture develops in a society of rights, more and more over time. Briefly stated, the trouble is that, despite its antipathy—well founded in both moral and existential considerations—to socioeconomic leveling, democratic culture appears to jeopardize human stature. The culture encourages and rewards exceptional endeavors in only some directions, but seems to exact a large cost in other directions.

There are two views in play here. The first is that justice, the public morality of justice, even apart from equal political rights, exists in a state of tension with the aspirations that make up the project of human stature. The second view is that the equal status of every individual exists in a state of tension with human stature, apart from morality, because human stature seems to require that elites make the people mere means for the elite's purposes, and override the people's own. If we harbor both thoughts, we face the possibility that human stature, the second and also existential component of human dignity, is jeopardized by democracy understood as the political-cultural system that alone answers to the moral and existential (or dignity) meaning and worth of equal human rights.

I have said that thinkers who subscribe to virtue ethics offer a critique of human rights in their absoluteness and finality, and do so most importantly in the name of a different conception of human dignity. (The moral critique found in virtue ethics is not the point in my discussion here.) We have already had to face, therefore, one sort of argument that is at odds with the idea of the equal status of all individuals, the dignity component in the defense of human rights. In the virtue ethics position, dignity has to be earned or deserved; it cannot be imputed to persons from the very fact of their common humanity. In Kant's theory, furthermore, dignity can be forfeited by wrongdoing. (My position is that dignity can be destroyed but not forfeited.) For the sake of human dignity, I tried to rebut the compound view that rights are tentative and probationary and that an administered paternalism is an acceptable principle to guide restrictions of rights. Now we must enter a field of problems in which the equal status of all individuals is challenged from within the same conception of human dignity, not another conception. The challenge is in the name of human stature. Thus, justice and equal status work together against the claims of human stature. Stature seems to be threatened from two directions.

Human Stature and Inequality

Our overall problem, then, is that societies without human rights, and that had few practices that worked to the same purposes as human rights, and were therefore marked by much injustice and oppression (leave aside totalitarian evil) and much unscrupulous use of the majority as mere means to the ends of the few, did further the project of human stature. These societies were capable of great achievements.

Is there an affinity between democracy and indifference or even hostility to human stature, and a corresponding affinity between oppressive and hierarchical societies and great achievements? Is the desire to discredit greatness and to credit naturalist reductions of the human species one of the hidden passions of democratic culture? On the other hand, is it possible that a mostly hidden motive of oppressive and hierarchical societies is to show what humanity is capable of, and to give the lie to those who want to reduce humanity's stature and make the human species just another species? Assume precapitalist scarcity: if the world had always recognized and respected human rights and on that basis set up democracies everywhere, would the loss as measured by the great achievements that oppressive hierarchies actually did accomplish have been exorbitant? As exorbitant in another way as the cost to the many who endured oppressive hierarchies? Would the reign of justice and dignity all through the history of scarcity have reduced human stature and worsened the human condition? Or would democracy much earlier have generated capitalism or something like it, and hence effected an enormous net reduction in scarcity for millions of people, and thereby displayed greatness, if only in the achievement of fantastic productivity?

Let us adopt for a moment a perspective provoked by Nietzsche, and look back at glorious societies in human history. In any given specimen, some talent obviously went to waste because of cruel and unfair practices, and some of those at the top were unfit for their position; the society was only partly meritocratic. But at least the few could use the many, could make or keep them poor and uneducated so that economic resources, and human beings themselves who were looked on as resources, could be concentrated and directed ruthlessly. A leisure class and an intellectual class (to use Mill's categories from an early essay, "State and Society in America," 1836) could be perpetuated. Only by means of a systematically malapportioned distribution of resources could a high culture arise, and could something fine for once be attained. Refinement could not otherwise be coaxed out of grossness; apparently wasted resources could be employed in adventures that revealed the audacity of the human spirit, or in apparently idle learning that came from intellectual curiosity that was not perverse a good part of the time; the arts could flourish, even if most people couldn't flourish and consequently had no use for the arts. Public life could bear the stamp of superior taste; there was no interest in accommodating what did not meet its standards. The private life of a few and only a few (some at the top, some in the middle) could give evidence of the creation of another world wholly different from that of the sordid lot of the rest of the population. Because only a comparative few could practice the arts, and artists and craftsmen had to appeal to the taste of those other few who could afford to support their endeavors, the culture as a whole seemed dedicated to excellence; excellence seemed to be its raison d'être. Resources were not dissipated in mediocrity or amateurishness, or in worrying too much about locating and nurturing submerged or incipient talent.

The usually implicit but insolent premise of hierarchical societies is that domestic elites know better than the people how the wealth created by the people should be spent. It is the same premise that drives leaders of colonial and other imperialist wars: the expansionist society claims to know better than the conquered population how to spend that population's wealth. "Better" means better of course for the conqueror's purposes, not those of the conquered.

Clearly, the project of human stature or human greatness was usually not deliberately pursued. There are moments in Athens, however, when a speaker defends or urges the project. Some examples include Thucydides' Pericles and Alcibiades, and Plato's Callicles; both democracy and antidemocracy spoke for the project. (Athens is the democratic exception, not the democratic model; it is beyond comparison or emulation; only its vices can be imitated.) But it is mostly by retrospective imputation that many endeavors are perceived as a project, when they were originally defended in commonplace language, or were launched in the confidence that nothing needed to be said in explanation or apology. The retrospective view, as articulated by thinkers like Machiavelli, Hegel, and Nietzsche, and numerous lesser figures, interprets the past as striving to attain awareness of the human stature and driven by the urge to manifest it. But the few at the top, apart from any theory, and amid their tangle of motives and purposes, must sometimes have had an intimation that the honor of the human race was at stake in maintaining a radically unequal society, and they were not deterred by a concern for the equal status of all individuals or equal consideration for the moral entitlements of all people. Throughout much of human history, great achievements in many fields of human endeavor have undeniably come about in defiance of what we now call human rights. If we praise aristocracies (or other oligarchies), we do not do so because their moral qualities were great or their respect for the dignity of people beneath them was in evidence. For them the discipline of mores was everything; their *virtù*—or less flatteringly, their masculine vices—were more prominent than their moral virtues.

For those at the top, the honor of the human race was maintained by the effort of some human beings, considered or considering themselves the best of humanity, and standing in for humanity in general, to demonstrate that humanity was existentially superior to animals and was not confined like them to the imperatives of nature. Humanity is better than all other beings on earth only when some people are able to show they are better than others. Humanity could transcend itself through confronting danger and taking risks when the imperatives of nature are temporarily silenced and a vision possesses the human spirit. When I say that the human species is the highest species, that its stature depends on its unique characteristics, and that these unique characteristics show that it is partly discontinuous with nature, am I adopting the traditional elitist view? No: despite my wish to make some use of it in defending the idea of human stature. I have no species snobbery, or try not to. Human stature must be affirmed in vanquishing snobbery toward animals by magnanimity.

That we are a higher species must be said because the facts about unique human traits and attributes rebut the theories of reductive science. We must begin and end in appreciation of nature, struggle as we must against many aspects of it. But the struggle for safety and sufficiency must not impede our wonder at, for example, animals in their profusion and variety, whether they are charismatic or not.

The movement in thought begins by insisting on total human superiority to animals, proceeds to define human greatness by reference to animal inferiority, and then locates greatness in achievements that require the subordination of the majority and even the assimilation of the underclasses to animals. Such thinking can no longer sustain the project of human stature. First, equal status of persons must be accepted and second, the sources of stature must be found, though not exclusively, in great achievements that serve nature. For the moment let us consider the service to nature.

Wonder is the antidote to snobbery. Animal species are so heterogeneous, it is as if no one mind, or group of fellow minds, no matter how transcendent, could have intended them. Only natural selection and random mutation could have produced them without anything in mind. They do not add up to one picture. The doctrine of intelligent design is even less plausible when we consider the complexity of animal species and their often antagonistic relations. Intelligent design would be incompetent design because the designer would be aesthetically debauched or confused. Animals want to survive but have to struggle to survive, while individual members and whole species often fail: this is not a pattern that bespeaks intelligence or even design. The case against intelligent design is even stronger when we take into account the fact that the living organisms, plants, and earthly matter that are now co-present did not emerge all at the same time to compose a supposedly harmonious whole, and the further fact that many things and species have appeared and disappeared as the earth has undergone many cataclysmic changes over three or four billion years or more. The wonder of the world in its endless mutations is greater for the absence of intentional design. The Book of Job conveys a radical theodicy of wonder, but for all its sublimity does not begin to approach the terrors found in the scientific story of the antiquity of the earth and of the changes of matter and life on it from its beginnings, not to mention the so to speak inhuman scale and dynamism of the universe.

Some species can strike us as miraculous, not only charismatic. Even so, human beings are not only animals. Because they are not only animals, they must not be treated as almost everyone, whether because of immemorial species snobbery or feelings much more crudely practical and exploitative thinks animals, perhaps except for pets, can be treated. Defenders of human stature must associate human greatness with the protection of nature, while still believing, though without snobbery, that because the human species is not a merely animal species it is the highest species on earth and, as such, is alone able to try to protect and revere nature. There is an affinity between regard for nature and the equal status of human beings. Let us recall Plato's description of leniently treated animals in democratic society: they moved around as if they were equal to citizens.

I do not say, like the practitioners and champions of the old order, that the great achievements of a few outweigh the moral and existential entitlements of the rest of the population. The concept of equal status itself would seem to require that a whole social system that eradicated most kinds of preventable human suffering but at the cost of substantially diminishing human capacities should be condemned. Some kinds and degrees of pain and suffering, some anxieties and risks, failure and losses are built into leading free lives. That is the price of honoring individual status and hence human dignity. The brave new world and societies that tend in its direction disregard human rights in the name of painlessness and contentedness. What is more, if the whole world were to tend in the same direction, human dignity would be on the way to extinction, and without moral complaint. In some cases, then, the two elements of human dignity, status and stature, are unified in a common struggle to defend human dignity against—it would be nice to call it—a distorted version of morality.

Now, in looking at the past, we see a different picture. In our partly (but only partly) anachronistic idea of what human beings are owed, we see that there was a struggle in which morality (or justice) and status, as we conceive them, were usually on the same side—either fighting together as equals or using each other as a supplementary conceptual force in the common fight—against the putative project of promoting human stature that was advanced on the opposite side. The really interesting point, if it is correct, would be that when we regard the past, and we wish to accept as our heritage many of the great achievements of the past, we would have to agree that, in general, there was and had to be, strife or at least serious tension between status and stature, the two concepts that make up human dignity, and that we beneficiaries of the past appear to come down on the side of stature against status and also against justice.

We want, in the name of human stature, to praise humanity for its indefatigable capacity to develop cultures or ways of life that defy constraining circumstances which are perceived as challenges, even perilous challenges, rather than as fate, and are treated not as a natural environment that inexorably selects for adaptation but as a protracted opportunity to be creative, ingenious, and able to change the terms on which life is given. Not to say that any group of people living together works on a blank canvas. It is only to say that people respond surprisingly, and do unpredictable things. What they do is never fully explainable by themselves or their contemporaries, or by later generations, by exclusive reference to what for other species would be the absolute force of the imperatives of nature. The variety of cultures is testimony to the brilliance of common humanity. The trouble is that we also want to pay tribute to the few. We want to cherish the knowledge and art heaped up by the few in all previous generations and seize them for our edification and that of future generations. We want, as well, to admire the traits and attributes, such as physical courage, tactical shrewdness, and strategic vision, that went into audacious enterprises of exploration and conquest, or defense and tenacity, even though they were manifestly unjust and oppressive and trashed the equal individual status of both the human instruments of oppression and its foreign victims.

But it is not only our admiration of the past that is at issue. Our continuous use of many of its achievements shows that we are willing to enhance ourselves by the achievements extorted from the labor of earlier generations, millions upon millions of people. Their coerced sacrifice and insolent inhuman treatment at the hands of elites created the wealth that helped make these achievements possible. Where there wasn't brutal exploitation of the many, there was immense indifference and neglect. There were always the terrible sufferings of war and occupation. However, not only do people in prosperous societies continue to benefit from the extorted achievements of the past, they also use their wealth in the pursuit of high culture and great achievements, when they could redistribute more of their wealth than they now do to alleviate the plight of the impoverished of the world. In the present, some people enjoy the human cultural inheritance and add to it; many others in their poverty can neither enjoy nor contribute. On a global scale, prosperous societies that respect rights at home address the suffering of others elsewhere insufficiently. Does this discrepancy, this inequality between societies, even when the result of neglect rather than exploitation, compromise us perhaps more than our use of what the oppressive past has bequeathed us? Or do we think, rather, that in regard to the past and the present the importance of stature should outweigh that of both status and justice? If so, what could we mean? Would we mean, among other things, that the contribution of the idea of human dignity to the defense of human rights in the present would become dubious, if one of the two components of that idea seems to undercut commitment to the other and hence to human rights? This conceptual instability is then intensified if we keep in mind the plausible belief that human beings are innately unequal in the uniquely human characteristics—to know and to appreciate—that contribute to human stature in general and, in particular, to the determination to serve as steward to nature.

In an effort to quiet the conceptual instability, I propose an oversimple solution. One question is whether the contribution of the idea of human dignity, in the form of equal individual status, to the defense of human rights becomes dubious once we praise great human achievements that have been attained through the violation of individuals in their rights and hence in what they are owed morally and existentially. For the last three and a half centuries, discourse about rights has been in circulation, and systems of rights have been established, even if falteringly and with backtracking. We have reached the point where we could not in good conscience say that a society can now endeavor to sacrifice people for the sake of the claims of human stature, as aristocracies and oligarchies once did. We cannot give precedence to human stature in its struggle with the allied arguments of individual status and the public morality of justice. But we should benefit from the past; it would be quixotic not to. At the same time, I do not see how the claims of stature in the form of great achievements *in the present* can be sacrificed to the project of redistributing as much wealth as possible to alleviate global poverty. It would seem that human dignity requires us to say no to the redistributive theory for reasons analogous to those that led me earlier to say no to Peter Singer's argument about personal economic self-sacrifice in "Famine, Affluence, and Morality." The general point is that there appears to be an important difference between initiating and maintaining an exploitative policy or condition (on the one hand) and neglecting to redress it when one does not have direct responsibility for it (on the other).

What I say about neglect rests, I know, on the debatable view that there is in fact a significant difference between exploitation and neglect. The counterclaim would be that what counts is remediable suffering, not the cause of it or responsibility for it. Mill offers, however, what I hope is theoretical assistance in *On Liberty* to rebut the counterclaim. He says that inaction in the face of dire need is culpable but "requires a much more cautious exercise of compulsion" than active infliction of harm. "To make any one answerable for doing evil to others, is the rule; to make him answerable for not preventing [or reducing] evil is, comparatively speaking, the exception" (*Liberty,* p. 225). If we can extend Mill's judgment from individual action in everyday life to international public policy, we can say that ignoring an immediate and widespread emergency is morally unacceptable, but undertaking a sustained international policy of costly amelioration is not morally compulsory. If what I say is wrong, then one must believe that a worldwide violent revolution would be permissible—perhaps obligatory—for the purpose of redistributing the world's wealth.

Perhaps the view that there is strife between the two components of human dignity is a mistake. But if this view is at least plausible, the only acceptable position, *for the time being,* is that the claims of the individual at the hands of the powerful must now beat out the claims of the species whenever the latter claims amount to the active and deliberate erosion of human rights for the sake of human stature. In our age, no people anywhere should be used or exploited by any given society, or neglected inside any society, so that high culture can flourish, much less to ensure that great adventures and enterprises that memorably demonstrate the unique capacities of the human species can be undertaken. Within the idea of human dignity, individual status must now constrain the project of human stature; morality then combines with the claims of individual status to reinforce the theoretical counsel of inhibition to the projects of audacious elites.

To resume the backward look: we cannot disown and fail to benefit from what the past has achieved. At the risk of parasitism, we could not even wish to undo the achievements. Compensatory or restorative justice to the earlier victims of the pursuit of high culture is impossible. Revenge taken on the past has been and would be cruelly self-destructive. Blowing up two great statues of the Buddha in Afghanistan was stupid as only religious fundamentalism can be; the Maoist Cultural Revolution in the name of a leveled equality and waged against people who embodied the culture of the past was an unforgivable organized and regimented series of thousands of particular crimes. (By the way, that is what any war is, too, whatever the purposes of any participant in the war. It is only when organized war is seen as a series of hundreds or thousands of discrete violent acts, one by one, and all of them crimes, or like crimes, that its horror will ever register properly on our felt experience or imagination.)

No, we atone for making use of what cost others too much when we remember the cost and refuse to fly over it without noticing it, and resolve not to persist in pursuing great projects at whatever cost to human rights. We must not be charmed or seduced by the great works of the past into forgetting the fact that without the labors of the many, most of the great achievements of the past would have been impossible. Yes, human beings are unequally endowed in their ability to initiate great deeds or create great works of mind and art, but they sustain what they cannot initiate or create. Their dignity, their equal individual status, is undamaged by their innate inequality in talent—as it is undamaged by their unequal virtue, as I have said.

In accepting the idea of human dignity and then wanting people in the present and future to benefit from the worth of the achievements of the past and to see them also as testimony to human stature, I hope I am not repeating an offense like the grave offense committed by the US government, for one example, when instead of destroying the records of atrocious "medical" experiments on prisoners performed by the Japanese during the Second World War, it decided after some discussion to keep the records in order to learn more about the limits of human endurance. The US government should have known better, but instead showed its contempt for both morality and human dignity by its readiness to keep the records and doubtless use the knowledge, as it has more recently used records of torture inflicted on US military and others by its adversaries, in order to facilitate the training of its own personnel and the infliction of torture on its adversaries in turn, whether guilty of earlier torture or not. The hokum of the "ticking bomb scenario" is used to mislead public opinion into accepting the need for torture.

The issue before us is similar to forbidden knowledge: using knowledge gained by an evil method, whether the method has been employed by the proposed user or some other agent, is morally prohibited. Is using the accumulated culture of the past like benefiting from torture? I do not think so. The principal aim of torture is to get the victim to agree with the assertions that the torturer makes about him, not to extract new truth. Most shocking of all, it seems as if the purpose of the torture inflicted by the US government on prisoners captured early in the recent wars against radical Islam was to force them to confess to what the torturers and the tortured knew to be false as if it were the truth, in the manner of Orwell's O'Brien in *Nineteen Eighty-Four*. They were being forced to say that Saddam Hussein was linked to the Al Qaeda attack on New York and that he was hiding weapons of mass destruction. Torture did not succeed in extorting these two falsehoods from them, but only other ones that had little use as propaganda. These cases are so extreme they add the evil of malignancy to the evil of torture, but they are not utterly discontinuous with the unjust and oppressive treatment of subject populations by elites in the past. Knowledge of the techniques and effects of torture only adds to the human capacity to inflict unjustifiable immediate pain and long-term physical and psychological suffering; it adds nothing to the enhancement of life, but makes life less worth living for all of us.

As one of the worst crimes, torture degrades those who do it or benefit when others do it, not only those who experience it. Using the knowledge extracted by torture makes vivid the plausibility of those views that scorn the idea of human dignity as a cruel joke, or a bit of deranged hubris, in the midst of human evil. Torture perpetuates itself and does not make even an unintentional contribution to something better than itself. Yet extreme evil, which cannot be outweighed by any consideration, also cannot allow the whole human record to be nullified by the worst that people have done. That would be to punish the great majority of people who are innocent of the worst, though they could predictably or unpredictably be capable of the worst, or at least capable of cooperating with it or letting it happen without any fuss.

The practical point is that the high culture of the past, with its feet standing on the mass of people, often prepares for its own eventual overthrow, even when its content is hostile to the people or otherwise reactionary. If we concentrate on the great achievements of the old order in works of art, thought, and literature, and even the conquest and adventure, we see that it would be foolish to refuse to engage with it. It is by now almost impossible even to regret its existence. To a significant degree, engaging with the achievements of the past is not like trying to benefit from torture. I am not defending the general principle that wrong may be done intentionally so that good may come of it, though I do think that the principle that doing the necessary and lesser evil or smaller kind of wrong than evil in order to prevent or remove a greater evil or wrong is tolerable, barely tolerable. Rather, in some cases, later generations may turn wrong to good against the intentions of those who did it. If in the past, good could not have come into existence except by exploitation and degradation of the majority, the result does not allow us in the present to justify or forgive the exploitation and degradation. But the high culture of the old order did inspire self-dissatisfaction and an uneasy conscience; it did inspire yearnings and give energy to move beyond the limits of the established order. Great and good art, thought, and literature are more than ideological justifications of the established order and not mere class-determined epiphenomena. Herbert Marcuse, a radical champion of human emancipation, was right to insist on the power for good of what came from conditions that we would never wish to see restored or wish with an easy mind that they had been established to begin with. I admit that we are dealing once again with a tricky matter about which anything one says will appear disingenuous.

Admiration of Nature and Admiration of Humanity

The hope is to enlist uniquely human characteristics in the stewardship of nature and thus associate human stature and hence human dignity with that stewardship. But even now stewardship cannot be the whole story. When uniquely human traits and attributes have been employed for the sake of achievements in art, science, and learning, and in audacious exploits and endeavors, stature has been insisted on and displayed. Human dignity must continue to depend on these achievements. Yes, we must acknowledge that these achievements have come and still do come at a terrible cost to human dignity in the form of the equal individual status of people and to morality as well. But the acknowledgment cannot prevent us, at whatever discomfort or risk of inconsistency, from admiring the manifestations of human stature that the human record puts at our disposal. If our ultimate commitment is to the stewardship of nature, we cannot disregard the human record of greatness in the enhancement of human life through the centuries, as essential testimony to human stature. We cannot serve nature on our knees. For all its crimes against humanity itself and all its destruction of nature, we should not want the human species to become extinct, as some radical environmentalists say they want. There is sufficient reason for willing human preservation, if there is no other: as far as we know, only the human species can record, know, and admire nature—the earth and the universe. Still, if this may be the most important reason to endure, it cannot be the only reason. The works of humanity are also admirable and justify themselves. Indeed how could the works of the highest species not be the most worthy objects of our admiration? More worthy than nature? Yes, insofar as human works are *works;* no, insofar as nature is just there, speechless and able to inspire speechlessness and then recovered speech in us. Is the human ability to know and appreciate nature greater than nature itself? Is the knower greater than the known, when the known is unknowing; is the admirer greater than the admired, when the admired is unknowing? Yes, if the human mind is the greatest thing in the universe; no, because without nature there never would have been mind.

Those who want to serve earthly nature are overwhelmed by its magnificence, by the beauty and complexity of creatures and plants, by the intricacy of the relations of dependence and assertiveness in nature, and above all just by its being there in its abundance when there could have been, for us, very much less. That there can be very much less in the future is what drives stewardship. One principal reason we should want to take on the stewardship of nature is that we appreciate and admire nature. The aesthetic receptivity to nature extends beyond the earth into the universe, beyond humanity's reach, and to a large extent, beyond humanity's close empirical observation. But those who admire nature should also admire the works of human greatness that testify to human stature. We should try to see that record as the record of the human species, even though the human species is not one collective agent; it is, instead, groups of people joined in cultures, who everywhere and all through human time account for the achievements in the human record. Groups have done evil, groups have done great things; much of the time, great things have been done on the basis of injustice and oppression and violation of individual status. (Can we call great any enterprise that was based on the evil of extermination or accompanied it? I am sure the answer is no, because we cannot admire it, even with a bad conscience.)

I guess that I am asking for a kind of Hegelian overview of the human species so far, without the goal of forgiveness and reconciliation, but nevertheless with an emotion, still intact, that must exceed even admiration. The emotion cannot be love or worship; it can scarcely be named. We have make do with wonder, awe, or reverence. If only for a moment, we should lose sight of individuals and groups; let our vision of them grow faint. Imagine the human species on the verge of extinction; let its great achievements, as if performed by one agent, pass before your mind as we drown. Take an external view of the human species, something we should never do with any individual member of the species. If talk about justification of nature is allowable, we could say that what justifies it is its capacity to bring out of itself what is not natural: animal consciousness, and human mind and self-consciousness. Nature cannot be justified as providential. Humanity cannot be justified as a species of preponderant moral goodness or existential respect for all its members. What justifies humanity is the extent of its being nonnatural: it is commendably, not only deplorably, anomalous. It is a species of great uniquely human achievements, but of one achievement as great as any: it alone is able to know that the earth and the universe exist, to provide knowledge of their workings, and to stand in awe of mere being (in Santayana's phrase). By this composite achievement, all the old false ideas of humanity on earth as being the center of the universe are replaced by the only truthful one.

Before going under, however, we should not love or admire nature to the exclusion of human achievements; we should not love nature so that we can hate human achievements; we should not admire nature so that we can overcome our disappointment at human failures of justice and mutual respect.

I have Thoreau in mind when I say these things. Thoreau's intensity of reception toward the particulars of nature is ever enlightening, and preserves the dignity of nature in a way that few other writers can match; but his misanthropic moods, also ever enlightening, are chilling. His mind is not at home in cities, but cities are among the greatest of human achievements, for all their concentration of vice and suffering; they are incomparably greater achievements than small tight communities. Some vices and suffering are inseparable from creativity. Thoreau's value is nevertheless immense for the reason that his misanthropy is largely caused by human brutality toward human beings, especially slaves and Native Americans. His aversion to the works of humanity (except for great literature) is occasioned by his sense of their cost in human rights. Thoreau's awareness of slavery, especially, poisoned his attitude toward social life, so great was the force of his commitment to morality (though a mostly negative morality) and the avoidance of human degradation. The commitment left him only nature to admire. He felt the existence of slavery as a personal trauma; the feeling had a depth that pays tribute to his moral imagination. But I think we cannot take Thoreau's position on the works of humanity as binding; and I hope the reason is not that we cannot feel trauma as deeply as Thoreau did—but perhaps that is the reason.

There is, however, a reverse current in Thoreau. There are passages in which his teaching is that human art prepares the way for the disinterested observation of nature, and that nature cannot exist for our reverence rather than exploitation until art refines our perception sufficiently to look closely at natural phenomena. With refined perception, what we sometimes see is that a natural occurrence has the qualities of art: he likens the surface of ice to silk, and thereby praises nature for its resemblance to human artifice (*Journal,* vol. 7, p. 180). He may not go the length of saying that nature does not exist for our reverence until human beings have first anticipated or reproduced it as art, but many of his descriptions of nature are not only exact but painterly. Thoreau can also congratulate the earlier Indian craftsman who ornamented the pestle he made and therefore indicated "fancy and taste" and hence a more "complete culture." Some "pure beauty" was added to "pure utility" (p. 180). Art does not justify human cruelty; it shows only that human beings are capable of more than cruelty.

If Nietzsche's early claim that the world can be justified only as an aesthetic phenomenon has worn out its charm by now, we can go to Walt Whitman for a less pugnacious and a more (so to speak) musical comprehension of the human record, which is Nietzsche's standard and aspiration and which Whitman, ignorant of Nietzsche but not of Hegel, reaches. Whitman seems to hold the human world before him, at a good distance, not to embrace it but only to allow it in its thousand facets to emerge as worthy of attention and appreciation. Of course Emerson is the teacher of Whitman, Thoreau, and Nietzsche, but unlike these admirers, he learned the lessons of Plato's Idealism perhaps a bit too well. We cannot dispense with any of these thinkers as instructors in the arts of attention and appreciation. And in an age when every individual's human rights are the paramount consideration, we still have to let the concept of the stature of the human species have its way in our perception of the past—up to a point. Not only the individual but also the species has human dignity.

Democracy and Human Stature: Exploits

The theory of human rights in its moral and existential foundation is there to remind us that we should now set limits on the pursuit of human stature, as shown in the human ambition for greatness. Only when we first judge the past, no matter how anachronistic or presumptuous our judgment, can we then decide deliberately to accept the achievements that accumulated from the pursuit of stature, when it was unconstrained by concern for the public morality of justice in its fullness and the equal status of every individual. There is no presumption in judging the present.

In the present, human rights must be recognized and respected. As I have said, the sole kind of government that meets the demands of the theory of rights is constitutional democracy. As time passes, human rights build up a culture, a democratic culture that is not only framed by rights but inspired by the spirit of rights. The great pursuits and projects must accommodate themselves to the constraints of rights. Human stature must be limited by both morality and individual status. In theory, the political-cultural system of democracy will gradually, sometimes reflexively, often intentionally, but of course incompletely, make human rights count for more than any ambition for greatness, any aspiration or policy that counts human stature more highly than equal individual status.

In theory, a democratic system will not concentrate resources in a few hands and direct that those resources be used in accordance with the purposes and standards of the few, and will not use the population as if it is simply a standing reserve of material resources and living instruments to be exploited for purposes that are not its own. The question returns: Does constitutional democracy, from its principles, so inhibit great but ruthless exploits and endeavors that it diminishes humanity as a whole? As rights spread worldwide, if only in aspiration, does this question become ever more insistent?

I think that the answer is obvious and mixed. Democracy unleashes the human ambition for greatness in some channels of endeavor while perhaps retarding it in other channels, but it is not always consistent with itself when it unleashes ambition or, perhaps, when it retards ambition. When democracy is combined with capitalism and imperialism it promotes the energies of competition and predation. (Racism is not intrinsic to imperialism, but it has often played a vital supporting role—surely in the case of the United States among democracies.) It is hard to imagine an imperialist democracy in modern times that is not also capitalist, though it is easy to find capitalist democracies that are not imperialist. Capitalism does not inhibit imperialism and may sometimes stimulate it, but it is hard to say that there is a necessary systemic connection between them, whereas this kind of connection does bind capitalism and democracy in modern times. (Scarcity of certain resources is a great problem, but not peculiar to capitalist or imperialist societies.) A state-socialist democracy seems an impossible system because it would concentrate too much state power in the hands of one bureaucracy, and it would threaten to be a monopoly of most kinds of initiative in society. It would be the one employer and thus command the resources of life. It would narrow unduly the right of property but also endanger almost all other rights as well.

Yet if there is no systemic connection between capitalism and imperialism, there is a psychological affinity. The affinity is between the mentality of the foreign policy elite and the mentality of those who lead large business firms or aspire to do so. The collective self of the imperialist elite begins in ambition, but after it is established a while it appears pathologically insatiable for as much control as possible of the affairs of the world, while the capitalist self dispersed among many firms appears pathologically insatiable for profits. I say appears, because the insatiability would be pathological if the motive remained ambition, whereas the endless pursuit of power or wealth eventually becomes—here is a different kind of pathology—a game with its own rules and logic that require that it be played without regard to the effects on people who endure the consequences. Undoubtedly, foreign policy elites even in countries with limited ambitions are eager for the game of international politics to go on forever. Perhaps some inwardly generated constraint could set a limit to political or economic ambition if ambition, collective or personal, were the constant motive. But the game, felt as a special kind of exalted game, runs on the motive of wanting to win or not wanting to lose; and no inwardly generated constraint can set a limit on such a motive, which we can regard as abstract or infinite. It is not an accident that these kindred mentalities facilitate the two-way movement between the elites of foreign policy and business. Immersion in one sphere of life is a preparation for involvement in the other. If this is not quite a systemic connection between capitalism and imperialism, it comes close.

Modern capitalist, imperialist democracy is agonistic. Athens, though not capitalist in our sense, was a commercially enterprising city and possessed by an expansionist spirit that was the wonder and dismay of the Greek world. There is something like a precedent in Athenian dynamism for modern times; as I have suggested, it is mainly the vices of Athens that force a resemblance to modern democracy. When the party or factional spirit is added to political life, the agonistic elements deepen. Again, it is hard to imagine modern democracy except on a partisan or factional basis.

Modern constitutional democracy should accommodate capitalism up to the point where socioeconomic inequality becomes steep enough not only to impair but to vitiate the citizenship of numerous people to the point of entrenched and apparently immovable plutocracy. In contrast, imperialism from its nature, in the modern age, contradicts the principles and spirit of constitutional democracy for several reasons.

This critique is directed at the United States; inevitably, American public opinion is largely unacquainted with the idea that the United States is an imperialist country; where acquainted, public opinion would deny the charge, even if some of the public thought the charge true. Let me try to say why imperialism—the tendency to dominate, intimidate, or influence disproportionately many countries by war, sanctions, and corrupt economic penetration—violates constitutionalism. The spirit of constitutionalism in a society must go beyond the boundaries of a society precisely so that the country's leaders do not undertake to act imperialistically beyond its boundaries. A globally active and interventionist foreign policy is anticonstitutional. No necessity requires it. The first principle of constitutionalism is always try to treat foreign citizens in a way that recognizes and respects their human rights—especially negatively, by way of abstaining from interventionist policies that introduce chaotic disruption and dislocation in their lives and dispossess them of life, integrity of body, material sufficiency, and the daily expectations of an unshocked and undisrupted life.

The first and most obvious reason for a constitutionalist denunciation of imperialism, then, is that an imperialist war or policy always violates the rights of the people whom it attacks or invades, or whom it coerces or corruptly influences. Every country in every war commits crimes against humanity and war crimes; large-scale war and, beyond that, a global foreign policy are a further aggravation of the evils of war and coercion. Indeed, the term *war crimes* is a timid euphemism because it hardly conveys the enormity of such acts as the firebombing and atomic bombing of enemy cities by constitutional democracies (the United States and the United Kingdom). War crimes are atrocious incidents, but these acts were not incidents, not incidental; these acts were crimes against humanity. The better side, committed to ridding the earth of the agents of monstrous crimes against humanity, committed them in the pursuit of that end. That some targets of intervention nowadays are societies that do not recognize and respect rights does not change the fact that violent intervention in their countries is a deep trauma. Second, the wars that issue from an adventurist foreign policy give pretexts for the abridgements of rights at home, and in the name of ever-urgent and ever-receding security. The abridgements are so considerable (and almost never fully reversible) that one has to ask whether the society is actually constitutional any longer. If we are not certain that it is, does that mean that we no longer live in a constitutional society? Third, the centrality of foreign policy distorts the original social contract by altering its terms. It changes from a contract for constitutionalism, for the public morality of rights and the recognition of equal individual status of all persons, and hence for limited and accountable government that has a fair degree of transparency and restraint, into an agreement for expansion and augmentation. Such an agreement results in a structure of government that becomes executive-centered in the manner of the old hierarchical order.

Government becomes ever more a web of thousands of discretionary acts performed by hundreds of civilian, intelligence, and military, bureaucratic officials, in the company of lobbyists and publicists; most of the acts are hidden, many of them secret. No one, no matter how well placed, knows the full extent of activity. From these bureaucracies come secret concerted long-term policies. In a global foreign policy, every change around the world registers as important or potentially important; nothing escapes attention; the benefit of the doubt is given to action over patient understanding. The ever-enlarged scope of policy makes it all the more abstract, and the more abstract it becomes, the more game-like it becomes and ever more distant from reality. In its remoteness from reality, the game authorizes an untroubled ruthlessness. Even when policies are announced, the steps on the way to decide them and the acts done to implement them are often obscure. The state in itself becomes a polity, ultimately hierarchical but vigorously participatory that sits on top of a mass of uncomprehending and therefore largely inactive or vicariously active citizens. Secrecy infects and lies dominate public discussion of foreign policy, while experts discountenance public opinion except when leaders find convenience in manipulating or inflaming it. The substance of public discussion gets wrapped up in technicalities and generalizations that cannot be grasped by ordinary abilities, except when caricatured; and the principals eventually get lost in their own deviousness or become hypnotized by their momentum. How can there be true accountability and reasonable popular control over the area of public policy that is most continuously significant and that wields the largest capacity to destroy lives and consume wealth ridiculously? How can constitutionalism accommodate the mixture of official criminality and selective tyranny that help to constitute imperialism?

It is generally true that the centrality of foreign policy signifies alienation by the people of its participatory, consultative, and supervisory powers in relation to government. When foreign policy becomes the most important field of public policy, constitutionalism becomes secondary at best. Foreign policy is a game that none of the players will ever want to end or want to imagine could end. In the people and the elites, team spirit is irrepressible, no matter how bloody the sport. The conduct of foreign policy involves the systematic attenuation, coercion, and manipulation of the consent of the people. If democracy runs on lies more than any other political system, except totalitarianism, because of the constant and partisan need to secure public acquiescence or active support of government policies, foreign policy makes this tendency worse, and imperialism and global foreign policy even worse. It is common to believe that what makes constitutional democracy imperfectly or questionably legitimate is the oligarchic nature of representation as such or the oligarchic reality where equality is nominal and formal but socioeconomic reality is full of inequality. These are fairly weighty considerations. But weightier yet is the mutation inflicted on constitutional democracy by an active and aggressive foreign policy that is insatiable for opportunities for involvement in and hegemony over the affairs of the world. The ancien regime is restored within the heart of modern democracy, but with ever more virtuosic and lethal military technology. It is no wonder that Kant thought that it approaches futility to establish a constitutional government in any one society unless as many constitutional governments as possible hasten to establish a world federation of constitutional governments that manages to abolish war and the preparations for war ("Idea for a Universal History with a Cosmopolitan Purpose" [1784], Seventh Proposition, p. 47). But the will to federate, even or especially among constitutional democracies, does not come easily, if it comes at all. Europe seems to have acquired it, and for the time being. But group identity, national identity in particular, solidified by religion and language, is always ready to stand in the way.

In short, the salience of foreign policy undermines the structure of government in a constitutional democracy, and an imperialist foreign policy subverts the values of constitutional democracy. Imperialism manufactures necessities and invites hostile reactions that guarantee emergencies, and by this always more intense dynamism promotes the further erosion of both the structure and the values. There seem to be no institutional remedies that can save constitutional democracy from forces and energies it has sponsored or accommodated.

The nonchalance of US imperialism is inadvertently displayed by Richard N. Haass, when he distinguishes between wars of necessity and wars of choice. Wars of necessity are waged when there are "vital national interests," which is as permissive a license for casual wars as could be imagined. But if that is what wars of necessity are, what are wars of choice? For one thing, they are "not inherently good or bad." Imagine thinking that a war could be inherently good and need not be inherently bad. This nonchalance grows out of the sort of intoxication that presages disaster. Wars of choice can be waged when "American interests are sufficiently important." This means that the United States can initiate wars of aggression—for what is a war of choice if not a war of aggression, as in the case of the US invasion of Iraq in 2003?—and think that it is doing something that may be *inherently* good and that need not be *inherently* bad; that is, it is free of any admixture of evil. The deaths, wounding, destruction, and dislocation—the whole monstrous dispossession—count for nothing ("In Afghanistan, the Choice Is Ours," op-ed, *New York Times,* August 21, 2009, A27).

One might say that all this is the cancerous growth of the project of human stature, an unlimited grandiosity, and it is enacted by the United States as a wealthy, technologically proficient, self-confident, and self-righteous democracy. This is a tragic pattern. Haass's sentiments are more nonchalant than those that most members of the establishment would be prepared to express publicly. The nonchalance is actually insolence of the most traditional kind: unpremeditated. If modern democracies without imperial or colonial ambitions do not typically war on one another, they may nevertheless be enlisted by imperialist democracies in wars where, inevitably, crimes against humanity and war crimes are committed, as if by a tyrant, and supposedly for the sake of eliminating tyranny.

Of course, it is easy to condemn, but there are times when it seems especially futile. The feeling of futility can make the condemnation appear quixotic or cranky to the critics themselves; the taunt of "beautiful soul" in Hegel's sense to those who are disquieted by power politics hangs in the air.

If adventures and exploits, including wars, bring out uniquely human capacities that would be wholly commendable if peacefully employed, and that are deplorably unique in war, then modern democracy contributes to the record of human stature, but in a way that is too much like the old order. In contrast, the tie to capitalism also allows modern democracy to bring out characteristics that, if not wholly commendable, are not wholly deplorable. The same goes for partisan and factional contest. As for largely peaceful capitalist democracies, perhaps we could say that consistently upholding the achievement of the public morality of justice combined with adherence to the requirements of human status, and without significant deviation at home or abroad, is so rare that we want to celebrate it as a great human achievement. This achievement, as such, gives testimony to the human capacity to defy the human record of injustice, oppression, and evil and to achieve, in more than a few societies, a political-cultural system that seems to go against the human grain itself. But how long can any such system last? How precarious must such a peaceful system be, as it is not only attuned to human aspiration but also goes against the grain. The more it is attuned to ideal human aspiration, the more it goes against the grain.

Democracy and Human Stature: The Life of the Mind

In the achievements of mind, modern democracy clearly has proved itself great in science and technology. In all fields of knowledge where past riches prepared the way but are not now in continuous use for instruction and stimulation, modern democracy excels. Science and technology are busy surpassing their antecedents; there is appreciable progress in scientific knowledge; past riches do not cast the shadow of "the anxiety of influence" on later practitioners, or lead them to feel that practically everything great has already been done. The accumulation of past richness does not inhibit present accomplishment. The field is wide open to greatness. There is nothing in modern democracy that would resist concentrating resources and applying standards of merit in social selection for talent in science and engineering. The competitive spirit can thrive without the achievers being thought guilty of odious condescension. No one resents the fact that some people know what most other people do not have the talent or will to acquire. The rights of free inquiry encourage the pursuit of almost all scientific knowledge; interests of every sort benefit from the pursuit.

Many forces thus cooperate in assuring that the distinctive human capacities to acquire scientific knowledge will flourish in modern democracy, peaceful or war-like, imperialist or cautious and law-abiding. Thus, the stewardship of nature by means of the history of nature and scientific knowledge of it are well served by modern democracy: these scientific endeavors constantly increase wonder, if one is disposed, at the splendor of nature on earth and in the universe to a degree that far exceeds any wonder instigated by religious thought about this splendor; the proposed theological answers to tormenting questions may actually stifle wonder, or at least direct the largest part of wonder toward the supposed creator and away from nature. But is the wonder felt in the wider culture? Does the culture sustained by human rights sustain, in turn, the admiration and appreciation, the enraptured yet disinterested reception that is owed to nature, and that the cultivation of the humanities most favors? And apart from the stewardship of nature, does democratic culture injure the humanities?

In contrast to the scientific learning accumulated in pursuing the history and knowledge of nature, the pursuit of the humanities, in literature and the arts, may endure democratic inhibition, or suffer from neglect, or be compromised by a sense that much greater profit lies in not trying to do one's best work but instead settling for doing work that most pleases the lowered standards that always prevail unless elitist pressure crowds them out. The question is, does democracy retard human ambition for greatness in the arts and in nonscientific thought to such an extent that it diminishes human stature below the level reached by past societies? We have already touched on this matter just by sketching the way in which the old order concentrated resources and imposed high standards on the creation of art, thought, and literature—standards that later generations ratified, even after the old order had passed on. Democracies can now afford a leisure class and a sizable learned class, to revert to Mill's terms, but this is a comparatively recent development in those democratic societies most devoid of remnants of the old order, like the United States, and is made possible to a large extent by the productivity of an unleashed capitalism. Even so, a leisure class and a learned class in a democracy do not have the weight that they do in unconstitutional and hierarchical societies that concentrate power, wealth, and prestige in a comparatively small number of people. But the story does not end there.

One of the principal missions of the fine arts has been to strengthen our desire to look at the world for the sake of its beauty, and for the sake of its interest, even when not beautiful. The interesting and the beautiful are not exactly the same, but they often coincide or instigate attention to each other. Recurrently, philosophy, under the influence of Heidegger, has tried to reinforce the teaching that it begins in wonder at the sheer presence of the world, but also in wonder at the way things move and affect each other, at the abundance of different kinds of creatures and plants and inorganic objects, at the natural spectacle that nature provides to the human senses that are permeated by knowledge and imagination, at the complexity of interconnection and dependence. Poetry also cultivates the faculty of attention in its readers. One of its lessons is that there is always more in the poem and in the world that is summoned by the poem than the first look notices. One must think again; one must be ill-disposed to overlook what might be crucial to taking in some phenomenon or other—including the poem itself—and noticing or distilling its point or meaning or the intricacy of its construction.

I think that democratic culture in the United States has done a good share of this humanistic work as a democratic culture. In line with the more extended significance of a culture of rights, humanist work has been done that excites interest in the world, a sense of its beauty, a feeling of wonder that the world is, and a more tirelessly perceptive eye. The achievements of Emerson, Thoreau, and Whitman are central. One could add quite a few others, especially those who learned from Emerson, such as Emily Dickinson, William James, Henry James, Robert Frost, and Wallace Stevens, or were profitably irritated by him, like Melville. Emerson provoked and inspired all of them. (Henry Adams and T. S. Eliot, armored in their snobbery, were two of the thinkers in this class not touched by Emerson's influence.) The Emersonian and anti-Emersonian traditions have made a distinguished contribution to define and elevate human stature and also prepare the way for directing the project of stature toward the stewardship of nature. They did their work attuned to the democratic spirit, but were also and necessarily troubled by it and disliked or were even disgusted by some of its manifestations.

Perhaps the democratic American contribution to the fine arts from the start has been minor, and its contribution to the literary humanities spotty. Of course, one can always say that the nineteenth and early twentieth centuries worked out all the best remaining potentialities in painting, architecture, and serious music, and that therefore in the last century or so, democratic culture, like any other kind of culture, is too late for great achievements in these fields proportional to the total population. But again let us say that the actual is not exhaustive evidence of the possible; better luck might have made a difference. But when was literature great, not just very good, the last time? Or when was the last time that philosophy was great but not technical? If there has been a dearth—not a total blank—of greatness, the cause is probably not the democratic culture of human rights, whether in the United States or elsewhere. Maybe part of the explanation is that the more people there are in competition, the more insignificant will creative minds in almost any field feel. It would nevertheless be odd that humanist creativity seems to have declined even as population continues to increase. Or, maybe the best literary and artistic talent goes into cinema, an art form that is comparatively new in the world. No doubt, enormous talent goes into moviemaking; still, shouldn't there be a lot left over for the traditional genres?

Perhaps democratic culture, the protector of the public morality of rights and of the equal individual status of every human being, does actually work against human stature in some important ways. If stature is demonstrated in the accomplishment of greatness in art and thought—leave aside undeniable greatness in scientific thought—that are unafraid to be complex and subtle, and aspire to durability (to mention just obvious principal standards) then democratic culture may be at fault. Democracy would be Janus-faced: audacious in political endeavors, splendidly brave in feats of exploration of the globe and outer space, brilliant in mathematics, science, and technology, but deficient in some of the humanities. It maintains or surpasses the level of achievement that nondemocratic and antidemocratic cultures have attained in every endeavor but the humanities. But the situation is less clear in the humanities. Where the humanities can feel pushed far away from the center of a culture's attention by popular culture and mass culture, the creators might suffer from their unimportance, as if the best achievements figure only as just another set of contributions in a world overfull of contributions, and count no more or even less than works that are accessible to an active, clamorous, and all-powerful popular and mass audience. Everybody is a consumer, everybody has an opinion, and everybody can spend money on culture. There can be no unanswerable hierarchy of taste in an unhierarchical society. One is almost driven to say: in the cultural battle between the few and the many, back the few; in the battle for human rights between the few and the many, back the many. Or, perhaps there is now no inconsistency between status and stature in the idea of human dignity, only a strain.

The Frankfurt school, especially Marcuse and Adorno, did much to force reluctant attention to the cost paid by the humanities in a democratic culture that seems so abundantly endowed with humanistic work in every discipline and mode. But the best work must struggle to appear because there is so much economic incentive not to do one's best work. Gifted people are discouraged from being as difficult as they know their best work would require them to be. A great deal of talent is therefore expended in satisfying popular and mass or middle-level expectations, in pandering and ingratiation. The talent is like the "knack" of the Sophists, who catered to popular taste, as it is described by a worried Socrates in the *Gorgias*. What is achieved is the astounding feat of creating a popular and mass culture that is rather good, good enough to appear to satisfy high standards part of the time, and even do the work that was once thought could be done only on the highest level. The fact is that many mass-distributed films, for example, have moments— moments only—of beautiful literariness or remarkable insight, of informal bursts of utopianism or dream-like juxtaposition or fluidity in action; or work out a pattern of action that is so delicate that you detect it only afterward. The best part of the talent goes into these moments and patterns. Films and TV have made a collective contribution to the subject of the vagaries of sexual desire, its uncertain direction, that has not been fully appreciated. Films made for smaller audiences are complex and subtle enough to deserve a long life. I do not want to quarrel with that or with the greatness of some jazz.

Still, I cannot accept the view passionately sponsored in a democratic culture that there is no line between high culture and popular culture. Yes, the line can be shifting and even momentarily invisible, but Bob Dylan is not a poet as Robert Lowell was; Cole Porter knew he was not Schubert. The high infiltrates the lower, and the lower can infiltrate the high; but when the lower has learned from the high, the lower traduces it in learning from it. The betrayal consists in attempted domestication, in presenting moments or extracts as if they were sufficient or as if they gain by being taken out of their original place and abridged or simplified and made more appealing in the process. The lower loses its own integrity when it tries to absorb the high. The situation is such that when the lower is raised, even when it does not invade the high, the high is lowered because its position is so minor; and the level of the whole culture must go down if the top is lowered, even if the average level is raised. In some arts, the standards are lowered so that more practitioners can reach them. Examples include installations, performance art, and graphic novels. To shock the audience seems a principal aim; the shock is supposed to come from understanding that this work, too, is art (though you didn't think so and don't want to), alongside whatever shock, if any, the content of the work supplies. But which of these works can be taken in repeatedly over a long period of time by the same person and by countless other observers over long periods of time because their richness and intensity require and repay close study and repeated efforts of interpretation that testify to inexhaustible interest? When this lesser kind of work is treated by representatives of the high as if it were up to old standards, the practitioners can think that their work is at the highest level. There is no way of compensating for loss at the top. The good is the enemy of the best because the good is not purely good; it is only pretty good and only some of the time. American popular music is a great achievement, but, to appeal to aesthetic criteria, is it complex, subtle, and durable? Yes, some of it is— durable, at least. Its success is musically instructive to serious composers, but isn't their greater instruction found in the hopelessness of reaching an adequate audience for their much more difficult work— difficult to do and to appreciate?

In a radical effort to efface the line between high and low art, the philosopher Arthur Danto has famously said in a rich and enlivening study that "Anything can be art" (*After the End of Art,* p. 114). One of his meanings is that anything presented by the artist as art and accepted by an appropriate audience or institution as art is art. But what is art? The answer is not clear, but Danto holds that the "aesthetic is in fact not an essential or defining property of art" (p. 112). I don't see how this could be right, despite all the gestures made by Marcel Duchamp and others. How many times did one want to look at a urinal, which is what Duchamp's "Fountain" was? In any case, Duchamp's gesture was wasted on anyone who was not acquainted with high art. It is true that art need not be beautiful by the standards of any particular time or place. But if we are to consider a work as a work of art it must be put forth as worthy of looking at or considering time and again, if not for its beauty then for its fascination or deep interest; aspires to last, not to be dismantled. Works of art appeal to aesthetic capacities like admiration and contemplation; other qualities than beauty can inspire these capacities. The motive of appreciation need not coincide with the original motive of the artist; for example, nonreligious people can appreciate religious art and find it compelling, just as nonreligious people can read religious texts and find them admirable though not literally believable. As it is, aesthetic considerations, independent of religious ones, must have played a role in the original creation, if what we now consider works of art and thought rather than works of religion have retained the power to compel continuous attention.

Imagine if all high art, by our accumulated standards, were suddenly unavailable, and all that was left was popular and mass culture. Then imagine the reverse. The absence of high art would be far worse, for those who are capable of appreciating both, than the absence of popular and mass culture. For a while, people would know what they were missing. There is no substitute for high art once a person is acquainted with it. It is made up of works that cannot be replaced. A completely successful cultural revolution of the Maoist sort is a nightmare to imagine, as it was a nightmare many times over for those who endured it. If a time came when people no longer knew what they were missing, the whole world would have altered—that is, shrunk. All I am doing is trying to apply Mill's Platonist doctrine of the higher pleasures—not to say of course that all that high culture is good for is to give pleasure.

Democracy, the New Media, and the Stewardship of Nature

The new media of communication, such as the cell phone and the internet, and new uses of the older media, like reality TV, give a powerful impetus to other tendencies in democratic culture that lower the higher, and also raise the lower and lower the lower even further. Or seem to lower the lower even further. These phenomena, however, are two-sided. Texting by cell phone and posting on Facebook, chatrooms, and Twitter on the internet offer unprecedented opportunities for self-display, but some of the self-display is unworthy; yet these modes indicate a sometimes passionate search for undramatized truth about oneself and others. Search engines give access to the world of information and knowledge, but also spread misinformation. Blogs permit ease of publication but also coat the world in incessant half-truths, rumors, false alarms, and gossip. Reality TV erodes the prestige of professionally produced and acted performances, and replaces popular art with amateur hours and freak shows, and adds the lure of prizes, yet it helps us remember the beggary of all performance on every level and in every medium: the urgent need to be looked at, to be loved, and to be praised by strangers.

Undeniably, the new media will multiply and be put to many uses, many unforeseen, some beneficial. I wish to single out two main aspects of these developments in democratic culture, which nurtures and welcomes the new media. The first is that they encourage the public expression of practically every conceivable facet of human beings: their tastes, temperament, peculiarities, experiences, random thoughts and fantasies. We now have a steady stream of inwardness made public; from a distance, it seems as if there is just a single inwardness in the world, a collectivized inwardness of some giant entity that is at once all too human, subhuman, superhuman, and always in motion, never to be completed or fulfilled. The infinite record is made accessible but cannot be encompassed. No one mind can take in all that is communicated; it can be stored but not processed. Yet if one were to imagine digesting it all at a given moment, one would think that one had frozen the flow and had present to mind all humanity and all its expression, and that all had been taken in and made sense of. One imagines oneself as the god conceptualized by Nicholas of Cusa in *A Vision of God;* he sees and understands everything, all inwardness and everything outward, all at once. (Nicholas has a vision of God's vision.) There is greatness in these human achievements, but some of the time, in Emerson's phrase, "for cheap ends," which are the purposes of exhibitionism. There is a pervasive and unembarrassed egotism, but perhaps mitigated by the equal opportunity, for anyone who wants, to take a turn in being egotistical. It is as if the audience for each person is not a group of recipients but a faraway and anonymous observer who knows better than oneself or anyone else what one really means and how good one really is. It is public confession as absolution, with no intermediate penance. What could be better? But what could be worse than the condition fostered by the new media in which popular sentiment, if not public opinion, has alienated to public surveillance some part of the right of privacy and weakened resistance to encroachments on other parts?

Above all, these developments achieve a kind of democratic consummation. The different facets of personality of each of us who take part in these new media are on display, and the facets of a vast number of people who take part in these media side by side give us a picture of the human species. Every experience we can imagine (and some experiences we couldn't) is mentioned or described as if it is of equal value with any other experience; everyone else's experiences are of equal value to ours; the self-exposure is, if not always perfectly matter-of-fact, then without shame. The irony is that what seems so trivial is actually an admission that an experience does not register until it is described and thus given a second life. Only the second time establishes the reality of the first time. One does not lead a life unless it is made into a continuously flowing written narrative; better, into a cubist narrative. People want a film of their whole lives and hope for an afterlife to watch it.

What is the complaint? Perhaps it is that the democratic consummation is the despotism of superficiality. Or, we can feel that what should be decently hidden is made casually visible. The rush to make inwardness public denies inwardness the chance to bide its time until it can do something worth doing, and weakens the inclination to be a receptive audience for works that are complex, subtle, and durable. If the audience grows smaller and smaller as the population increases, perhaps the will to create such works gets weaker.

The other main aspect of the recent techniques of communication I want to discuss is related to egotism and superficiality, but is not the same. Those who tweet and text may be exhibitionist, but they are also implicated in a phenomenon that is somewhat better than superficial. The best sense that I make of it is that numerous persons have found a way of suggesting that every human being has innumerable facets that deserve to be recorded because they are all valuable, they are all parts of the person. Furthermore, one's life is a kind of production that is more serious than any professional theatrical production; recorded fully, it doesn't have the shape of a play or movie, but it is more important: it is a chronicle that will change with time into an open-ended epic. The more fully recorded one's life is, the more of a hero one is. I detect the hints of a wish to believe that the only greatness is being oneself; one's greatness will be known when one is much more fully disclosed; to be known is to be found more interesting and perhaps appreciated, even admired. The old order had to think that human stature came from rare great achievements; they had no way of seeing greatness in the most ordinary, or at least no interest in doing so. James Joyce was prescient when he changed aristocratic Ulysses into Leopold Bloom and needed eight hundred pages to cover one day in his lower-middle-class life.

The democratic point of the new media and new uses of older ones is not for an artist to turn life into art but for us to see, if possible, that life is already worthy to be apprehended as art, but not art that incipiently resembles the art that great and good artists make of life by changing it into formal works of literature, painting, and other modes, or even the deliberately ephemeral works of some contemporary artists. But notice a bare possibility. Human everyday life, processed through the new media, though of course discontinuous with nature, nevertheless provides a perhaps useful model (or analogy) for the aesthetic appreciation of nature. I have said that human stature would be at its most commendable if human creative energies were turned more to the effort of preserving nature from further damage; but if that is just beginning, the human efforts to record and know nature already constitute some of the most praiseworthy achievements that the human species has ever accomplished. Serving nature, however, also includes an aesthetic part—appreciating and admiring it. The aesthetic part is the least developed. I think that if people in greater numbers could extend to nature the fundamentally democratic urge to include everything in its embrace; to lavish attention on natural particulars as if each had importance; to perceive nature as possessing innumerable facets that beg for appreciation; to feel that other species are precious, not as people are, but precious still; that human beings are, in Whitman's phrase, leaves of grass (or in Homer's phrase, the generations of human beings are like leaves [on the tree of life]) and that the natural leaves of grass in their indefinitely large number are separately valuable as human beings are—if we could do all this, if our aesthetic cultivation were, in some of its aims, democratically cultivated, then our effort to protect nature from as much human depredation as possible would become more passionate.

No, we cannot take a census of the leaves of grass; we cannot notice every sparrow that falls on the ground; we believe that every single human being is absolutely valuable, while members of other species and other species as wholes are valuable, but cannot be absolutely so; and that the aim is to preserve other species, not necessarily every individual member of them, while the aim is to preserve if possible every human being from a miserable life or a premature death. In his *Journal,* Thoreau records his encounters with every kind of tree, flower, weed, bird, and land-creature that he comes across in his wanderings, as if each species had a dignity that entitled it to mention by name and a close attention to its distinctiveness. He nourishes the wish to hold the preciousness of nature as an aspiration, which, if necessarily distinct from the feeling of preciousness we should bestow on human beings, is not completely discontinuous with it. He wants us to see the "perfect success" of a pine tree as it achieves its being by "lifting its evergreen arms to the light," rather than looking at it only as material to be cut up in boards and used in making houses. He says, "the pine is no more lumber than man is," and the poet who loves it "as his own shadow in the air" uses it rightly by letting it stand (*Journal,* vol. 7, pp. 131–132). But he also knows, two days later, that "Cultivation exterminates the pine but preserves the elm," and that there "is not enough of the garden in the wilderness" (p. 139). He mourns any tree that is cut down, but also believes that its right to exist cannot be absolute.

The properly aesthetic response to human works includes a capacity to be both detached and impersonal, but when transferred to nature, it can be based on sympathy with nature, when nature is not a mortal threat to human beings. The sympathy is an extension of democratic fellow feeling to nature; in Whitman's poetry it is extended even to what is inorganic. The project of recording the history of nature and acquiring ever more careful and ample knowledge of nature needs little further encouragement. But the aesthetic motive for wanting to serve nature can lead by a winding road to a desire to protect it because it is appreciated and admired for its own sake. We know that nature cannot reciprocate, and that it cannot even know that it is appreciated and admired. That should make no difference. The bleak truth, however, is that a democratic society that is also joyously capitalist and unrepentantly imperialist is not the best suited to teach reverence for nature.

Democracy's largest contribution to human stature would come when it led the way in teaching that preserving nature is the greatest achievement and that sympathy and fellow feeling for it ease the way to appreciation and admiration. The strain between the two components of human dignity, between status and stature, would be less. Concern for equal individual status, which now in the name of human rights constrains the project of stature, would help, by analogical extension to nature, to inspire it. Species snobbery would be sublimated into appreciation and admiration if a species not wholly natural and partly discontinuous with nature experienced sympathy and fellow feeling with it, despite its inability to reciprocate. In a bad mood, we could misapply Sartre's words about humanity's condition to humanity's appreciation and admiration of nature: it is a useless passion, and then get past the bad mood.

I also am aware, however, that sometime in the future, the project of serving nature for its own sake would probably entail abridgements of some human rights. A voracious consumerism that grows out of and drives capitalism, and that is nourished by the democratically encouraged love of sensory adventure, change, and novelty, may necessitate restrictions on doing what one wants and living as one likes. The most important restriction may be in reproductive rights. In order to reduce the rate of population growth, China has imposed a limit of one child that parents can ordinarily have. China may simply be ahead of the world. The policy is a terrible abridgement of fundamental personal liberty. But appalling as it is to invoke a value that conflicts with liberty, when most such invocations in the past have been cynical, there will be too many people alive for any purpose, including mass survival, if growth is not checked, by coercion if need be. The wasteland would grow even larger, would grow vast: new wars and further natural destruction would make life chaotic. People would demand regulation far more extensive and destructive of rights than the regulation of reproductive rights. This sort of regulation would, however, reintroduce a terrible tension between human rights and human stature.

A state policy of population control is not only an abridgement of fundamental human rights but also a further assault on the core of human dignity. The policy's premise is that there can be too many of us for the good of the species and the earth, and that in fact, those who say that there are already far too many of us may be right. The meaning of the latter point is that everyone now alive should feel a twinge of regret merely at being alive. What matters is that the species should go on in an environment that can sustain it and that is not ravaged ever more intensively. The species has an imputed interest in its perpetuation and this interest is different from the interest of any individual in not dying prematurely and from the same interest of all those living at any given time. I do not mean that many human beings must be put to death so that the human species may survive. The interest of the species belongs to the unborn generations indefinitely into the future; yet the number of unborn must be greatly reduced. The stewardship of nature promotes this species interest while also promoting the perpetuation of the natural environment for the sake of nature and thus demonstrating the greatness, the stature, of the human species. Thinking about this prospect is demoralizing. But how would people manage to live immersed not in the feeling of life's precariousness—that has always been common—but rather in the feeling that human life is dangerous to nature and must be rationed in numbers and consumption in order to make it less dangerous to nature? Would some think that it is better to end it all through wanton expenditure than to go on so carefully and meagerly? Is there hope in the thought that people as always can get used to anything, provided they lose sight of the better condition of their predecessors?

The species, not the individual, becomes the center of thinking about human dignity, and we are threatened with being thrown back to earlier times before the concept of equal individual status had the central place or any place at all, and stature did practically all the work in dignifying and elevating human beings in their own eyes. Inevitably, the policy of placing limits on population opens up the question of deliberate genetic selection for superior types, not merely for the sake of avoiding terrible diseases and deformations. In China, free choice has led to disproportionate selection for male children. The concept of equal individual status has so far been developed on the assumption that the human race should not be culled for any purpose of the species. The concept of status could not withstand such a practice. Those who urge the unrestrained pursuit of human stature for certain existential purposes would have no objection, but a defender of human rights wants stature constrained by status. For any person to feel unnecessary and even a burden on the earth is not compatible with individual dignity. If many began to feel that way, a mood would descend on humanity that would signify a dismal alteration in human self-conception. Thus, individual free reproductive choice leads to disaster, while stewardship of nature, the summit of human stature, seems to require strong restrictions on human reproduction and hence on equal individual status. The long-term interest in species survival would ally itself tightly with considerations of stature. I cannot see my way to the terms of decent compromise between status and stature, let alone reconciliation. The problem seems awful beyond tragedy. What I can say is that the beneficiary of resolving the contest between human status and human stature in favor of human stature would not be the few, as in the past, but the whole species and its future.

Stature in the Face of Death

Sophocles wrote for the Chorus in Antigone an unequalled celebration of humanity (*Antigone,* pp. 170–171). The celebration is painfully mindful of the human implication in wrongdoing—some of it helpless and some of it showing a human proclivity to do excessive wrong once it is set in a direction that appears to be laid out for it—and is enunciated amid calamitous events. (*Antigone* is in plot sequence the third of the three plays about Oedipus and his family, though produced first.) The Chorus says (sings), "Many the wonders but nothing walks stranger than man." Wonders are always somewhat strange; the strangest wonder is man. Why is man supremely wondrous? The Chorus proceeds to tell of the ways in which humanity tames and uses nature, whether the natural elements or the domesticated animals. "He can always help himself. He faces no future helpless." Humanity can do what no other species can, and does it in part at the expense of other species. Humanity is master, for good and bad. He is "clever beyond all dreams." But, "there's only death that he cannot find an escape from."

The puzzle is that in the second play in the plot sequence (but produced last) of the so-called Theban trilogy, *Oedipus at Colonus,* when Oedipus is near death, the Chorus says that it is best never to have been born and second best to die early. The Chorus, however, never praises suicide, never counsels freely dying before one's time; nor does it suggest, to begin with, that a person's soul ever has a choice to be born or not and that a person can therefore regret being alive as the result of one's own mistake. (Obviously, no one alive ever remembers making a choice.) In Oedipus's family, Jocasta commits suicide, but only after the worst truth has been disclosed to all; Antigone chooses suicide perhaps because she would rather kill herself than be killed by another. Suicide is a way of minimizing the accident of one's existence. But both mother and daughter lived as long as they thought they could; it is not clear that either ever believed that it would have been better for them not to have been born, despite the events they lived through, or even comprehended the Chorus's verdict on the abysmal worth of life. Isn't the implication of the Chorus that what is good for every individual is good for the species? Better for humanity never to have come into existence? One possible inference we could make is that humanity would show it is master only in a self-imposed extinction like Antigone's and then it would prove, but with supreme irony, that it is master only of itself. Does this implication cancel the ode to human greatness that appears in *Antigone?* No; it sets up a polar antagonism, which can be resolved, but not neatly, and certainly not within the plays, by the thought that even if continued existence is not good for humanity, it is of surpassing importance for the earth and the universe, when there are no gods or other species to know and admire nature.

Humanity is master of nature but not of death. The Chorus in *Antigone,* however, does not let death force it to abandon its awe before the human race. Can a species, itself almost certainly mortal, and made up of individuals all of whom are mortal, be an object of awe? "All flesh is grass," says Isaiah (Authorized Version, 40:6). Can we attribute the highest stature in the universe to a species that will turn into nothing, while the universe goes on and on, or gives way to another universe, which gives way, in turn, and so on forever? Being is eternal, but humanity is not. If there were an afterlife, the situation would be different. But secularists think that any notion of an afterlife that we could desire is merely wishful thinking. The Greeks did not desire the afterlife they said they believed in: everyone but Socrates found abhorrent the thought of Hades' kingdom, in which the shades (whether or not they are disincarnated souls awaiting reincarnation) bitterly regretted their absence from earthly life, which they also knew was often bitter. If they were not sorry that they had ever been born, even though, when alive, they knew they had to die, the reason could be that they refused to think the matter through, as perhaps Socrates did. As secularists, we cannot escape the finality of death.

But suppose it was said that unless human beings were immortal, it would be unimportant if a person were deprived unjustly of life and was made to die at an early age. How could it matter that the person, any person and all persons, died, since once a person is dead he or she could not possibly regret being dead and yearn, as the souls in Hades' kingdom yearned, for life on earth. In Hades, even brave Achilles, who chose to die young for glory, craves life on earth so much that he would settle for another earthly life on the worst terms; he would choose to be born. When he was alive he had not been able really to imagine how much he would miss life after he died. But once dead, we are nothing and therefore have no regret at being dead. So, what difference does it make to a clear-eyed person that he is going to die or even that his right to life is not respected and that he dies before his time and for unacceptable reasons? He has to die anyway. It seems that only an afterlife, especially one that is inferior to earthly life, can make being alive so desirable that the system of human rights takes on its full significance.

In response to this line of thought, we could say that yearning endlessly in an afterlife for the earthly life a person once had gives solidity to the thought that it is better never to have been born, even though the ancient Greeks refused the Socratic temptation to entertain that thought. All that secularists have to say is that there is one life, that one life is better in most cases than none, and that mortal human life is better when the system of rights is in place. A decent life is better than a bad life and also equips us to think that it is good to have lived, even if we could not have known what we were missing if we the living had not been born, and even though once dead we are nothing again.

Facing death honestly could be everyone's heroism. I think that other candidates for heroism like seeing humanity as lonely and abandoned in a vast and indifferent or hostile universe, or learning to live without the conviction that there is a higher and intended meaningfulness, design, or purpose in the world, fade in importance beside the fact of death. The ability to live in an unenchanted world should ideally come as a matter of course. The wish to blame the world for its not having been created or shaped by divinity and sent into existence for the sake of going about God's business must be given up. Then, too, divinity must not be given credit for the beautiful mathematical regularities in nature or for attuning human senses and faculties to life on earth. To say that there are regularities, beautiful or not, is only to say that there is a world; how can there be a world without natural regularities? To say that we are attuned is only to say that we are able to survive in the world, not that humanity was made for the world or the world made for it. Furthermore, any view that disdains taking refuge in likening the universe to a harmonious cosmos, a choir of diverse voices or an orchestra of diverse instruments, is welcome. Better is a view that sees the universe as designed to sustain itself through a tense struggle of discordant amoral elements that achieve equilibrium, but that story, though aesthetically compelling, is still not good enough. We need to stay true to what we know—the immensity beyond immensity of space and time and the universe's purposeless waste—because that knowledge is an incomparably superior encouragement to wonder. It lets go of the idea that the universe is a display of omnipotence by an inscrutable magician, and it therefore serves the secular purpose of providing for wonder that is warranted. No matter how good a story theology is—one theology or another—the stature of adulthood is better than any story. Yes, the human mind, the only mind, has not yet encompassed the universe; perhaps it never can.

The concept in Sophocles' play of human stature as demonstrated by mastery and exploitation of nature cannot be ours. What once served humanity did not despoil nature so badly as to threaten its continuation in the forms humanity knew, but rather helped humanity to gain a life, built on audacity, that climbed to ever greater complexity of self-consciousness. "Language, and thought like the wind / and the feelings that make the town / he has taught himself." What now serves humanity as humanity desires threatens nature and itself with much ruin. But death remains constant as the fact that humanity cannot honestly get around. If in no other way, we can be in agreement with the Chorus: we do not let the fact of death force us to abandon commitment to the idea of the stature of the human species. In fact, persisting in life despite knowledge of the finality of death is further testimony to human uniqueness and hence stature. Add that except in the most terrible conditions, some people persist not in life merely, but also in their efforts to elevate the human stature by striving to do more than persist in life.

We should not want to live forever on earth or some other place. What would it mean? We can't conceive of it; there is no plausible, let alone desirable characterization of immortality. Augustine's speculations in *The City of God* (22.29–30) about immortal life with God are made vapid by their wish to be imaginative. The immortal gods of the Greeks would have perished without the spectacle of human acts. One of Blake's proverbs of hell, and none the worse for that, is that "Eternity is in love with the productions of time" (*Marriage of Heaven and Hell*, p. 253). Only a rare philosophical spirit could find existence endlessly interesting. Even to want to live much longer than what is now advanced old age is foolish. There is no mind without a brain and no brain without the sense organs and no sense organs without a body, and an intact mind with a shriveled body is an unwelcome idea, as Tithonus learned. Why want to drink life to the dregs? He was also wrong to have wanted to live forever. How would he have filled the time? What does experience signify without death? Experience is intertwined with death, even in good health; after a certain age it is tinged by thoughts of death. We can have infinite passions only because we are not immortal. If *per impossible* we were immortal as human beings, experience, good and bad, would scarcely register on us. Everything would just pass through us insubstantially; that is, the accumulated weight of experience and the burden of interpreting it—a burden that is constant, sometimes heavy, and sometimes unendurable—would not exist. But there is no human life without interpretation. It is close to meaningless to posit an immortal personal identity. Even Socrates would tire of the unending burden of interpretation. If death is not good, immortality is worse. The immortality of the human species would be another and much better condition: mortal generations of individuals giving way to mortal generations, forever. Death does not make living futile; awareness of it without illusion and acceptance of it without resentment would make human beings yet more wondrous.

Bibliography

Adorno, Theodor W. *The Culture Industry*. Ed. J. M. Bernstein. London: Picador, 1991.

Althusser, Louis. "Contradiction and Overdetermination: Notes for an Investigation." In *For Marx*. Trans. Ben Brewster. New York: Vintage, 1970.

Arendt, Hannah. "The Conquest of Space and the Stature of Man." In *Between Past and Future*. 2nd ed. New York: Viking, 1968.

———. *The Human Condition*. Chicago: University of Chicago Press, 1958.

———. *The Origins of Totalitarianism* (1951). 2nd ed. New York: World, 1958.

———. "Some Questions in Moral Philosophy" (1965–1966). In *Responsibility and Judgment*. Ed. Jerome Kohn. New York: Schocken, 2003.

Aristotle. *Nicomachean Ethics*. Trans. Martin Ostwald. Indianapolis: Bobbs-Merrill, 1962.

———. *Politics*. Trans. Ernest Barker. New York: Oxford University Press, 1958.

Auden, W. H. "Vespers." In *The Shield of Achilles*. New York: Random House, 1955.

Augustine. *The City of God*. Trans. Henry Bettenson. Baltimore: Penguin, 1972.

———. *Confessions*. Trans. R. S. Pine-Coffin. New York: Penguin, 1961.

Beitz, Charles. *The Idea of Human Rights*. New York: Oxford University Press, 2009.

Bentham, Jeremy. *A Fragment on Government* (1776). Ed. F. C. Montague. Oxford: Clarendon, 1891.

————. *An Introduction to the Principles of Morals and Legislation* (1789). Ed. J. H. Burns and H. L. A. Hart. London: Methuen, 1982.

Berlin, Isaiah. "The Concept of Scientific History" (1960). In *Concepts and Categories*. Ed. Henry Hardy. New York: Viking, 1979.

————. *Four Essays on Liberty*. New York: Oxford University Press, 1969.

Blake, William. *The Marriage of Heaven and Hell*. In *The Portable Blake*. Ed. Alfred Kazin. New York: Viking, 1946.

Bourne, Randolph S. *War and the Intellectuals: Collected Essays, 1915–1919*. Ed. Carl Resek. New York: Harper, 1964.

Brennan, William. "In Defense of Dissents." *Hastings Law Journal* 37 (January 1986).

————. Concurrence in *Furman v. Georgia* 408 US 238 (1972).

Brettschneider, Corey. *Democratic Rights: The Substance of Self-Government*. Princeton: Princeton University Press, 2007.

Bromwich, David. *Hazlitt: The Mind of a Critic*. New York: Oxford University Press, 1983.

Burke, Edmund. *Reflections on the Revolution in France* (1790). New York: Penguin, 1968.

Cameron, Sharon. *Writing Nature*. New York: Oxford University Press, 1985.

Cassirer, Ernst. *The Individual and the Cosmos in Renaissance Philosophy* (1926). Trans. Mario Domandi. Oxford: Blackwell, 1963.

Cavell, Stanley. *The Senses of Walden* (1972). Expanded ed. San Francisco: North Point Press, 1981.

Coetzee, J. M. *Elizabeth Costello*. New York: Viking, 2003.

————. *The Lives of Animals*. Ed. Amy Gutmann. Princeton: Princeton University Press, 1999.

Connolly, William. *Pluralism*. Durham, N.C.: Duke University Press, 2005.

Conrad, Joseph. *The Heart of Darkness* (1899). New York: Norton, 1971.

Danto, Arthur. *After the End of Art: Contemporary Art and the Pale of History*. Princeton: Princeton University Press, 1967.

Dworkin, Ronald. *Freedom's Law*. Cambridge, Mass.: Harvard University Press, 1996.

Eliot, T. S. "Hamlet and His Problems." In *Selected Essays*. New York: Harcourt, Brace, 1950.

Emerson, Ralph Waldo. *Essays and Lectures*. New York: Library of America, 1983.

Fitzgerald, F. Scott. *The Great Gatsby* (1925). New York: Scribner, 1953.

Fodor, Jerry. "Against Darwinism." *Mind and Language* 3 (February 2008).

————. "The Trouble with Psychological Darwinism." Review essay on books by Steven Pinker and Henry Plotkin. *London Review of Books,* January 15, 1998.

Foucault, Michel. *The Care of the Self.* Trans. Robert Hurley. New York: Pantheon, 1986.

————. *Discipline and Punish.* Trans. Alan Sheridan. New York: Vintage, 1979.

————. *The Use of Pleasure.* Trans. Robert Hurley. New York: Pantheon, 1985.

Freud, Sigmund. *The Interpretation of Dreams.* (1900). Trans. James Strachey. New York: Avon Books, 1965.

Frost, Robert. "For Once, Then, Something," and "West-Running Brook." In *Collected Poems, Prose, and Plays.* New York: Library of America, 1995.

Fukuyama, Francis. *Our Post-Human Future.* New York: Picador, 2002.

Gray, John. *Straw Dogs: Thoughts on Humans and Other Animals.* London: Granta, 2002.

Green, T. H. "Liberal Legislation and Freedom of Contract." In *The Works of Thomas Hill Green.* Vol. 3. Ed. R. L. Nettleship. London: Longman's Green, 1891–1894.

Haass, Richard N. "In Afghanistan, the Choice Is Ours." Op-ed. *New York Times,* August 21, 2009, A27.

Hauser, Marc. "Aspects of 'Humaniqueness' Differentiating Human and Animal Cognition." *Medical News Today.com,* February 18, 2008.

Hegel, G. W. F. *Introduction: Reason in History.* Ed. Johannes Hoffmeister. Trans. H. B. Nisbet. Cambridge: Cambridge University Press, 1975.

————. *The Philosophy of History.* Trans. J. Sibree. New York: Dover, 1956.

Heidegger, Martin. *Discourse on Thinking* (1959). Trans. J. M. Anderson and E. H. Freund. New York: Harper, 1966.

————. *An Introduction to Metaphysics.* Trans. Ralph Manheim. New Haven: Yale University Press, 1959.

————. "Letter on Humanism" (1947). Trans. Frank Capuzzi and J. G. Gray. In *Basic Writings.* Ed. David Farrell Krell. New York: Harper and Row, 1977.

————. *Poetry, Language, Thought.* Ed. and trans. Albert Hofstadter. New York: Harper, 1975.

————. *The Question Concerning Technology.* Trans. William Lovitt. New York: Harper, 1971.

————. *What Is Called Thinking?* Trans. F. D. Wieck and J. G. Gray. New York: Harper and Row, 1968.

Hobbes, Thomas. *Leviathan* (1651). Ed. Richard Tuck. New York: Cambridge University Press, 1991.

Honig, Bonnie. *Emergency Politics: Paradox, Law, Democracy.* Princeton: Princeton University Press, 2009.

Hume, David. "Of the Standard of Taste" (1757). In *Of the Standard of Taste and Other Essays.* Ed. J. W. Lenz. Indianapolis: Bobbs Merrill, 1965.

———. *Treatise of Human Nature* (1739–1740). Ed. L. A. Selby-Bigge. Oxford: Clarendon, 1951.

Huxley, Aldous. *Brave New World.* New York: Harper, 1932.

Ignatieff, Michael. *Human Rights as Politics and Idolatry.* Ed. Amy Gutmann. Princeton: Princeton University Press, 2001.

Jonas, Hans. *The Imperative of Responsibility.* Chicago: University of Chicago Press, 1984.

Kant, Immanuel. *Grounding for the Metaphysics of Morality* (1785). Trans. James W. Ellington. Indianapolis: Hackett, 1981.

———. "Idea for a Universal History with a Cosmopolitan Purpose" (1784) and "Perpetual Peace" (1795). In *Kant's Political Writings.* Ed. Hans Reiss. Trans. H. B. Nisbet. Cambridge: Cambridge University Press, 1970.

———. *Metaphysics of Morals.* (1797). Trans. Mary Gregor. New York: Cambridge University Press, 1991.

Kolbert, Elizabeth. "The Sixth Extinction?" *New Yorker,* May 25, 2009.

Lincoln, Abraham. "House Divided," speech at Springfield, Illinois, June 16, 1858 (vol. 1), and letter to Albert G. Hodges, April 4, 1864 (vol. 2). In *Writings and Speeches.* 2 vols. New York: Library of America, 1989.

Locke, John. *Essay Concerning Human Understanding.* Ed. Peter Nidditch. Oxford: Clarendon, 1975.

———. *Second Treatise of Government.* In *Two Treatises of Government.* Ed. Peter Laslett. 2nd ed. New York: Mentor Books, 1965.

Macedo, Stephen. *Liberal Virtues.* Oxford: Clarendon, 1990.

Madison, James. "Speech in Congress Proposing Constitutional Amendments" (1789). In *Writings.* New York: Library of America, 1999.

Marcuse, Herbert. *The Aesthetic Dimension.* Boston: Beacon, 1978.

———. *Counter-revolution and Revolt.* Boston: Beacon, 1972.

———. *One-dimensional Man.* Boston: Beacon, 1964.

———. "Repressive Toleration." In Robert Wolff, Barrington Moore, Jr., and Herbert Marcuse, *Critique of Pure Tolerance* (1965). 2nd ed. Boston: Beacon, 1969.

Marx, Karl. "The Meaning of Human Requirements," "Private Property and Communism," and "Critique of the Hegelian Dialectic and Philosophy as a Whole." In *Economic and Philosophic Manuscripts of 1844,* in *The Marx-Engels Reader.* 2nd ed. Ed. Robert C. Tucker. New York: Norton, 1978.

Mayerfeld, Jamie. *Suffering and Moral Responsibility.* New York: Oxford University Press, 1999.

Melville, Herman. *Moby-Dick* (1851). New York: Rinehart, 1948.

Mill, John Stuart. Letter to Emile Acollas, September 20, 1871. In *The Later Letters of John Stuart Mill 1849–1873.* Ed. F. E. Mineka and D. N. Lindley. In *Collected Works.* Vol. 17. Ed. J. M. Robson. Toronto: University of Toronto Press, 1972.

———. *On Liberty* (1859). Ed. J. M. Robson. In *Collected Works.* Vol. 18. Ed. J M. Robson. Toronto: University of Toronto Press, 1977.

———. "State and Society in America" (1836), and "Civilization" (1836). In *Collected Works.* Vol. 18. Ed. J. M. Robson. Toronto: University of Toronto Press, 1977.

———. *Utilitarianism* (1861). Ed. J. M. Robson. In *Collected Works.* Vol. 10. Ed. J. M. Robson. Toronto: University of Toronto Press, 1969.

Montaigne, Michel de. *An Apology for Raymond Sebond.* Trans. Michael Screech. New York: Penguin, 1987.

Nagel, Thomas. *The Last Word.* New York: Oxford University Press, 1997.

———. *Partiality and Equality.* New York: Oxford University Press, 1991.

———. "What Is It Like to Be a Bat?" In *Mortal Questions.* New York: Cambridge University Press, 1979.

Nehamas, Alexander. *Nietzsche: Life as Literature.* Cambridge, Mass.: Harvard University Press, 1985.

Nicholas of Cusa. *The Vision of God.* Ed. Evelyn Underhill. Trans. E. G. Salter. New York: Dutton, 1928.

Nietzsche, Friedrich. *The Birth of Tragedy* (1872), *Beyond Good and Evil* (1886), and *The Genealogy of Morals* (1887). In *Basic Writings of Nietzsche.* Trans. and ed. Walter Kaufman. New York: Modern Library, 1968.

———. *Twilight of the Idols* (1889), and *The Anti-Christ* (1895). Ed. and trans. Walter Kaufmann. In *The Portable Nietzsche.* New York: Viking, 1954.

Nozick, Robert. *Anarchy, State, Utopia.* New York: Basic Books, 1974.

Nussbaum, Martha C. *Liberty of Conscience.* New York: Basic Books, 2008.

Orwell, George. *Nineteen Eighty-Four.* New York: Harcourt, Brace, 1949.

Paine, Thomas. *The Rights of Man* (1791, 1792). Ed. Eric Foner. New York: Penguin, 1984.

Pascal, Blaise. *Pensees.* Trans. W. F. Trotter. London: Dent, 1908.

Pettit, Philip. *Made of Words.* Princeton: Princeton University Press, 2008.

Pico della Mirandola, Giovanni. *On the Dignity of Man* (1486). Trans. Charles G. Wallis. Indianapolis: Hackett, 1988.

Pinker, Steven. "The Stupidity of Dignity." *New Republic,* May 28, 2008.

Plato. *Apology* and *Crito.* In *The Trial and Death of Socrates.* Trans. G. M. A. Grube Indianapolis: Hackett, 1975.

———. *Gorgias.* Trans. Donald J. Zeyl. Indianapolis: Hackett, 1987.

———. *Republic.* Trans. G. M. A. Grube. Rev. C. D. C. Reeve. Indianapolis: Hackett, 1992.

Pogge, Thomas. *World Poverty and Human Rights.* Cambridge: Polity, 2002.

Popper, Karl. *The Poverty of Historicism.* Boston: Beacon, 1957.

Rawls, John. *A Theory of Justice.* Cambridge, Mass.: Harvard University Press, 1971.

Robinson, Daniel N. *Consciousness and Mental Life.* New York: Columbia University Press, 2008.

Rorty, Richard. *Philosophy and the Mirror of Nature.* Princeton: Princeton University Press, 1979.

Rousseau, Jean-Jacques. *Discourse on Inequality.* Trans. Roger D. Masters. New York: St. Martin's Press, 1964.

———. *Emile or On Education.* Trans. Allan Bloom. New York: Basic Books, 1979.

———. *Essay on the Origin of Language.* Trans. John H. Moran. New York: Ungar, 1966.

———. *On the Social Contract.* Trans. Judith R. Masters. New York: St. Martin's Press, 1978.

Sandel, Michael J. *The Case against Perfection: Ethics in an Age of Genetic Engineering.* Cambridge, Mass: Harvard University Press, 2007.

Sarat, Austin. *When the State Kills: Capital Punishment and the American Constitution.* Princeton: Princeton University Press, 2001.

Sartre, Jean Paul. *Being and Nothingness* (1943). Trans. Hazel Barnes. New York: Washington Square Press, 1992.

———. *Saint Genet* (1952). Trans. Bernard Frecthman. New York: Braziller, 1963.

Schoolman, Morton. *Reason and Horror: Critical Theory, Democracy, and Aesthetic Individuality.* New York: Routledge, 2001.

Schopenhauer, Arthur. *On the Basis of Morality.* Trans. E. F. J. Payne. Indianapolis: Bobbs-Merrill, 1965.

Shklar, Judith N. *American Citizenship: The Quest for Inclusion.* Cambridge, Mass.: Harvard University Press, 1991.

———. "The Liberalism of Fear" (1989). In Shklar, *Political Thought and Thinkers.* Ed. Stanley Hoffmann. Chicago: University of Chicago Press, 1998.

———. *Ordinary Vices.* Cambridge, Mass.: Harvard University Press, 1984.

Singer, Peter. "Famine, Affluence, and Morality." Available online at www .utilitarian.net/singer/by/1972/htm.

———. "The Groundwork of Utilitarian Morals: Reconsidering Hare's Argument for Utilitarianism." Unpublished manuscript. 2009.

Sophocles. *Antigone.* Translated by Elizabeth Wyckoff. In *The Complete Greek Tragedies: Sophocles.* Ed. David Greene and Richmond Lattimore. Chicago: University of Chicago Press, 1959.

———. *Oedipus the King.* Translated by David Greene. In *The Complete Greek Tragedies: Sophocles.* Ed. David Greene and Richmond Lattimore. Chicago: University of Chicago Press, 1959.

———. *Oedipus at Colonus.* Translated by Robert Fitzgerald. In *The Complete Greek Tragedies: Sophocles.* Ed. David Greene and Richmond Lattimore. Chicago: University of Chicago Press, 1959.

Stalin, Joseph. "Marxism and Linguistics" (1950). In *The Essential Stalin.* Ed. Bruce Franklin. New York: Anchor, 1972.

Stevens, Wallace. "Esthetique du Mal." In *Collected Poetry and Prose.* New York: Library of America, 1997.

Strauss, Leo. *Liberalism Ancient and Modern.* New York: Basic Books, 1968.

Strong, Tracy. *Jean-Jacques Rousseau: The Politics of the Ordinary.* Thousand Oaks, Calif.: Sage, 1994.

Taylor, Charles. *A Secular Age.* Cambridge, Mass.: Harvard University Press, 2007.

———. *Sources of the Self.* Cambridge, Mass.: Harvard University Press, 1989.

Tocqueville, Alexis de. *Democracy in America* (1835, 1840). Trans. Reeve, Bowen, and Bradley. 2 vols. New York: Vintage, 1954.

Thoreau, Henry David. "Civil Disobedience" (1849). *Thoreau: Collected Essays and Poems.* New York: Library of America, 2001.

———. *Journal, vol. 7: 1853–1854.* Eds. N. C. Simmons and R. Thomas. Princeton: Princeton University Press, 2009.

———. *Walden.* In *Thoreau's Works.* New York: Library of America, 1985.

Tubbs, David. *Freedom's Orphans: Contemporary Liberalism and the Fate of American Children.* Princeton: Princeton University Press, 2007.

Villa, Dana. *Socratic Citizenship.* Princeton: Princeton University Press, 2001.

Waldron, Jeremy. *Law and Disagreement.* Oxford: Clarendon, 1999.

———. *Liberal Rights: Collected Papers 1981–1991.* Cambridge, Mass.: Cambridge University Press, 1993.

Webb, Adam. *Beyond the Global Culture War.* New York: Routledge, 2007.

Weisman, Alan. *The World without Us.* New York: St. Martin's Press, 2007.

White, Stephen K. *Sustaining Affirmation*. Princeton: Princeton University Press, 2000.

Whitman, Walt. *Leaves of Grass*. In *Whitman: Poetry and Prose*. New York: Library of America, 1982.

Williams, Bernard. "The Human Prejudice." In *Philosophy as a Humanistic Discipline*. Ed. A. W. Moore. Princeton: Princeton University, 2006.

Wilson, Edward O. *The Diversity of Life*. Cambridge, Mass.: Harvard University Press, 1992.

Index

Evil, 68; immorality compared with, 16, 39; definition of, 39; right to life and, 39; using knowledge gained from, 185–187

Evolution, 128–129, 140, 180

Exhibitionism, 206–209

Existential values/perspective: moral perspective compared with, 12–17, 21–24; on inhuman treatment, 21; on individual equality, 30; on absoluteness of rights, 32; government and, 36–40; tension between moral perspective, 40–43. *See also* Stature of the human species

Exploitation: of nature, 4, 215–216; by governments, 38–39; initiating vs. neglecting, 183–187

Extraterrestrial perspectives, 148–149, 158

Facebook, 205–209

Factions, 1–2, 193–194, 198

False consciousness, 19–21

"Famine, Affluence, and Morality" (Singer), 55–56, 183

Fear, 63–64; in morality, 66–67; egocentrism and, 69

Fitzgerald, F. Scott, 149

Foreign policy, primary importance of, 193, 194–198

"For Once, Then, Something" (Frost), 144

Foucault, Michel, 35–36, 101

Fragment on Government (Bentham), 80

Frankfurt school, 202–203

Free agency, 14, 20, 41, 143, 168–172

Freedom: value of, 12; instrumental value of, 22; security vs., 31–32; paternalism and, 99–109; Mill on, 103, 104; Green on, 104–106; Rousseau on, 135–136; inner, 165;

experimentation and, 170; pain and suffering in, 181

Freedom's Law (Dworkin), 29–30

Free will, 172–173

French Revolution, 3, 67–68

Freud, Sigmund, 156–157, 168

Frost, Robert, 144, 201

Frustration, pain of, 102

Fukuyama, Francis, 132

Furman v. Georgia (1972), 14–17, 39

Gay rights, 72–73

Genealogy of Morals (Nietzsche), 145

Genet, Jean, 155

Genetic engineering, 132

Genetic selection, 211–212

Golden rule, 51, 52–59, 67, 72; justice compared with, 59–60

Golding, William, 150

Good Samaritan, 54, 55, 56

Gorgias (Plato), 203

Government: oligarchic, 2, 37; individual status and, 8; Brennan on, 15; manipulation by, 19–21, 41–43, 84–85, 181; moral vs. existential perspective of, 22; individual rights and, 28–31; abridgment of rights by, 29, 30–32, 34–36, 63–64, 90–92; equality under, 29–30; legitimacy of, 33–34, 71–73; constitutional, 33–35; morality and, 33–36, 50–52; tyrannical/despotic, 34–37, 68; existential defense of rights and, 36–40; property rights and, 51–52; moral heroism and, 57–58; coercion implicit in, 60, 62–63; revolutions against, 60–64; consent to, 69–73; world vs. nation-state, 77–79; utilitarianism on, 80; virtue ethics and, 95–97; paternalism in, 97–109; obedience vs.

free choice and, 105–106; Hobbes on, 121, 122; foreign policy and, 193, 194–198

Gray, John, 116

Greater good, 66, 88–90

The Great Gatsby (Fitzgerald), 149

Greek myths, 25, 157, 214

Green, T. H., 104–106

Group rights, 11–12

Haass, Richard N., 197–198

Habits, 172

Hades, 214

"Hamlet and His Problems" (Eliot), 155

Happiness: manipulative societies and, 41–43; utilitarianism on, 79–92; as goal, 84; virtue and, 92–94

Hare, R. M., 82

The Heart of Darkness (Conrad), 139

Hegel, Georg Wilhelm Friedrich, 178

Heidegger, Martin, 114, 132, 200

Hereditary rank, 11

Heroism, moral, 54, 55–58, 215

History, 124–126; admiration of human, 182; use of knowledge from, 182–187

"History" (Emerson), 124

Hobbes, Thomas, 120–122

Hodges, Albert, 68

Homer, 25

Homogeneity, 78

"House Divided" speech (Lincoln), 74

Human dignity. *See* Dignity, human

Humanities, 199–205

Human nature, 131

"The Human Prejudice" (Williams), 57

Human rights: human dignity as basis of, 1–5, 42; sources of opposition to, 2; literature defending, 2–3; group, 11–12; as instrumental, 21–22; moral vs. existential perspective on, 21–24,

40–43; animal rights vs., 22–23; statements of, 28–29; individual status and, 28–112; government abridgment of, 29; equality of, 29–30; as absolute, 29–33, 90–92; interpretation of, 30–31; conflicts between, 31, 52, 110–111; insufficiency of moral defense of, 33–36; justice and, 59–65; coercion in support of, 60–63; revolutions based on, 60–63; fear and, 63–64; egocentrism and, 65–79; individual vs. group, 66, 89–92; poor use of, 66; defending those of others, 67–68; consent for, 69–73; political, 70; judiciary in determining, 73–77; as revocable privileges, 90–92, 107; consciousness of, 163–164; abridgment of in stewardship of nature, 210–212

Human traits and attributes, 113–173; benefits of to nature, 113–119; achievements, 115, 123–131; philosophical reductions of stature and, 119–123; sources of, 126–127; philosophical anthropology and, 131; agency, 132; language, 133–134, 136–139, 141–142; discontinuity with nature, 140–141, 142–143; thought, 143–145; knowledge, 145–160; maker's knowledge, 150–160; motivation, 153–160; incomprehensibility, 158–160; self-consciousness, 160–169

Hume, David, 46–48, 49

Huxley, Aldous, 41, 42, 84, 132

Hypocrisy, 45–46

"Idea for a Universal History with a Cosmopolitan Purpose" (Kant), 124, 196–197